PRIMORDIAL LEADERSHIP

PRIMORDIAL LEADERSHIP

*Unleash the Results Animal
in You and in Others*

LAWRENCE D. DUCKWORTH

NEW YORK

PRIMORDIAL LEADERSHIP
Unleash the Results Animal in You and in Others

© 2014 **LAWRENCE D. DUCKWORTH**.

Published in New York, New York, by Morgan James Publishing. Morgan James and The Entrepreneurial Publisher are trademarks of Morgan James, LLC. www.MorganJamesPublishing.com

The Morgan James Speakers Group can bring authors to your live event. For more information or to book an event visit The Morgan James Speakers Group at www.TheMorganJamesSpeakersGroup.com.

FREE eBook edition for your existing eReader with purchase

PRINT NAME ABOVE

For more information, instructions, restrictions, and to register your copy, go to **www.bitlit.ca/readers/register** or use your QR Reader to scan the barcode:

ISBN 978-1-61448-763-0 paperback
ISBN 978-1-61448-871-2 hard cover
ISBN 978-1-61448-764-7 eBook
ISBN 978-1-61448-765-4 audio
Library of Congress Control Number:
2013945992

Cover Design by:
Rachel Lopez
www.r2cdesign.com

Interior Design by:
Bonnie Bushman
bonnie@caboodlegraphics.com

In an effort to support local communities, raise awareness and funds, Morgan James Publishing donates a percentage of all book sales for the life of each book to Habitat for Humanity Peninsula and Greater Williamsburg.

Get involved today, visit
www.MorganJamesBuilds.com

Habitat for Humanity®
Peninsula and
Greater Williamsburg
Building Partner

PRIMORDIAL (adj.) \prī- mor-dē-el\

1. a. first created or developed: primeval

1. b. existing in or persisting from the beginning (as of a solar system or universe)

1. c. earliest formed in the growth of an individual or organ: primitive <primordial cells>

PRIMAL (adj.) \ prī-mel\

1. original, primitive

2. first in importance: primary

DRIVE (v.)

To press or force into an activity, course, or direction

Source: *Merriam-Webster.com*

TABLE OF CONTENTS

ACKNOWLEDGMENTS

My profound admiration goes to corporate leaders and entrepreneurs. They are the ones who take risks, invest, innovate, work long and hard hours, hire people, pay taxes, take Wall Street analysts' guff, raise educated families, and provide many other benefits to our small planet. Thank you for leading us to the strongest economic system in the world. I hope this book reveals new thinking and methods so your results can be even better.

I wish to thank my parents for giving me the values, curiosity, and giving nature that provide the context for this book, and the energy required to begin writing a book while still being CEO of a company.

My wife deserves a civilian Medal of Honor for putting up with my periods of thinking intensities and "zoning." Plus, she has raised three great, successful children while I have been leading business adventures for twenty-plus years.

I want to express my great respect and love for my brother Roger, a retired West Point "O6" bird colonel, a leader, and a hero to me. He reflects the best in America (and is a better fly fisher than I am). He penned the military leadership ideas in chapter 8.

I have had many mentors who saw something in me, whom I thank. These included; Dr. Tom Coyne, head of the economics department at Marshall University; Dean Billy Mitchell at Virginia Tech,; Dr. Sang Lee, my advisor at Virginia Tech; Ed Harvey, my first business boss; and Dave Davis, a now deceased boss whose frequent Pennsylvania Dutch saying, "Too soon old, too late smart," made me stop and think many times before acting incorrectly.

Acknowledgments go to the many other leadership authors over the years for their contributions, and to the college professors who teach management and leadership and have also written books on these topics. This education is vital to arm potential leaders with the skills they need to succeed. Keep doing it! I hope these insights and real-world applications help further knowledge.

I thank Morgan James Publishing for choosing this book as one of the small percentage they publish, and for working closely with me. Relatedly, Amanda Rooker's editing provided wonderful clarity to my ideas, insights, and experiences. My good friend Ruth King deserves thanks for pushing me for years to write this book while mentoring her.

PREFACE

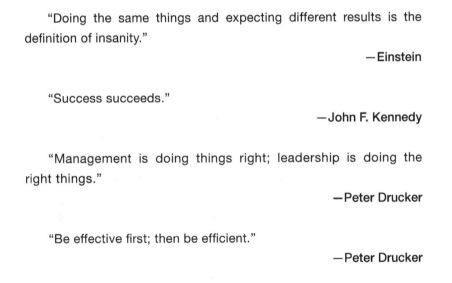

"Doing the same things and expecting different results is the definition of insanity."

—Einstein

"Success succeeds."

—John F. Kennedy

"Management is doing things right; leadership is doing the right things."

—Peter Drucker

"Be effective first; then be efficient."

—Peter Drucker

Great leadership, which is very different from "management," is ages old and, in fact, Primordial. The role of leader naturally emerges when human animals are together, whether with official or unofficial "pecking orders" of power. The same factors that contribute to leadership success have existed from the dawn of humankind—and even before that in other animals (and probably back to Homo erectus more than two million years ago, which preceded Homo sapiens, a.k.a. us).

Luckily, in modern times, intellect and attitude have replaced physical prowess as determinants of leadership success. Nevertheless, leadership rights, like respect, are still *given* to those who most deserve them based on the followers' perception of who best meets *their* Primordial Drive and enabling Primal Drive needs. Leveraging those needs via the Judo Principle is key to standout leadership success.

> "Effective leadership is not about making speeches or being liked; leadership is defined by *results*, not attributes."
>
> —Peter Drucker

> "Business is simple. Management's job is to take care of employees. The employees' job is to take care of customers. Happy customers take care the shareholders. It's a virtual [and the author would add, virtuous] circle."
>
> —John Mackey, Whole Foods CEO

General Patton once noted that "The secret to winning is not to lose." While running a business is not exactly the same as being in a war like Patton was, there are many parallels. Threats such as competition, constraints, and constant change must be overcome. Failing to address these threats has grave consequences. Failing to be proactive has many consequences as well, because the old "grow or die," "change or die," and "differentiate or die" mantras are true. So is "the best defense is a good offense."

Today, key factors that determine who holds the designation of "leader" include being the person who:

- Best manages himself
- Has the best vision for improving the future based on best understanding of the Why of things, and then the resulting "What" and "How" actions required for success
- Gets the most out of others by harnessing their Primal Drives

Better Leverage Change

Famed sci-fi author Isaac Asimov observed that "the only constant is change." Business author Tom Peters observed that "excellent firms don't believe in excellence—only in constant improvement and constant change." Everything around us is changing every day, as reflected in this graphic, and the impacts are multidimensional and inevitable. Changes impact objectives, entities, and roles in complex, constantly evolving, disruptive ways. Change cannot be stopped, so it must be leveraged. In the movie *The International,* the question is asked, "What do you do when you have no way out?" The answer: "Go further in." The standout leader must *proactively* leverage change as a competitive advantage, like others are increasingly doing.

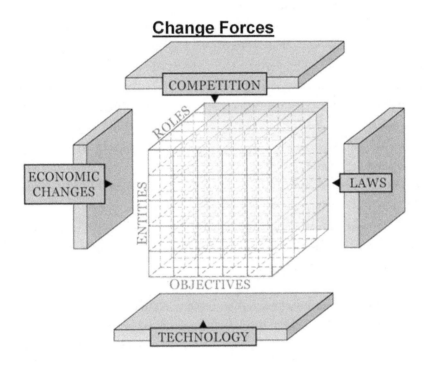

Constant change means that today's strengths will certainly become tomorrow's weaknesses. Doing things the old way will not work; the coefficients have changed in the causation (R^2) formula. With the rise of the Internet and mobile technologies, new opportunities arise every day and are quickly snatched, and the pace of change will become ever faster, even in the quickly increasing expectations of Millennials and Gen Xers versus Boomers. Whoever both executes with excellence and also eats their own young the fastest stays ahead. "Attack yourself before others attack you," we are told by Trout and Reis in *Marketing Warfare.* And as Robert Kiyoski, author of *Rich Dad Poor Dad,* notes, "It's not what you have to 'do' that needs to change. It's first how you 'think' that needs to change." Using the Primal Drives is the *new way of thinking*, as will be shown.

Do You Qualify?

You should only read this book if you are on a constructive, perpetually dissatisfied, personal quest to progress toward being what Jack Welch termed an "A-player" entrepreneur, leader, or manager. You need to be on a personal, compelling quest for the "impossible dream" of leadership excellence as an end, "no matter how hopeless, no matter how far…" as Don Miguel de Cervantes Saavedra urged us all in his classic *Don Quixote de la Mancha.* Think of his sweet "Dulcinea" as your family, employees, customers, shareholders, and partners (i.e., "stakeholders"), with total commitment to them ahead of your own self-interest, and then they to you. It is true that the leadership excellence journey, rather than the destination, is a more important reward, but the destination is good also, especially for those who depend on us.

Also, like the two buzzards on a limb, you need the "Patience my a__; I'm going to kill something" conviction to proactively put new learning, ideas, and tools to work using the Primal Drives (via the Judo Principle). Stay on the balls of your feet and keep competitors on their heels. If you are hitting them, they are not hitting you. With employees, be courageous and help them be on the balls of their feet; the payoff will be wondrous because you are leveraging their Primal Drives for you. It is the Judo Principle in action. Everyone wins.

> "Without ambition one starts nothing. Without work one finishes nothing. The prize will not be sent to you. You have to win it."
> —Ralph Waldo Emerson

The Book's Flow

In front-to-back order, the contents are as follows:

Chapter 1 is a brief history of leadership evolution in the last one hundred years. It shows the progression from harsh leadership in subsistence times to more positive leadership being espoused and increasingly practiced. This evolution directly results from more economic plenty over time, resulting in more safety, and the room for a less-stringent leadership style. Also, the expectations of workers evolved to require more positive approaches, as their economic job opportunities grew.

This chapter tracks classical leadership views from Herzberg, Maslow, McGregor, Drucker, Goleman et al, and others, and shows how their views actually *derive* from the core Primal Drives. Their principles were (and are) correct and are still taught today in MBA programs, but now the reader will have a deeper understanding of the underlying, causal Primal Drives behind them. The chapter also reviews how "observations" are usually used by authors versus actual practice.

We capture a bridge by conquering both ends simultaneously (and thus avoid Collins's "tyranny of the [either/]or"). Before we show in chapters 4 through 8 how to apply our envisioning capability, our values, and our and others' Primal Drives to specific leadership contexts, chapter 2 provides a summary, Cliffs Notes-type excerpts of the more detailed Appendix A, as illustrated in the earlier "iceberg" graphic.

In chapter 3, special focus will be on the critical "spatial thinking" capability in the tier of cognition, and how it contributes to the all-important *envisioning* capability. Values are also reviewed, and a self-assessment construct is provided as an Excerpt from Appendix B.

These summary insights are intended to give you just enough background to optimize your understanding of the leadership ideas presented in subsequent chapters, and thus your leadership success potential. This is consistent with Sun Tzu's famous observation that a battle's outcome is determined "before the first clash of steel."

Note: The reader is encouraged to spend time reviewing Appendices A and B before chapters 4 through 8, and/or afterward. Many more rich human behavioral insights are provided for leadership use.

Chapter 4, "You Can't Manage Others until You First Manage Yourself," is inwardly focused. It applies the Primal Drives to one's own life as entrepreneur or leader or manager; and as a person who always interfaces with subordinates, family, friends, cohorts, peers, prospects, customers, suppliers, investors, community members, and others. Some self-assessment constructs are provided. Not To Do insights are given.

Given that our most precious asset in an organization is our people, in chapter 5 we will explore high-impact, To Do leadership and management techniques to get the highest commitment and productivity from our people via leveraging their Primal Drives. We will help mitigate the tongue-in-cheek truism that "Running a company would be easy if it wasn't for people (or customers)." You'll learn how to make positive and negative forces work for you (and not against you).

Chapter 6 provides leadership execution insights, methods, and To Do tables and templates for leadership actions using the Primal Drives. Its power if applied is incalculable, as the way to solve a complex problem is to break it into its parts and address each element. Specific tools, like the simple but powerful table below, are provided for use in each interpersonal or business process situation.

Program/Audience Focus:		
Date:	By:	
Not To Do's	Primal Drives To Leverage	To Do's
	1.	
	2.	
	3.	
	4.	
	5.	
	6.	

Chapter 7 covers the key areas of planning processes and managing change. These key topics are constantly discussed at almost any session on leadership, management, "business excellence" and "business (or continuous) process improvement." We will see how the typical obstacle of change resistance can be turned into a change-seeking energy source. As Darwin reported, whoever best adapts (to constant change) wins.

Chapter 8 provides some leadership guidance for special situations, specifically for female leaders, older leaders, leaders who are engineers or accountants, military leaders, non-profit leaders, government leaders, turnaround leaders, and more.

Appendix A goes further and deeper than the brief summary in chapter 2 in applying neuroscience and sociobiology insights to leadership, for the leader truly committed to self-improvement.

Appendix B is a more complete look at an example self-assessment tool for leadership insights.

Enjoy. Carry on.

"Do you want to know who you are? Don't ask. Act! Action will delineate and define you."

—Thomas Jefferson

"It's not the size of the dog in the fight; it's the size of the fight in the dog."

—Mark Twain

"Lead, follow, or get out of the way."

—Thomas Paine

HOW TO *CONSISTENTLY* WIN THE BUSINESS BATTLES BETTER THAN OTHERS

I'm going to begin this book with perhaps an important suggestion, for context. I want you to embrace, and leverage, the fact that you, and all of your stakeholders, are *animals*. As animals, science has taught us that the deepest Primordial Drive™ at the core of all of us is to perpetuate our species' genes, no matter what. More than any other drive or motivation we may experience in life, this Primordial Drive is the most powerful, pervasive drive of all.

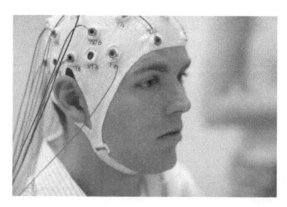

As we will learn in this book, the Primordial Drive is enabled by consistent, powerful Primal Drives™, and all can be leveraged via the Judo Principle™ for results-generating leadership. Effectively "unleashing the animal" in you and in others will yield many results, benefits, and rewards by taking your leadership to the next, A-player level.

An old story is told about a cheetah and a gazelle both waking up each day with the imperative of running. It's a good metaphor for today's leader. Which one do you want to be: the eater, or the eatee? My advice: You are in the race no matter what, so why not be the hunting cheetah?

In the pages of this book you'll learn how to be a different and better leader—faster, smarter, and still standing at the end. The results animal in you, and the others you lead, will be unleashed.

> "The person who knows how will always have a job. The person who knows why will always be his boss."
>
> —Alanis Morissette

The Primordial Drive and the enabling Primal Drives represent the key, *deepest possible* "Why" behind our behavior. When an understanding and leveraging of the Primal Drives is combined with the power of envisioning and values, the improved leadership results can be remarkable. A "bridge" to optimal results is provided.

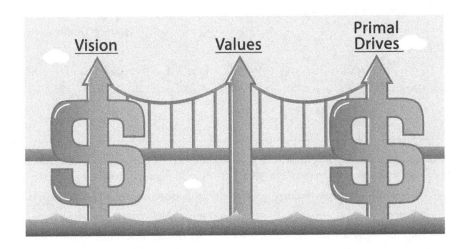

"Effective leadership is not about making speeches or being liked; leadership is defined by *results*, not attributes."

—Peter Drucker

"The inner mind resides in all of us, and we often go through life not knowing that it is even there. The shocking thing is that all of us go through the existence that we have been given on this earth only using a percentage of our potential."

—Greg Frost, *How to Unlock the Subconscious Mind and Access Your Full Potential*

This book is dedicated to helping the entrepreneurial or larger enterprise leader develop new thinking in order to be highly successful in spite of the tough counterforces, constant change, fleeting opportunities, and the inevitable challenges from Murphy's Law. You're going to learn how to better self-manage, lead, plan, and attack intelligently in a powerful, differentiated way that few others have yet figured out. And you're going to learn how to ethically and morally gain a compelling, sustainable advantage with a winning, "no prisoners," give-to-give (not just give-to-get) mindset—with a practical focus on actionable steps *that work in the real world.*

"The best time to plant a shade tree was twenty years ago; the next best time is today."

—Source Unknown

When you start using the Primordial Leadership principles and methods presented in this book, you will better achieve the Type-A example results and avoid the Type-Z example results below.

Type A Results	Type Z Results
• Your management team is cohesive, has a common focus, and is synergistic. • Your market share percentage is steadily growing.	• Good people leave, and the exit interviews reflect it's because there's more opportunity elsewhere. • No matter what your solution's advantages are, the decider wants to go another direction.

Type A Results	Type Z Results
• The board supports a new program even if new criteria and resourcing need to be adopted.	• The draft plan or report submitted to you has thinking gaps and oversights.
• Your "top-of-the-funnel" lead generation marketing efforts are creating the quantity and quality of leads wanted.	• The sales team consistently misses its projections.
• Your sales win ratio is very high, per unit sales costs continue to go down, and market share is rising such that you are becoming a defacto leader in your space.	• People click on your webpage but only a very small percentage request information.
• Employee turnover is very low.	• Company turnover is higher than it should be, at great cost (tangible and opportunity costs included).
• Trust pervades the organization.	• Politics pervade the organization.
• Unasked personal extra effort is the norm.	• People are hunkered down.
• A commitment to results drives initiative.	• Little self-initiative exists.

As business leaders, we are after Type-A results and are on a constant quest to better achieve those results. Developing our envisioning capability, applying core values, and leveraging the below six Primal Drives, with provided methods and tools, are a way to consistently do so, when used in self-management, leadership, marketing, sales, and other relationships. Relative to the Primal Drives, we have heard the individual words before, but the constructs, and their power, are critical to perceive. (The word "Word" is a word symbol for an underlying powerful software program we use. Likewise, metaphorically, each Primal Drive word(s) below represents a powerful, deeply hidden "software program" that controls us in every action; that will be revealed.) The six Primal Drives are:

1. Safety
2. Self-Interest (including greed)
3. Hope and Transcendence
4. Honesty and Trust
5. Energy and Time Optimization
6. Sociability

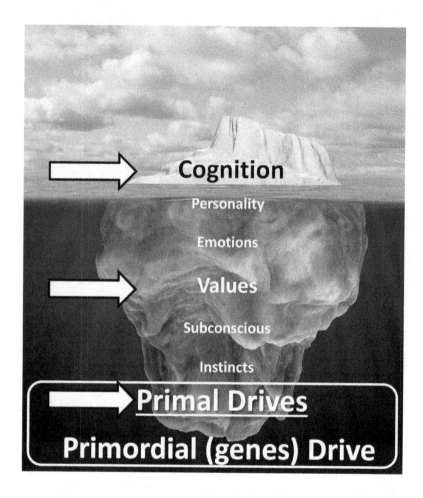

My observation is that the first three, in order, are the most powerful and prevalent, and the second three slightly secondary in power. Different combinations of the Primal Drives, or a "marbling" of the Primal Drives in varying combinations, will exist in different situations. The "art" of leadership lies in understanding what kind of marbling achieves results per situation.

It is important that Judo-leveraging the Primal Drives is combined with the power of envisioning, and with leadership values. They form the earlier "bridge" needed for optimal results, to get from here to there.

Learn from the Scientists

As a serial C-leader, I was compelled to discover the deepest motivational factors, or what I call the "Why," behind human behaviors I observed. Also, I sensed that even deeper, more powerful Why factors existed behind, and underlying, the observations by other famous authors. That launched me into an investigation into brain science and other sources to learn more about the Why causations. The Primordial Drive and the enabling Primal Drives observations resulted.

"…neuroscience could certainly enlighten our understanding and add substantially to our knowledge of what are the best practices in leading people."

— *Vision.org*, 2009

"We now also know that the brain changes as a function of where an individual puts his or her attention. The power is in the focus."

— *Training Media Review*, 2006

Sociobiology: "Systematic study of the biological basis of social behavior. The concept was popularized by Edward O. Wilson in his Sociobiology (1975) and by Richard Dawkins (b. 1941) in The Selfish Gene (1976). Sociobiology attempts to understand and explain animal (and human) social behavior in the light of natural selection and other biological processes. A central tenet is that the transmission of genes through successful reproduction is the central motivator in animals' struggle for survival, and that *animals will behave in ways that maximize their chances of transmitting their genes to succeeding generations (aka the Primordial Drive as defined in this book).*"

— *Britannica Concise Encyclopedia*

In his much-debated book *The Selfish Gene*, famous scientist Dr. Richard Dawkins observed that "Intelligent life on a planet comes of age when it first works out the reason for its own existence…the argument of this book is that we, and all other animals, are machines created by our genes…We are survival machines—robot vehicles blindly programmed to preserve the selfish molecules known as genes…."

As a scientist, he was attacked by fellow scientists for the lack of a rigorous scientific method standard versus his observations, and for just focusing on one gene being perpetuated: the selfishness gene. I believe the critics did not see the forest for the trees, and missed the idea "donut" for the strict scientific method "hole." They missed the key issue of the all-controlling genes perpetuation

Primordial Drive in us, and its unequaled importance for understanding its affecting behavior in us and others.

Using insights from neuroscience, psychonomics (laws of the mind), sociobiology, and my own decades of hands-on C-level leadership experience and practice, this book will explore how the bedrock of human motivation wells from the deepest mechanisms in our brains—and how you can understand and use those mechanisms to your unique advantage.

These motivational insights go beyond even Abraham Maslow, Douglas McGregor, Herzberg, Stephen R. Covey, Jim Collins, Daniel Goleman et al, and many other popular leadership authors. Most of these have never directly led a company but have been good observers and authors (Douglas McGregor did lead Antioch College for a time). Also, more recent neuroscientific and sociobiological sources are introduced specifically for leadership contexts.

The Judo Principle, applying the principles of Judo/Jujitsu, means proactively harnessing the power of the key, basic Primal Drives *for* you, rather than letting them overcome you. The Judo Principle can also be used for <u>all</u> forces you encounter, pro and con (the latter for turning problems into opportunities). "Let the force be with you!"

The leader who understands the true, underlying, controlling Why of behavior motivation, and then Judo-leverages the insights, is the one who will achieve better, deeper, more powerful Type-A results. All leaders and managers—whether in small or large organizations; in private, public, or government sectors; male or female; thin or fat; marketing minded, financial minded, or engineer minded; and young or old—can benefit.

"Successful people do what unsuccessful people are not willing to do."

—Jeff Olsen, *The Slight Edge*

Understanding the Primal Drives

"Sociobiologists do not believe that animal or human behavior can be explained entirely by 'cultural' or 'environmental' factors. They believe that in order to fully understand behavior it must be analyzed with some focus on its evolutionary origins... then evolved behavioral mechanisms that allowed an organism a greater chance of surviving and reproducing would be more likely to survive in present organisms. Many biologists accept that these sorts of behaviors are present in animal species."

—*fact-index.com*

In accordance with the insights below, Primordial Leadership also helps leaders achieve unfair advantages (that are moral):

> "...Social relationships 'are merely byproducts of behavior originally (genetically) selected to avoid our being eaten by predators' [or today, being beaten by competitors, technological change, changes in the economy, or changes in the law—author's add]."
> —**Dr. Michael Gazzaniga,** Director of the SAGE Center for the Study of the Mind at UC Santa Barbara

In the parlance of Kevin Maney's *Tradeoff*, this book is focused on the "fidelity" (quality and comprehensiveness) end of the tradeoff spectrum. Trout and Reis noted in *Marketing Warfare* that all battles are fought in the mind and the mind is "80 percent emotional." The Primal Drives are even more powerful than our emotions (and even instincts), because they are the *source* of our emotions, instincts, and more. Thus leveraging the Primal Drives will drastically improve your leadership effectiveness versus past teachings and practices.

Special Notes for the Reader

In order to effectively teach and apply a shift in mindset, and recognizing that many people read books on an intermittent basis, any repetition or redundancy is intentional. This includes some key quotes and graphics. My goal is to ensure you fully understand and can fully apply this new knowledge, even at the risk of repeating what you already know.

Due to the inescapable structure of the English language, at times the masculine "he" is used for convenience when referring generically to individuals, but this book is equally written for and applicable to female leaders. Envision he/she.

Many quotes are from years ago and the attribution has been lost at times. I apologize for this, but the information is valuable for leadership use so we will proceed anyway.

Like the complexity of the brain's neurons, leadership is complex. Numerous chapters' cross references are provided for greater ease in navigating ideas.

||||||||||||||||||||||||||||||||||||||||||||||||||||||||||||||||||||||||||||||||||||||||||||||||||||||||||||||||||||||||||||||||||||||||||||||||

Example: Earnings Multiple Twice as High as Competitors!

It can and has been done, and much more. Why would an acquirer, whether private or public, pay for such high value that can only be realized in the future?

Simple. Their Primal Drives were heavily triggered...on purpose!

||||||||||||||||||||||||||||||||||||||||||||||||||||||||||||||||||||||||||||||||||||||||||||||||||||||||||||||||||||||||||||||||||||||||||||||||

Also, it's important to note that this book's "applied method" is based in real-world *direct observations* of my and other leaders' actions and subsequent results (or the lack thereof). Most other studies and views are based on *indirect observations*, usually by smart, well-intentioned academics with little direct leadership experience as to what does and does not work. Nevertheless, the indirect observations (many of which are cited in this book) are helpful, are used, and are built upon here.

My hope is this book will inspire more academic and scientific research and subsequent publications regarding the Primordial/Primal Drives and how they affect leadership success (or failure), related leadership attributes, and more.

You see, great leadership provides great value to all, including society at large. My hope is that the Primordial Leadership approach can be used to help you become a different and better leader.

"Leadership is getting someone to do what they don't want to do, to achieve what they want to achieve."

—Tom Landry

"The greatest leader is not necessarily the one who does the greatest things. He is the one that gets the people to do the greatest things."

—Ronald Reagan

Chapter One

Unleash The Results *Animal* in You...and in Others

A BRIEF HISTORY OF WESTERN LEADERSHIP THOUGHT IN THE LAST ONE HUNDRED YEARS

P olitical activist Marcus Garvey once noted that "A people without the knowledge of their past history, origin, and culture is like a tree without its roots." To establish the context for the new art of Primordial Leadership, we must first summarily trace the evolution of leadership thinking in the last one hundred years in the industrial regions of the world, especially the West. The shift of views and methods has been material, and is proceeding in the right direction (thanks to growing economic and political safety). As will be seen, leadership insights need to go one level deeper than past views, and how-to methods must be added.

In particular, we will notice a seminal evolution/revolution in "modern" leadership thinking, which started in America in the early twentieth century and continues to develop today. This context will show why this book's focus on the Primordial Drive and its enabling Primal Drives is the next step in continual leadership excellence.

Historical Summary

The wretched status of non-noble peasants and the like in the Dark Ages and Middle Ages is well known. Even apprentices to masters often endured harsh conditions.

During the Industrial Revolution, workers were treated as veritable servants. Prior to more modern sensitivities, workers up until the early to mid-1900s were very typically subjected to low status, harsh roles, abusive conditions, poor pay, and even physical danger and death.

The result of subsistence living and unequal powers between workers and owners were a recipe for economic (and occasional physical) abuse by today's standards. Workers' status was utilitarian only, with Self-Interest being the controlling Primordial Drive of most owners, alongside low concerns about workers' needs. Famous classics like Charles Dickens' *The Tale of Two Cities*, Victor Hugo's *Les Miserables*, and others depicted a squalid society for the non-privileged masses in Europe in the 1800s. Woody Guthrie's movie *Bound for Glory* and John Steinbeck's novel *The Grapes of Wrath* revealed abusive conditions for rural America workers into and after the Great Depression. For centuries until the mid-1900s, coal miner deaths were very high owing to lack of care by distant owners (my father was a coal miner in the late 1940s in West Virginia who was injured several times by mine falls due to poor mine safety standards being in place by owners).

"One evening little Gavroche had had no dinner; he remembered that he had had no dinner also the day before; this was becoming tiresome. He resolved that he would try for some supper."
— Victor Hugo, *Les Miserables*

"How can you frighten a man whose hunger is not only in his own cramped stomach but in the wretched bellies of his children? You can't scare him — he has known a fear beyond every other."
— John Steinbeck, *The Grapes of Wrath*

Attempts to unionize to gain power for the workers started to gain traction in the late 1800s, originally often by women. In the later 1800s and early 1900s in the US, Samuel Gompers (Cigar Workers' Union) and others eventually founded and confederated labor unions—i.e., the AFL (American Federation of Labor) and CIO (Congress of International Organizations), who later merged. They began to fight for more worker power against the top-down, one-sided impositions of industrialists. Using political power to augment workers' economic powers, federal administrations supported efforts to give more power to workers via passing the Clayton Act of 1914 and the Norris-LaGuardia Act of 1932. The Franklin Roosevelt administration then supported this trend via many labor laws, which included establishing the National Labor Relations Board (through the 1935 Wagner Act) to better protect workers. It was becoming recognized that a strong middle class, founded on power-based rewards sharing via union power to offset powerful, wealthy owners, was important to America's future strength.

||||||||||||||||||||||||||||||||||||||||||||||||||||||||||||||||||||||||||||||||||||||||||||||||||||||||||||||||||||||||||||||||

Early Labor Credo

"The trade union movement represents the organized economic power of the workers... It is in reality the most potent and the most direct social insurance the workers can establish."

—Samuel Gompers, early US labor leader

"(For) The Middle Class"

While recently at a Starwood hotel in San Francisco, the desk clerk had a Teamsters pin. When I commented on Teamsters being in the hotel business, his immediate reply was, "Yes, sir. We're making sure there is a middle class." While this is obviously a union talking point, he was fully invested in it.

||||||||||||||||||||||||||||||||||||||||||||||||||||||||||||||||||||||||||||||||||||||||||||||||||||||||||||||||||||||||||||||||

In Europe, political support for workers and union organizing somewhat lagged behind the aggressive pace in America initially, due to the fact that tradition was an even stronger force there. But eventually it surpassed even the US in terms of greater workers' rights and unionization. Today, while changing somewhat, politics and labor unions under generally quasi-Socialist political banners have major sway in some European countries.

In third-world countries, with more subsistence living, workers' rights generally continue to be weak, which contributes to economic disparity in many locations. In some, like present-day Venezuela, Bolivia, and other countries, socialists have politically garnered major worker reactions to wealth gaps to supposedly provide some power balance for more wealth equity. The success or failure of socialism is still being determined. (Generally, wealth gains based on redistribution without self-improvement and increased personal output efforts have not worked well.)

Dictatorships, monarchies, and theocracies of different types generally favor the powerful, who are needed to support the leaders and not revolt. North Korea is a good example. Workers suffer greatly.

An American Leadership Evolution Occurs

More modern leadership views began evolving in the early to mid-twentieth century in the West. As economic strength increased (and thus a sense of economic safety), there were more societal pressures for owners to be more compassionate and flexible. Owners also saw more margin of error and room to be less stringent. Many laws were also passed to help workers.

In the 1920s, the oft-cited and famous Hawthorne Studies of the Western Electric pieceworkers assembling phones were commissioned for the purpose of improving productivity. Up until that time, workers were considered automatons who would be managed according to Frederick Taylor's utilitarian, lowest-cost "Scientific Management."

The studies found that when workspace lighting was improved, productivity went up. When the lighting was lowered, surprisingly, productivity also went up. Why? It was finally understood that the motivating force behind the increased productivity was the fact that the researchers were *paying attention* to the workers, as though they were important and appreciated—and was not the changes in lighting.

It became apparent that more forces were at work than just physical ones. Many positive Primal Drives were being triggered, including Safety (if I'm important enough to be researched, my job might be important), Self-Interest (I might get more rewards), and Hope. Productivity improved. Success reports went far and wide. Slowly leaders began to think differently.

Then, in the 1930s and 1940s, modern leadership mores and insights began to actively take hold in the universities. Lectures and books began to portray workers as having more than one dimension.

Abraham Maslow and His Famous "Hierarchy of Needs"

The mid-twentieth century work of Dr. Abraham Maslow was a major breakthrough in beginning to better understand human behavior in the workplace (he observed his academic colleagues with great insight). This graphic and the below excerpts from Simons, Erwin, and Drinnien's *Psychology: The Search for Understanding* (West Group, 1987) provide important insights into his seminal work.

Humanists (Maslow and others) focus upon potentials. They believe that humans strive for an upper level of capabilities. Humans seek the frontiers of creativity, the highest reaches of consciousness and wisdom. This has been labeled "fully functioning person," "healthy personality," or as Maslow calls this level, "self-actualizing person."

Maslow has set up a hierarchic theory of needs. All of his basic needs are instinctive, equivalent of instincts in animals. ...Maslow's basic needs are as follows:

- Physiological Needs
- Safety Needs
- Needs of Love, Affection, and Belongingness
- Needs for Esteem
- Needs for Self-Actualization

As can be seen, Maslow importantly described the *impacts, or the results,* of the underlying (yet unidentified) Primal Drives, including a flow of needs as each lower level was met, and thus by identifying their symptoms well got close to the lower, causative Primal Drives, and even named one (Safety). Self-Interest, Transcendence, Sociability, and more are indirectly reflected in this two-dimensional needs "hierarchy." The truth of this is revealed when we ask: Why are these hierarchy drives like they are, and what caused them? Answer: The Primal Drives, located one level lower than Maslow took us.

Frederick Herzberg's Two Factors Theory

Dr. Frederick Herzberg, a psychologist and professor, helped us understand even more about human motivations, and his findings closely align with the lower-level Primal Drives we'll cover in this book, including how combinations can be "marbled" in their effect.

As explained by Joseph Gawel of the Catholic University of America:

"In summary, *satisfiers* describe a person's relationship with what she or he *does*, many related to the tasks being performed. *Dissatisfiers* ('Hygiene Factors'), on the other hand, have to do with a person's *relationship to the context or environment in which she or he performs the job. The satisfiers relate to what a person does, while the dissatisfiers relate to the situation in which the person does what he or she does.*"

The two groupings are:

Satisfiers	Dissatisfiers (Hygiene Factors)
Achievement Recognition Work itself Responsibility Promotion Growth	Pay and benefits Company policy and administration Relationships with co-workers Supervision Status Job security Working conditions Personal life

These have been very helpful to leaders who paid attention and used the observations. In terms of the Primal Drives, Herzberg missed the deeper Why causal factors, but he did reflect the marbling nature and impacts of them in varying, complex situations. Value was added.

Douglas McGregor's Theory X and Theory Y

Dr. Douglas McGregor was another master of leadership study, with *The Human Side of Enterprise* being his most recognized work. As a president of Antioch College, in addition to being a management professor, he brought unique "in-the-seat" experience to his observations. The experts at *Management Guru* provide a good overview:

His book *The Human Side of Enterprise* (1960) is a seminal work in management as it introduces a humanistic approach to the business perspective. McGregor's view was a critic on what we perceived as erroneous assumptions of the 'human relations' approach that was popular after the Hawthorne experiments.

...It was also clear to McGregor that prevalent management practices of 'bossing' workers through control and direction were also wrong and counterproductive.

...This McGregor termed 'Theory X' and the perspective assumed:

The average human being has an inherent dislike of work and will avoid it if he can...

Because of this human characteristic of dislike of work, most people must be coerced, controlled, directed, and threatened with punishment to get them to put forth adequate effort toward the achievement of organizational objectives...

The average human being prefers to be directed, wishes to avoid responsibility, has relatively little ambition, and wants security above all.

Reminiscent of Follett, McGregor argued for a shift of perspective towards one that emphasized the 'integration of individual and organizational goals.' This view of humans he termed 'Theory Y':

The expenditure of ...effort in work is as natural as play or rest. The human being does not inherently dislike work...

External control and the threat of punishment are not the means for bringing about effort... Man will exercise self-direction and self-control in the service of objectives to which he is committed.

Commitment to objectives is a function of the rewards associated with their achievement. The most significant of such rewards, e.g. the satisfaction of ego and self-actualization....

The average human being learns, under proper conditions, not only to accept but to seek responsibility. ...

The capacity to exercise a relatively high degree of imagination, ingenuity, and creativity in the solution of organizational problems is widely...distributed....

The intellectual potentialities of the average human being are only partially utilized.

The McGregor insights were very well received, but they still stopped short of the Whys behind them.

These and other professors' observations and writings provided the mid-twentieth century breakthroughs that have spawned perhaps scores of different books on management and leadership since. They allowed us to evolve from prior autocratic methods, where Theory X–type negative practices were predominant worldwide.

Dr. Peter Drucker Was Unequaled

Dr. Peter Drucker of Harvard has been called the most influential management thinker of the twentieth century. His advice was heeded by more leaders than any other person. His dozen or more books were, and are, devoured by leaders. Such important bromides as the following resulted:

- The effective executive achieves results.
- Be effective first; then be efficient.
- Do the right things first; then do things right.
- The purpose of a business is to create a customer.
- A manager is responsible for the application and performance of knowledge.
- A manager does things right. A leader does the right things.

He stressed five key things:

- Managing time
- Choosing what to contribute to the organization
- Knowing where and how to mobilize strength for best effect
- Setting the right priorities
- Knitting all of them together with effective decision making

Drucker's "Five Most Important Questions" were:

- What is our mission?
- Who is our customer?
- What does the customer value?
- What are our (target) results?
- What is our plan?

Notice that successful leadership yields *results*. He says to focus on the key areas that will make the biggest difference, picking only the key ones as important, communicating the Whys (including why the rejected alternatives are not as strong), gaining emotional support, and executing to exceed plans.

Getting the right people into the right jobs and organizing to strengths are emphasized. Ability versus schmoozing must be identified, nurtured, promoted, and supported. Meritocracy is enhanced culturally.

‖‖

No "Creeping Meatballs" Allowed!

Dr. Ed Maaze at Virginia Tech often gave examples of "face men" (vs. true leader athletes) being promoted due to socializing skills vs. true abilities. He derisively called them "creeping meatballs." The author has observed this dynamic, and some nepotism, in multiple companies. In one, a key, high-hubris P&L leader, in way over his head, literally put a Fortune 100 company so deep in the losses hole that, coupled with other accompanying problems, the company never fully recovered. He would preen and schmooze, but he was not only clueless, he was wrongheaded. Disaster resulted.

‖‖

"Creating a customer" is a key Drucker imperative, using marketing and innovation. The importance of the "knowledge worker" is a key, early Drucker focus. This includes developing a knowledge organization.

Self-management is an important leadership attribute as well, according to Drucker. Staying true to one's own self while also listening to conflicting, and even dissenting, opinions before deciding is an important success attribute.

Primal Leadership

Primal Leadership, the 2004 evolutionary book by university professors Daniel Goleman, Richard Boyatzis, and Annie McKee, got the closest yet to the key Whys behind how to successfully get the most out of yourself and others. It presents many compelling scientific studies and surveys linking the brain's functions to management, and has many good recommendations, but it still leaves important room for these deeper, more powerful Why elements to be revealed.

The pronouncements are materially correct and very helpful. An important exception is on page one of the book's preface, when the authors say that the "fundamental task of leaders… is to prime good feelings in those they lead." I believe they are confusing "means" and "ends." Dr. Drucker (and I) says that *results* are the fundamental task of leaders. Positive, motivated, "resonant" employees are certainly key means to those ends, and the preferred means if possible, but they are still just a means. This is why scores of actions that do not result in employees' good feelings happen every day—to achieve leadership results in the real world. To be fair, the authors later do show that negatives sometimes have to control a leader's decisions on behalf of real-world results.

The authors use the term Emotional Intelligence (EI) and Emotional Quotient (EQ) throughout. Their views are that leaders need to be emotionally sensitive and provide "meaning" and "resonance"[1] to the organization; leaders are also the key to Transcendence as "emotional guides."

The importance of humor is highlighted, which will be seen as a key Safety-releasing Primal Drive.

Much emphasis is made on "what" leaders do to lead. (Some mention of the importance of vision is noted, but not sufficiently in my view.) Positive feelings do not last long if the company is being beaten in the market due to a poor vision and resulting plan, and workers' jobs are at risk.

In an exciting and pioneering way, much time is devoted to the brain, its limbic system, the amygdala (shown here as part of the central limbic system, with the small, round amygdala containing fully 20 percent of the brain's synapses and controlling emotions), memory, reactions, and other brain processes—including the interactions with the prefrontal lobe (emotions). The authors seem to stress

---

1   Braksick in *Unleash Behavior—Unleash Profits* also talks about the importance of "discretionary (voluntary) performance," which is similar to "resonance." I fully agree.

the importance of the emotional areas over the neocortex ("thinking brain"). (I generally have the reverse view.)

An "open loop" brain is discussed, and how we make connections with others' brains to form "contagions" and to "latch." All the information is documented with many research studies and is useful to know as we move forward as leaders. Research showing the positive impacts of "upbeat" cultures, or "climates," are documented.

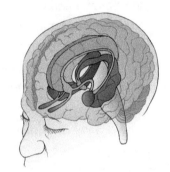

Perhaps too much emphasis is put on "good moods," upbeat styles, and more; however, as Gen Y and the Millennials enter the workplace, such styles are becoming increasingly expected. Based on documented studies, the authors show how "discord" (fear) causes a "flooding [increasing] of heartbeats" as the negative reaction. They note that "dissonance" (negatives) can be used when needed but will have short-term impacts only. They did not explain Why, however.

Four domains of EI and its sub-elements are reviewed, summarized as follows:

- Self-awareness
- Self-management
- Social awareness
- Relationship management

Leadership styles are structured in six groups that are also reviewed:

- Visionary
- Coaching
- Affiliative
- Democratic
- Pace-setting
- Commanding

A major, correct emphasis is on choosing A-players. Competency profiles are needed, objectively based on the best performers. Identify those with high potentials and move them up the ladder at the right pace. This fosters meritocracy also.

||||||||||||||||||||||||||||||||||||||||||||||||||||||||||||||||||||||||||||||||||||||||||||||||||||||||||||||||||||||||||||||||||||||||||||||||||||||||

Generally Terminate the Lowest 10 Percent

This mantra of Jack Welch received much resistance, but he persevered because he knew it would harness the Self-Interest and Safety needs of a person to not be in that 10 percent, thereby boosting performance individually and collectively. Also, the bar would naturally be constantly raised as a result for all.

But make sure objective criteria and due process are used!

||||||||||||||||||||||||||||||||||||||||||||||||||||||||||||||||||||||||||||||||||||||||||||||||||||||||||||||||||||||||||||||||||||||||||||||||||||||||

While *Primal Leadership* has been criticized for few *How* ideas to actually use, it does move the leadership evolution forward towards brain-centered Primordial Leadership, and it is recommended reading.

Many Other Leadership Insights Exist, But . . .

Ken Blanchard, Warren Bennis, Jim Collins, Stephen Covey(s), James Champy, Malcolm Gladwell, and many others provide excellent indirect observational insights to leadership, organizational development, change management, re-engineering, and other aspects of effective leadership. Max Dupree's *The Art of Leadership*, though irreverent, also has many practical insights and ideas from a leadership practitioner. Many situational insights are provided.

All of their ideas are sound—and all over the board. The proscriptions are many and are generally difficult to consistently implement in the myriad of situations that leaders encounter daily. They provide many good "What" and some "How" ideas, but they consistently fall short of the key underlying, more powerful Why factors explained by the Primal Drives.

Direct vs. Indirect Observations

The *direct* observations in this book are similar, but are more practiced than, the *indirect* observations by the authors listed below. For the purposes of this book, direct observations are those that have been also directly and personally practiced, while indirect observations are simply observed. Yet these indirect observations are still valuable. Even if Dr. Dawkins's observations in *The Selfish Gene* are just indirect observations by a very smart student of people and the universe, they are valuable.

For example, Abraham Maslow's Hierarchy of Needs was based on indirect observations, as were Herzberg's six Motivator Factors and eight Hygiene

Factors. McGregor identified Theory X and Theory Y via direct and indirect observations.

Trout and Reis in their classic *Marketing Warfare*, based on both direct and indirect observations, defined and organized the *four* different marketing warfare types:

- Offensive, if you are not the leader
- Defensive, if you are the leader
- Flanking, to create a new, differentiated value space
- Guerilla warfare, to hit and run

Using his indirect observations, Covey's *Seven Habits of Highly Effective People* identified *seven* key habits particularly useful for leaders and provided other key insights.[2] The Seven Habits are:

1. Be proactive
2. Begin with the end in mind
3. Put first things first
4. Think win/win
5. Seek first to understand, then to be understood
6. Synergize
7. Sharpen the (personal) saw

Stephen M.R. Covey's *The Speed of Trust* was based on his mostly indirect observations and life experiences. The works of Tom Peters, Warren Bennis (who, like McGregor, actually ran a university), Peter Drucker, and Ken Blanchard were based on their direct and indirect observations of leaders. Max Dupree's *The Art of Leadership* was based on his in-the-trenches C-level leadership observations, as a leader himself.

Gil Schwartz, a CBS communications director, provided many indirect observations in *What Would Machievelli Do?* under the pen name of Stanley Bing.

The ideas in Collins's and Porras's *Built to Last* were based on smart academics' insightful yet indirect observations of Citicorp, Procter and Gamble, Philip Morris,

---

2   Additional insights particularly important for leaders are (1) balance the P = PC equation (production = production capacity), (2) long-held paradigms can be self-limiting, and (3) maturity is the "balance" between consideration (for others) and courage (for helping yourself). All of these observations have advanced the art of leadership, including self-management.

American Express, Johnson and Johnson, Merck, General Electric, Nordstrom, 3M, Ford, IBM, Boeing, Walt Disney, Marriott, Motorola, Hewlett-Packard, Sony, and Walmart. They opined these recommendations:

- Practice clock building, not time telling
- Avoid the tyranny of the (either-) OR
- Focus on more than profits
- Preserve the core/stimulate progress
- Set big, hairy, audacious goals
- Foster cult-like cultures
- Try a lot of stuff and keep what works
- Support home-grown management
- Good enough never is

In *Good to Great*, Jim Collins studied, indirectly and observationally, Abbott Laboratories, Circuit City, Fannie Mae, Gillette, Kimberly-Clark, Kroger, Nucor, Philip Morris, Pitney Bowes, Walgreen, and Wells Fargo. He identified several key factors:

- Level 5 leadership
- First who...then what
- Confront the brutal facts
- The hedgehog concept
- A culture of discipline
- Technology accelerators

He observed that a Level 5 leader is "a paradoxical blend of personal humility and professional will." He endorsed internal promotions, opining that outsiders are "concerned more with their own reputation for personal greatness" and less so on "setting the company up for success in the next generation."

In *Crossing the Chasm*, in regard to marketing, Geoffrey Moore mostly indirectly and observationally defined five new product adoption phases:

- Innovator
- Early adopter
- Majority adopter

- Late adopter
- Laggard

Elements of each and examples were provided. It is a sort of Bible for technology marketers today.

As noted, the six Primal Drives are based on my own in-person, *direct* observation, research, and actual practice in the contexts of leadership, planning, marketing, and sales. The "actual practice" element is especially important and is consistent with "kinesthetic" learning, or "learning by doing," endorsed as the most effective by Confucius: "I hear; then I forget. I see; then I remember. *I do; then I understand.*" Directly seeing what does and does not work is priceless.

The key difference, backed by scientific research, is that *these observations have been both studied and practiced and not just theorized.* They can be, and need to be, applied in all aspects of self-management, leadership, marketing, sales, and other relationships.

Moving the Ball Forward

In addition to being based on direct observation, Primordial Leadership moves the ball forward from these great minds by addressing the very deepest Why behind behavior and providing powerful, practical tools and insights.

The next chapter, "Summary of the Primordial Drive and the Enabling Primal Drives," provides important context before the five chapters on implementation. The Primal Drives are the key, most basic, and most powerful Why factors that can be Judo-leveraged by leaders. Note: many books would spend their entire length on explaining the Primal Drives, and perhaps a chapter or two on implementation or application. I have done the reverse: I am spending just a chapter or two on the basic principles (supported by the more extensive Appendices A and B), and the bulk of the book on the implementation. In my experience, this will be far more useful to you as a practitioner in real-world business. Chapters 4 through 8 explain how to implement the principles and findings in chapter 2.

"One of [sociobiology's] central tenets is that genes (and their transmission through successful reproduction) are the central motivators in animals' struggle for survival, and that animals will behave in ways that maximize their chances of transmitting copies of their genes to succeeding generations. Since behaviour patterns are to some extent inherited, the evolutionary process of natural selection can be said to foster those behavioural (as well as physical) traits that increase an individual's *chances* of reproducing."—*brittanica.com*

"...Social relationships 'are merely byproducts of behavior originally (genetically) selected to avoid our being eaten by *predators*' [or today, being beaten by competitors, technological change, changes in the economy, or changes in the law]."—Dr. Gazzaniga, director of the SAGE Center for the Study of the Mind at UC Santa Barbara

Chapter Two

Unleash The Results *Animal* in You...and in Others

SUMMARY OF THE PRIMORDIAL DRIVE AND THE ENABLING PRIMAL DRIVES

(see Appendix A for more detailed information and leadership examples)

A s Trout and Reis noted in *Marketing Warfare,* all battles are fought in the mind of the participants. Also, the mind is "80 percent emotional." While they were generally right, the true power levers are even below our conscious mind, our emotions, our subconscious mind, and even our instincts—and it is where we will go, to the Primordial Drive and its enabling Primal Drives.

Who wins the Why wins. The best end results control, and people will rally around the best ends for their Primal Drives benefits. The Whys are the high ground, the pinnacle. The Covey "end."

This section will shine a beacon light on the key Whys for leadership success, referencing recent neuroscientific findings using brain science methods.

> "The number one thing that we have to do in order to increase our mind power and become aware of our true potential is to realize that we are capable of being number one!"
>
> —Stephen Hughes

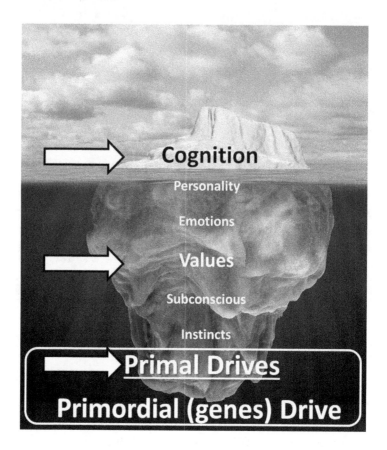

This section contains the Paul Harvey-like "reessstt of the story" six Primal Drives... six (of eight) key Primal Drives that serve and directly enable and protect our most basic, Primordial, DNA-level "engine." The Primal Drives can be then be powerfully, consistently, and purposely harnessed by applying the Judo Principle.

Learning from the Scientists

Infosource.org explains the genes perpetuation drive as follows: "*Genetic imperative* refers to the instinct of an organism to pass on its genes or reproduce. The phrase can be used to describe the behavior of specific organisms or a species as a whole."

In 2008 *Neuromarketing* observed that "...neuroscience is creeping into many areas of business endeavor. In a few years, a manager discussing Neuromarketing may find that she shares a common vocabulary with other managers attempting to adapt traditional management methods to the findings of brain science."

Dr. C. George Boeree of Shippensburg University stated that "There are certain *patterns of behavior* found in most, if not all, animals, involving the promotion of oneself, the search for status or raw power..."

According to Dr. Gazzaniga of UC Santa Barbara, "The human brain is a bizarre device, set in place through natural selection for one purpose—to make decisions that enhance reproductive success."

According to *public.wsu.edu*, "...an animal doesn't necessarily have to survive on its own. Another aspect of personal survival is the forming of social groups within a species. When staying alive is not just the responsibility of the individual, but other members of the species help the individual to survive, and vice versa, all members' chances are enhanced...The purpose of a social group and the level it takes is often dictated by how well it serves to promote the survival of the members."

Thus the Primordial imperative is to survive the very competitive, unsympathetic "natural selection" process that is required *for survival and to perpetuate the genes of the species,* which is the most basic, "primordial," DNA-level drive of all.

Thus, we need to proactively understand, appreciate, and leverage that core drive and its enabling Primal Drives in all human interactions—as an imperative.

The Six Key Primal Drives Contexts for Differentiated Leadership

Advantageous social behavior to get the most results via people is the strength-in-numbers vehicle! Per the preface, in a hypercompetitive, people-to-people social world like ours, we must find ways to stand out as better, different leaders from those around us and competing with us, in order to get them to respond in a desired way. We need a *differentiated advantage!*

Many additional Primal Drives quotes could be provided, but the above from very smart people help us to realize *several very important, useful, Judo-leveragable things*:

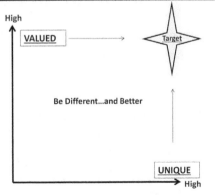

Differentiated Value Positioning

- There is indeed a deep, primordial "factory" or "engine" that drives our genes survival probability.

- Along with strong, spatial cognitive envisioning skills, and values, leveraging the Primal Drives provide strong, *differentiated* capabilities relative to those less knowledgeable. This allows us to stand out as different and more valuable.
- While we may know the term "Primal Drive," until now we have not deeply understood and applied on a purposeful basis the unequaled powers of the Primal Drives for better and different business results.
- Although we may not have been consciously aware of them, *the Primal Drives are even more pervasive and powerful to utilize than leadership training and management books to date have identified!* New insights allow new skills and actions.
- In our professional race for success *versus competitors and obstacles, and for potentials,* who best learns the underlying, genes-perpetuation-enabling Primal Drives (called the "proximate mechanism(s)" structure by the sociobiologists), and harnesses them proactively (via Judo leverage), have better, stronger leadership action levers to push and pull *than others.*

As noted, think of the Primal Drives as being the quiet but all-powerful "operating system software" that secretly manages everything we do, but well below the conscious/awareness level. While this is disconcerting in regard to being controlled in reality, it *can* be harnessed with awareness and purposeful actions. The payoffs are many.

Through my direct observations and experience, I have identified eight Primal Drives, but two are not readily leveragable for leadership (but do drive much of our autonomic systems):

- The reproductive drive
- The will to live (that drives the autonomic system)

The six key, leveragable Primal Drives, to be further explained below, in approximate power order, are:

1. Safety
2. Self-Interest (including greed)
3. Hope and Transcendence
4. Honesty and Trust
5. Energy and Time Optimization
6. Sociability (including altruism)

My observation is that the first three, in order, are the most powerful and prevalent, and the second three slightly secondary in power. "Marbling" (interacting) combinations in certain situations will be important to understand for situation correctness. The "art" of leadership is in the correct marbling for results.

Each Primal Drive will be reviewed below, including many sub-Drives and examples for each. These are generally ordered in importance. In given situations several will be involved, in a "marbled" sense. Their mixture and weightings will vary according to the situation and will be determined by what best assures the perpetuation of the genes. *Learning to assess each situation's Primal Drives hierarchy and marbled combinations is a skill that needs to be mastered, and the results applied.* Specific tables can be used in all human interaction areas to assess how to leverage the Primal Drives in each situation. Examples are in chapter 5.

1. Safety

This from LiveSciences shows just how pervasive and controlling the Safety Primal Drive is: "The brain's 'fear center' doesn't need to be working for an animal to learn to be afraid...If the region is damaged, another area can take the reins and allow the brain to continue to form fear-driven, emotional memories."

> "Fear is a universal emotion. New research...has begun to explain how this part of our brain works...two studies have shown how the central amygdala encodes memories of fear and controls learned responses to fear."
> —*LiveSciences*, **November 2010**

> "Freezing in the face of danger is an old, emotional response which probably was evolutionarily adaptive in our ancestral past."
> —*LiveSciences*, **December 2005**

Safety is the most controlling and pervasive Primal Drive we have, and it needs to be proactively harnessed *at all times;* yet its power and pervasiveness are usually not sufficiently understood, or not used strongly and purposefully enough. It is the elephant in the room, and we must *always* harness it to avoid getting trampled.

When change or a new opportunity or a challenge comes up, we will, far below the conscious level, instantly *first* determine if the contemplated action or situation is

Safe or not—or if not acting is perhaps even more unsafe. The scope and importance of the issue will determine the degree to which this factor plays.

Some aspects of how Safety deeply and quietly, but controllingly, works in specific situations include:

Job Commitment Safety

Do I work for a giver that will be fair and positive, or a taker that I cannot trust? Does management find the right first? Does management take credit and pass blame, or the reverse? Will merit prevail, or brown-nosing? Is inward political jockeying and undercutting the operating rule and an open opportunity for selfish opportunists? Will we be allowed to learn from mistakes, or get our head handed to us in a basket, possibly accompanied with a pink slip? Is management visionary to protect us from the future? Does management respect and protect the Safety power of quality? Is management fast to act or hide-bound? Do they listen and heed advice from those on the front line? Is decision making decentralized to give us some control, reflective that top management is trusting? Does honesty prevail at all levels? Does management truly appreciate new ideas and challenges, or not? Can I bring bad information to management and survive? Can I meet my autonomy needs as long as I produce well? Can I self-determine a future if I perform? Should I make an emotional commitment to the company versus just showing up and holding a spot?

Buyer's Personal Resources or Career Safety

When selling a product or a service solution to a buyer's decision team, the seller probably will not get a bonus for a good decision, but can get career-sanctioned, and even fired, for a bad decision. Thus there is not much room for Safety error in marketing and selling, especially B2B. In all such purchases the buyer's career Safety factor needs to be carefully identified and thought through beforehand, and harnessed via the Judo Principle. When the prices and/or features are about the same, Safety will be the determinative elephant in the room, and often hidden.

Product or Service Use Safety

For consumer and business purchasers, products/solutions Safety is always a key, even if an unspoken concern. Car warrantees (now up to 100,000 miles from some), home warrantees, electronics warrantees, products' money-back guarantees, conditional service payments, "claw-back" contract provisions, and product return policies are just a few examples.

Investors' Safety

For potential investors, will the Safety concerns offset the Self-Interest (greed) drive when considering an investment? Will the cash be enough to get to net cash critical mass, even if a downturn occurs? Will "liquidation preferences" for investors exist? For public companies, these types of considerations are really what is going on related to the P/E multiple, often unspokenly. The major types of risks investors look at are:

- Market/growth risk
- Competitive risk
- Financial risk
- Management risk
- Valuation risk
- Syndication risk
- Legal risk

Other Safety Arenas

Is the bank's debt loan going to be safe in the bank's eyes (are the key financial ratios solid, and is the "Times Interest Earned" net income factor large enough for Safety)? Are the covenants sufficient? Does solid collateral exist that can be monetized? If personally guaranteed, what assets exist, what is the credit score, etc.? Hundreds of other Safety areas exist.

These and many other such Safety "reads" are taken many times per day by each employee, by prospects, by partners, by investors, and by others at the Primal Drives level. How should we harness the near-manic need for Safety? If we do not, resistance will arise: although often unspoken, it will be determining in many situations.

‖‖‖

Use "Avoids" Positioning to Harness Safety Factors for You

It is amazing how strong the "avoid" approach is versus getting people to do things for normally the right, positive reasons.

This works with employees, partners, prospects, customers, and others. Facts and perceptions need to support the view, or major backlash will result. People hate to be falsely scared.

Note: This path is especially strong when dealing with "takers." They are very sensitive to avoiding negatives for themselves, far more so than are "givers." (More on this later.)

‖‖‖

Communicate Safety!

Leaders need to be conscious of Safety perceptions 24/7/365. Many methods exist, to be applied situationally. For change management, see chapter 7.

Humor is a very strong tool to use, including pursuing a fun environment. This communicates Safety in multiple ways. Touching is good (appropriate touching). Smiling is Safety bearing. Be upfront about the fears, and they may well go away. The real key is inward confidence and courage, to feel Safe yourself.

2. Self-Interest, including Greed, Selfishness, Self-Realization, and Some Narcissism

Adam Smith spoke of the Self-Interest drive in his 1776 *Wealth of Nations*, noting "the invisible hand of self-interest" as being pervasive and vital to success. He was correct.

Even though second in power of the Primal Drives to Safety, Self-Interest is the most controversial Primal Drive, especially if no Sociability is involved (taking into account what is also good for others) as a brake. Self-Interest (greed) is a derided Primal Drive, but it is a key to business, democracy, and capitalistic prosperity. It is key to wealth being generated for others, versus all being at subsistence levels (again). The envious and their protectors deride it. If marbled with other Primal Drives such as Sociability, then perceived reasonableness can occur.

Without Self-Interest and Hope overriding Safety, no investment would happen, and the result would be stagnation. Instead of the "pie" growing larger for wealth sharing, destructive arguments over the sharing of a fixed, or even shrinking, pie would ensue. Not pretty, or productive.

Personal drive seems to be centered here. See chapter 5 for more insights.

Self-Interest is vital and well practiced by all in varying degrees, with some being less constrained than others by Sociability and values. Therein lives destructive greed. Narcissism also resides there. Larceny and deception also, combined with weak Honesty and Sociability drives. Jealousy and envy are rooted here. But, we must protect our Self-Interests.

Be Prepared to Walk Away

When once negotiating a multimillion-dollar deal as president of a public company (who needed the deal for quarterly results!), we were assigned the number-two purchasing manager for a large organization that had figured out that "it made its profit on the buy." Buying was a bloodsport.

Leading a team of four, he was going to get our scalp, and kept the offer at about 15 percent of where we should have been.

After about five hours of this "we've got the gold so we rule" folly, I turned to our sales rep and said (in front of all), "Ken, this deal is not going to work, and let's catch an early flight home." Very graciously, I thanked the five buyers for their time, expressed sorrow we could not close the deal, closed my portfolio, and went out to call Delta—half with resolve and half feigning. I was prepared to leave if there was no fair deal on the table.

As I was changing the reservation, the chagrined buyer leader came out and asked me to come back and get the deal done. We quickly did, for what it should have been. Then we went to have a very cordial dinner with him and his team, after changing evening flight reservations back to the next morning.

"Taking" is in all of us to some degree, to get something for as little as possible—perhaps, in some, even if moral dishonesty is involved (determined by how strong the Sociability and Honesty Primal Drives are—or are not). However, taking does not wear well long term, so never give in to it becoming ingrained. Per Covey, balance courage and consideration.

Narcissism is an aspect of Self-Interest, defined by Twenge and Campbell in *The Narcissist Epidemic* (following *Generation Me*) as "having an inflated or grandiose sense of self."

They also note that the narcissism trend is worsening: "We know that narcissism has increased over time among individuals based on several datasets."

Ego in our personality mainly rests in/on Self-Interest. An egotist is self-absorbed to the detriment of sensitivity to others.

Hedonism is an aspect of Self-Interest, where wanton self-indulgence without any regard for the needs or perception of others, or common sense, prevails.

Autonomy is an aspect of Self-Interest (and Safety also), to not have to deal with others' pressures or Self-interest risks.

Envy of others is centered in the Self-Interest drive and is never productive. Envy is one of the worst aspects of human behavior, and is Self-interest based.

The differing values of different generations with varying Safety contexts and resulting varying Self-Interest and Sociability drives is a dynamic where increasing macro or aggregate Safety allows individual Self-Interest-based narcissism, etc., to emerge, to overcome Safety-enhancing Sociability restrictions. While not meant to be pejorative, the Millennials and "Gen Y" generations are great examples, and to lesser degrees each the Gen X and Boomers groups. Each had more contextual Safety than their parents before them due to continually improving surrounding economic circumstances and world events. "Me" over "we" is a resulting dynamic that must be managed.

In the 1950s, Isaac Asimov in his famous *Foundation* series coined the term "psychohistory" to reflect this dynamic in human behavior. In summary, in difficult times good decisions were made, and in times of plenty less good decisions were made.

With increased Safety also comes more Transcendence potential, which helps explain, in addition to more Safety due to more prosperity and opportunities, the younger generations' openness (and some would say drive) to change jobs versus their elders' higher level of Safety-based loyalty.

As shown, Self-Interest is a Primordial need in all of us. Leadership challenges have continued to evolve as a result of the generational changes due to increased Safety, the ascendance of Self-Interest, and the higher Hope and Transcendence needs. The great thing is that these Self-Interest drives are very easy to leverage. Proactively Judo-leveraging Self-Interest is a great opportunity in virtually all situations. Selfish persons are easy to leverage. Using "avoid" positionings is often needed to get them to do the right things as the "the lesser of the evils."

Compensation, recognition, autonomy, "avoids," and many other needs exist to be leveraged. Herzberg's findings (see chapter 1) highlighted this. Chapters 4 and 5 review what not to do and what to do in this regard.

3. Hope and Transcendence

I consider these linked drives to be a forward-looking Primal Drive that leads to Safety and Self-Interest *in the future*, recognizing that change is inevitable over time. It is like the brain intrinsically knows that "the only constant is change" and wants to Judo-harness it for Safety and Self-Interest later. It is impressive how strong it is in our "primordial soup" ("hope springs eternal"). I have seen it trump seemingly impossible Safety dangers. Short-term Self-Interest can be put aside due to future Hope. Energy calories are purposely expended now on the Hope of a better result later. When consulting I have seen employees stick with a seemingly failing company because they sensed that there was Hope (often versus change Safety risks). Employees will stay with a visionary, destructive leader due to near-term success Hope (but only for a short period usually, unless results occur).

Leadership that evokes a vision, hopefully correctly, automatically communicates Hope. The loss of Hope is when most relationships finally end, including at work—and home as well.

Transcendence is a Primal Drive for constant change and improvement over time, again to help assure improved Safety and Self-Interest in the future so that change will be protected against. Abraham Maslow picked up on the impacts of this in his "Hierarchy of Needs," but did not explain the underlying Why of the Primal Drives.

Among labor negotiators it is well understood that no matter how lenient and benevolent management has been in the past, a "what will you do for me now?" commanding Hope force will exist to support Self-Interest and job Safety. The rank and file want to consistently Transcend from where they are for Self-Interest, etc., even if it is currently better than the average.

The Transcendence Primal Drive provides a change openness mentality if properly positioned and explained. A key is to credibly paint a vision of what the planned actions will *avoid* in the future, or even now.

I believe that *curiosity* is a derived sub-force to help with Transcendence to situations that are more Safe, have more Self-Interest potential, and benefit other Primal Drives.

Ambition is sourced in Hope and Transcendence.

Likewise, *boredom* seems to be centered here. We need to continually transcend. "Wanderlust" is probably located here also.

Power seeking is Transcendence based, to position for more Safety and Self-interest gains.

Power Is a Means

Whether the Primordial Drive "marbling" is led by Safety, Self-Interest, Hope, or others, power is a key success factor for achieving these drives.

In business, the one who controls the power forces has a distinct competitive advantage—and more chance of the Primal Drives being served. Seek power but use it well. Lincoln once noted that a test of a person's character is how he uses power.

|||||||||||||||||||||||||||||||||||||||||||||||||||||||||||||||||||||||||||||||||||||||||||||||||||||||||||||||||||||||||||||||||||||||||||||

4. Honesty and Trust

|||||||||||||||||||||||||||||||||||||||||||||||||||||||||||||||||||||||||||||||||||||||||||||||||||||||||||||||||||||||||||||||||||||||||||||

Elvis Had It Right!

"...we can't go on together with suspicious minds..."

|||||||||||||||||||||||||||||||||||||||||||||||||||||||||||||||||||||||||||||||||||||||||||||||||||||||||||||||||||||||||||||||||||||||||||||

I believe these drive elements are protectors of Safety, Self-Interest, Transcendence, and Sociability, today and tomorrow, and are kind of a "third-dimension" protective Primal Drive for managing results via people relationships over time. These are powerful drives and important to Judo-leverage, but truth must be pervasive to be successful. The Honesty and Trust drive results in all of us having a good barometer of the character and thus dependability (Safety) of other parties in a relationship relative to our own self-interests. Others' self-interest (Safety, Self-Interest, etc.) will unconsciously calibrate our own trustworthiness, and they will react accordingly. A relationship without Honesty and Trust will be a weak one over time and not fulfill its promise for any of the parties. Thus, being dishonest and untrustworthy hurts the untrustworthy person also, and most.

Stephen M. R. Covey's *Speed of Trust* (as summarized by Gather.com) states that:

After summarizing why trust is so important, Covey explains the Four Cores of Trust: integrity, intent, capabilities, and results, and how these Four Cores of Trust will impact the way people view you and trust you. The Four Cores of Trust are part of the first wave in the Five Waves of Trust model. The first wave is Self-Trust. In the Five Waves of Trust, Covey explains each wave in detail and what makes up each one, using examples and even in some cases giving charts for readers to fill out. The other Four Waves of Trust are: Relationship Trust, Organizational Trust, Market Trust, and Societal Trust. In the second wave, Covey explains the thirteen behaviors that make up a trustworthy person, varying from talking straight to creating transparency, to showing loyalty, and to simply clarifying your expectation of someone, among others that are just as important.

The fact that "the truth hurts" has led some to believe that being evasive or dishonest is the easier path. However, other people have very rich "antennae" and will subconsciously quickly pick up honesty and trustworthiness concerns (women are especially good in assessing this; a result of their role in genes-perpetuation Safety, as explained in chapter 8). Goleman et al called it "latching." How we "walk our talk" over time will constantly be calibrated by others in terms of trustworthiness, or not. A negative rating will cause caution and possibly even rejection. Potential impacts will be diminished. Those that unconsciously reflect "do as I say and not as I do" will be quickly found out and diminished. That "95 percent of communication is nonverbal" will reveal the truth rather quickly.

Use Lesser of the Evils to Control "Takers," Who Are Often Dishonest Due to Character Flaws

They are figuratively dangerous. They are often contrarian, and need to be outmaneuvered or cordoned off where no harm can result.

Once a CEO friend asked me for advice about handling a negative, contrarian board member. I told him the key was to position the CEO's ideas as lesser of the evils from the start, and what we (and the board member) did not want to happen. Once the "avoids" circle is drawn very well, the contrarian will self-manage so worse outcomes can be avoided—and the right things then are agreed to. He said it worked.

The imperative for ethics, and unconditional ethics, is centered in the Honesty and Trust drive of others, marbled with the Sociability and Safety drives for strength in numbers. Always.

It should be noted that if a non-trust situation is seen to be short term and will end, the other person's Self-Interest and other Primal Drives may override this concern. This will not endure, however.

For self-management, leadership of others, marketing, sales, and other relationships, Honesty and Trustworthiness are critical to sustained personal success (Safety, Self-Interest, Hope, etc.) on a consistent basis. In reality, "the truth will set you free!" As a small example, if you make a mistake, as we all do, be the first to openly raise it. That act takes energy out of the problem, reflects character, and will automatically increase your Trustworthiness quotient. The obverse is true also if you try to protect what everyone knows was a mistake.

Honesty and Trustworthiness are powerful Primal Drives to be Judo-leveraged, for you and not against you. Such drives must come from the core of individuals to be received as real and not just "put on."

5. Energy and Time Optimization

The Energy and Time savings Primal Drive is responsible for very innate, DNA-level, important sub-drives such as laziness, procrastination, continually seeking easiness and convenience, taking shortcuts, and saving time. There is a drive in us that says to save Energy calories for emergency use when needed, and to do so purposely. Thus, laziness and procrastination are no accident; they have a core, DNA, genes-protection purpose. Saving Time has the same imperative.

When the Energy or Time cost is worse than the gain, we do not act, which may seem lazy or procrastinating, but it is deeply calculated. It is Primordial.

We constantly strive to get more results from our Time use. We see Time as a priceless resource and try to optimize its use for gain. We understand the truism of *tempus fugit*. The truism that "time is money" is also reflective. We constantly look for more results in a time period. We also understand that "timing is everything." It is an underlying Primal Drive.

What are some everyday examples? (Think about the Why behind each of these.)

- Easy-open packages
- Fast-food drive thrus
- Mouse and icons vs. a keyboard (Windows vs. DOS; Mac vs. PC)
- Speech-to-text software vs. keying
- Express lanes in the store
- Shortcuts through lawns or bushes vs. using the sidewalk
- Self-checkout lanes
- Pre-packaged foods
- Meals Ready To Eat (MREs)
- Microwaves and microwave products
- Jets vs. prop planes
- Bullet trains
- Express buses

- HOV lanes
- Quick Install instructions vs. the full manual
- FedEx or UPS vs. USPS
- Fax, e-mail, and now IM, texting, Twitter, Facebook, etc.
- Elevators and escalators vs. stairs
- Cruise control
- Bookmarks vs. typing URLs
- Welfare vs. work for some (even if self-liberties are surrendered)
- The "nanny state" where everything is done for us, until George Orwell's *1984* "Big Brother" world exists
- Many more examples could be listed for Ease, Speed, and Time savings actions.

All of these and hundreds more save us Time and mental or physical Energy. IT IS IMPORTANT TO NOTE THAT THESE ABOVE EXAMPLES DID NOT JUST HAPPEN. THEY WERE *CAUSED* TO HAPPEN BY THE LOW-LEVEL ENERGY SURPLUS/TIME SAVING PRIMAL DRIVE.

Habits are a result of this Energy Optimization Primal Drive. Habits allow proven, automatic actions with no mental calories or Time delay needed to act. Net "input-output" gains result.

Comfort zones also form due to ease and Energy savings control—and Safety probably, since the present outcome is pre-known versus variable. These comfort zones become the enemy over time due to changes constantly occurring. We get comfortable with the status quo (where perceived Safety, Self-Interest, and Energy saving also reside), and do not want to expend the energy to change or accept the risks.

Comfort Zones Can Be Dangerous

Pavlov's frog experiment is reflective. If we throw a frog into hot water, it will quickly jump out. But if we put it in ambient water and then slowly heat it, the frog can stay until it dies.

Comfort zones that do not register the dangers in surrounding changes can quickly yield similar results.

Related *Complacency,* the anti-zeal, is partly lodged in the Energy and Time Optimization Primal Drive. We get lazy to save Energy. The problem is that when an emergency arises due to complacency, as it always will, the problem is far advanced and much more expensive to resolve—and it may not be resolvable.

Paradigms are derived from the Greek *paradiegma* (pattern) and defined in *Dictionary.com* as "… (a) set of forms all of which contain a particular element…a display in fixed arrangement of such a set…an example serving as a model; pattern…"

Paradigms are centered in Energy saving also, with some Safety (proven) and Self-Interest marbling also. Paradigms are pattern-based filters that allow situational views and judgments to be made with no mental (Energy) effort. Covey's *Seven Habits of Highly Effective People* warns us that paradigms can become our single biggest impediment to correctness in a situation. Constantly check and validate your paradigms.

I believe that the *"memes"* concept is based in Energy saving, similar to paradigms. These ideas that become viral are an Energy-saving way to organize the mind with certain beliefs in a low-energy use way.

Acronyms are a purposeful Energy-saving element. Ask the military (e.g., DoD, DLA, JSOC, TRADOC, SOCOM, NATO, SEAL, AFCENT, and thousands more). In business, terms like SOX (Sarbanes-Oxley), IRR, NPV, ROI, SBA, SEC, IRS, VC, CEO, COO, CFO, VP, EVP, ERP, HRIS, and thousands of others exist to get a point across with near-zero mental calories or Time used.

Shortcuts and summaries save Energy. Cliffs Notes, executive summaries, briefs, PowerPoint slides versus full documents, etc., are used to convey core information with optimal Energy and Time saving value.

As noted, in *Blink*, Malcolm Gladwell referred to the Primordial nature of the unconscious mind for making correct assessments very quickly, in a blink, and drawing on (lower-level) non-conscious (Primal Drives) sources to do so. This "blink" is an instantaneous, low-Energy and Time-use "read" by the Primal Drives construct in a given, marbled situation.

Kinetic energy in people ("a body in motion tends to stay in the same motion; a body at rest tends to stay at rest," per Isaac Newton) is a result of the Energy-saving protection drive, probably with Safety and Self-interest elements as well. A pattern or process tends to move forward as it has in the past. Changing a direction is very hard to do, but often vital. Getting it started is hard and requires a "compelling" reason to expend Energy and Time resources (that may become "the lesser of the evils").

As seen, the Energy and Time Optimization Primal Drive is pervasive and affects all that we do, far below the conscious level.

6. Sociability (Constraints on Self-Interest, to Enhance General Safety)

Sociability has a genes-perpetuation purpose far beyond just being nice. Per Dr. Gazzaniga of the UC Santa Barbara Center for the Study of the Mind, "...Social relationships are merely byproducts of behavior originally selected to avoid our being eaten by predators" (or today, being beaten by competitors, technological change, the economy, or legal changes—author's add).

The below excerpt from the *Associated Press* (December 2010) reviews findings about that part of the brain that controls Sociability. But what drives it to do so? Answer: the Sociability Primal Drive.

> NEW YORK—Do you spend time with a lot of friends? That might mean a particular part of your brain is larger than usual.
> It's the amygdala, which lies deep inside. Brain scans of 58 volunteers in a preliminary study indicated that the bigger the amygdala, the more friends and family the volunteers reported seeing regularly.
> "That makes sense because the amygdala is at the center of a brain network that's important for socializing," says Lisa Feldman Barrett, an author of the work published online Sunday by the journal *Nature Neuroscience*.
> ...People have one amygdala in the left half of the brain and another in the right half. The findings of the new study held true for each one....

Sociability is not a whim or accidental. It is a key survival drive, varying in intensity across individuals, is most strong in trying situations, but is the weakest Primal Drive generally. The power of "strength in numbers" causes us to protect Social circles and ties that can contribute to our Safety, Self-Interest, Energy saving, and Hope/Transcendence. This drive requires us to obey mores, customs, ethics, etc., such as the Ten Commandments, the Golden Rule, and the Pillars of Islam. Elaborate rituals and practices exist to keep the Social fabric strong. It provides some control over our Self-Interest excesses.

Owing to nurture variances, some are obviously better than others at Sociability, and some need it less than others due to the confidence and comfort of operating alone, or having insecurity about being around others. Some even have an anti-Social personality, perhaps because they were "potty-trained at gunpoint" when growing up, in a negative environment where they had to emotionally pull within themselves to psychologically survive.

Cultural Sociability norms (and values) vary by region of the world and even in regions of the US. For example, "Southern hospitality" is a truism. Evolving from a history of agrarian-based poverty in the South versus the more industrial, richer North, Social interdependence needs were higher in the South, so the Sociability norm was higher. "Southern hospitality" is the result, and it is real even today.

That there is sociology, the study of groups, attests to the existence of the Social Primal Drive. Social drives will exist inside a company (a key for "organizational development," or OD). When the informal organization is actually in control, Social factors are very strongly at work in a company, for good or bad (for good if top leadership is flawed, and bad if leadership is correctly focused but burdened by a bad culture it has inherited). The existence and strength of a "grapevine" reflects Social drives at work. Political cliques are the Social drive in action, and strength in numbers for Safety and Self-Interest.

Driven by Safety, Self-Interest, Hope, etc., "pecking orders" form in all animal species' Social orders, reflecting how the Primal Drives interact. Pecking orders are true in households, communities, businesses, governments, and among nations. In formal or informal organizations, different sub-drives determine the power pecking order for each. A striation of power and influence will form and generally be accepted by most (for their net Safety, Self-Interest, Hope, etc.). The combination of vision, ability and goodness, together, will prevail. Negative structures cannot sustain in the long run (due to the Safety and Self-Interest needs of others that will prevail over time to punish threats and dismantle negative pecking orders). Managing this force is important, with merit-based goodness ("meritocracy") prevailing.

Altruism is centered in the Sociability arena. There is Safety strength in numbers by helping others, and getting the rewards indirectly by contributing to causes others will reward. Note, however, this force is far down the power list versus other Primal Drives, so in general cannot be depended on consistently versus stronger Primal Drives such as Safety, Self-Interest, Hope/Transcendence, etc. Altruism often fades quickly when higher-order Primal Drives are controlling, which is a special challenge to volunteer and charity organizations (see chapter 8 for some action insights).

To repeat, Sociability has a genes perpetuation purpose far beyond just being nice.

Summary

As business leaders we are after results, and we are on a constant quest to better achieve those results. The *combination* of understanding the importance of the Primal Drives (that enable the Primordial Drive for genes perpetuation), envisioning, and values, and executing this understanding via the Judo Principle is a 1 x 1=4 combination. Each without the other is incomplete. The combination is essential to optimal results. Weak insights/visions/ideas, even well executed, cause weak results. Good ideas poorly executed cause weak results. Together, good insights, visions, and ideas that are motivational to others are powerful and provide a path to success. As Drucker noted, "Do the right things first, then do things right."

The Primal Drives, to enable the core Primordial Drive (genes perpetuation):

1. Safety
2. Self-Interest (including greed)
3. Hope and Transcendence
4. Honesty and Trust
5. Energy and Time Optimization
6. Sociability

Chapter Three

Unleash The Results *Animal* in You...and in Others

THE IMPORTANCE OF ENVISIONING AND VALUES FOR LEADERSHIP

P er the earlier "iceberg" graphic, the other brain tiers are important and complement the Primal Drives. This is especially true for cognition's "spatial" thinking for envisioning, and for a leader's values (which affect others' Primal Drives).

Other brain-tier elements are affected by personal (nurture) experiences, so are not as consistently and broadly usable. The reader is referred to many sources for understanding each. "Instincts" are the sensory-response mechanisms to put the Primal Drives' needs into action in a specific sensory or cognitive situation.

Spatial Thinking and Vision

Stephen Covey suggested that we "begin with the end in mind." That great sage Yogi Berra observed that "You can't hit 'em if you can't see 'em." We will see that whoever has the best resulting vision and values (for others' Primal Drives) will be at the top of the inevitable "pecking order" that always forms (in all animals).

Differentiated leadership requires an innate ability to intangibly and spatially *envision an end beforehand*, and the path to get from here to there (or from there to

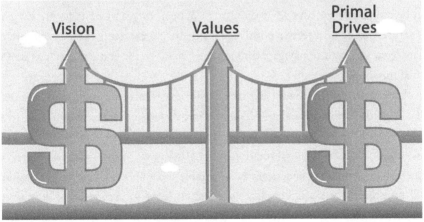

here, like working a maze backwards, as I do—notice the speed difference). Relatedly, one source wrote long ago that many professional golfers will walk a new course *backward* before playing the first round.

Being able to spatially and temporally "see" into the future, without even consciously thinking about it, is an important gift, and it can be honed by processes in chapters 5, 6, and 7. Its presence is an unfair advantage. Being able to "see" an end before beginning, and what should not happen to get there, is highly valuable. By natural processes, affective positive and negative forces along the way will present themselves, so a path to navigate through the "rocks" to the end will result as well via spatial thinking.

A group at the UC Santa Barbara Center for Spatial Studies found that "At a basic cognitive level, spatial thinking is three-dimensional perception and recall. Strong spatial thinkers can easily recognize the same assembly of blocks in different positions (in so-called 'mental rotation' tests). They always turn in the right direction when leaving buildings and never have trouble locating their cars in parking lots. Well-developed spatial thinking leads to spatial literacy—the capacity to learn about, analyze, and explain the natural and social worlds through spatial visualization, technologies..."

These UCSB studies tend to have a physical relationship focus. However, spatial thinking by leaders is 100 percent intangible, perceptual, and time-in-motion. For leaders it is about the ever-moving, constantly evolving understanding of:

- What are the end-in-mind objectives, both positive and negative (i.e., what needs to be avoided)?
- Prioritization
- What are the affective input-output forces relative to objectives?
- The cause-effect relationships of forces
- The motion and flow of forces
- Time-based changes in forces over time, and the impacts
- Experience
- Common sense of things
- Outside-in sensitivity, empathy, and insight (on a give-to-get basis)
- Risk assessment
- Resulting plan elements
- Communicating and persuading
- Executing, monitoring, and rewarding
- Constant recalibration, but staying the course with perseverance unless material events call for change ("simultaneous tight and loose properties").

Great athletes envision success and then execute to the vision. Creative people, like architects, composers, and others, envision the result *before* they start. A leader must do the same. A literal back-to-front "roadmap" vision in the mind is needed. Its motivating force is palpable. Yogi was right.

Being able to quickly "read" a map is a spatial/visual skill, like quickly figuring out the very confusing London subway system. A strong spatial mind is like having an internal GPS and gyroscope.

Having employees tell you that they would follow you across a minefield is a metric of your envisioning capability. The other-side end objectives are valuable to them (justifying the risks), and they know that you know how to navigate all of them through the risks and resistances that will be encountered on the journey.

Once the end is defined, the road to it is automatically more clear. For leading a project, program, or entity, moving *right-to-left* is smart when planning:

1. Establish the right end: List goals, and what should *not* happen
2. Then move sequentially to the left:
   a. Key Success Factors
   b. Strategies for KSFs

    c. Tactics for strategies

    d. Organization

    e. Assignments for tactics

    f. KPIs

    g. Deadlines

    h. Resources

    i. Measurement

    j. Rewards

3. Note that this is a Why, What, How, Who, When flow. *Always* use it.

Also note that this flow generally supports SMART (Specific, Measurable, Action-oriented, Resourced, Time-based) goal setting, for more Safe performance to plan.

It is amazing what specific, goals-focused, and time-based accountability will do to protect results. Per Jack Welch, "What gets measured gets achieved."

Intuition, foresight, prescience, etc., are critical in a leader, and result to some degree from spatial skills. *eHow.com* notes that "Whereas left-brain or linear thinkers excel in sequential tasks such as logic and math, visual spatial thinkers often have what many call *intuitive* skills. These skills include making cognitive leaps from seemingly disparate things. There doesn't necessarily have to be a logical order or explanation for the understanding. Visual spatial thinkers can often connect dots, so to speak, by intuition."

Women's Intuition

As explained in chapter 8, women have especially strong intuition skills, especially about people. Listen to it!

At a recent Chief Strategy Officer (CSO) conference, many of the excellent CSO presenters were women, from Dell, SunTrust Bank, AMC theatres, and more.

Foresight, or seeing ahead, is critical in a leader.

According to *Thesaurus.com,* the synonyms for foresight are: "anticipation, canniness, care, carefulness, caution, circumspection, clairvoyance, discernment, discreetness, discretion, economy, far-sightedness, foreknowledge, forethought, insight, long-sightedness, perception, precaution, precognition, preconception, premeditation, premonition, prenotion, prescience, prospect, providence, provision, prudence, sagacity." The antonyms are: "hindsight, ignorance."

Prescience is an intangible foresight ability. *Merriam-Webster* defines prescience as: "an act or the power of foreseeing" and "foreknowledge of events."

While some say the left brain/right brain definition is too simplistic, a leader needs to have both—but especially the right-brained "spatial" capabilities. Left-brained details can be delegated.

In *Seven Habits*, after he advises us to "Begin with the end in mind," Covey suggests that only 1 percent have such spatial capabilities. Perhaps his estimate is a little low, but the percent is small regardless. Being able to synergistically combine *all of* the Why, What, When, How, Who, and How Much aspects over time to achieve results is a powerful, differentiating combination of left and right brains. The more conceptual, commanding Why must come first, and it is always intangible and futuristic to some degree.

Without the ability to conceptualize an end, and the optimal path before starting, then "any road will take you there," as the Mad Hatter told Alice in Lewis Carroll's satire *Alice in Wonderland,* when she asked for directions but did not know where she wanted to go. "MBO" (Management by Objectives) programs use this ends-focused principle, but can have many shortcomings in practice. Chapter 6 provides the "MAP" (Milestones Achievement Progress) program as a better end-in-mind leadership approach. (This includes for cross-departments' inter-dependencies management, which is often overlooked.)

The Rand Corporation's General Foods Hypothesis that envisioning-based good strategy is more important than good tactics reflect that spatial "gray matter" is a very precious commodity and essential to leadership. Without the right focus/vision/ picture, execution excellence will not help much.

Therefore, in any meeting, when planning or conceptualizing, the ability to first correctly conceptualize the correct *end(s) and the optimal path to get there* is an important leadership intangible. Being able to "see" how things fit together, and correct cause-effect associations, without even thinking about them, is an insight art and a blessing. People will sense it and follow. (Chapter 6 provides a "Dynamic Programming" tool to help with this thinking style, even if it is not native to you.)

Higher-purpose "should be" envisioning versus "as is" thinking is a key to motivation.

Also, projecting the impacts of the power forces in the above "change cube" graphic over the planning horizon is important. New projects will take quarters or years to gestate and prove to be successful or not. All of today's success and risk and affective factors will have changed by then. Thus, future "vectoring" of value positioning and time-based changes is critical. This is consistent with Wayne Gretsky's famous statement: "I skate to where the puck will be, and not to where it is."

In *Managing at the Speed of Change,* Connor observed that "Effective leaders are capable of reframing the thinking of those whom they guide, enabling them to *see* that significant (continual) changes are not only the imperative, but achievable."

Predicting and harnessing inevitable change impacts over time is vital. Chapter 7 provides some forecasting and planning tools.

Like in the actual example below, outside-in thinking needs to be combined with inside-out learning, memory and realities, with spatial management of the interactions.

No vision can be strong without "both ends of the cognitive and Primal Drives bridge" being simultaneously applied, with Values, and in a bidirectional and auto-correlative manner. This means that each element actively influences the others, and the sum or dividend or product is a result of that interaction.

Example Desired Vision Positioning*

Market Opportunities

Desired Position

Capabilities For Achieving Vision

*From the Chief Strategy Officer Summit, May, 2013

Knowledge Is Critical to Have and to Continually Gain

Socrates noted that "There is only one good, knowledge, and one evil, ignorance." Sir Francis Bacon opined that "Knowledge is power." Drucker observed that "A manager is responsible for the application and performance of *knowledge*."

Knowledge is critical for spatial thinking and memory development. It is important for execution success as well. Without knowledge there is no frame of reference for envisioning, decision making, executing, monitoring, and more. Knowledge quality is a key differentiator. Get it. Perhaps hire or contract it. Use it.

||||||||||||||||||||||||||||||||||||||||||||||||||||||||||||||||||||||||||||||||||||||||||||||||||||||||||||||||||||||

An Example of Both Knowledge Types

As an analogy, the captain (leader) of a Navy vessel must know *all* of the following:

- General people motivation and leadership
- General Navy procedures and regulations
- General battle strategies and tactics (sea, air, and land)
- General logistics
- General organization
- Every specific system and process on the ship, how they interact with each other, and how the personnel interact with the systems
- The specific mission that has been assigned to the ship

||||||||||||||||||||||||||||||||||||||||||||||||||||||||||||||||||||||||||||||||||||||||||||||||||||||||||||||||||||||

There is no one best answer for the ages-old question about being a knowledge generalist or a specialist. Each has strengths and weaknesses in alternative areas. Optimally, having *both* is an advantage: general business excellence knowledge, and specific knowledge about the industry, the solutions, and the duties of a role.

In their Summer 2013 article "The Wise Leader," Booz and Company stated that the leader has to balance both broad and narrow vision. This is true; however, I believe that generalist knowledge is better long term. Specialist knowledge can be more easily hired.

Memory Is Important to Great Envisioning, Tactically and Strategically

If you don't have it, get it. Or hire it (including using consultants). It is important to have correct reference frames for ideas envisioning, whether strategic or tactical. Knowledge and memory are the fonts of such references. Bring in others' memories (and their related knowledge) and listen to them. Many memory and knowledge-improving books exist for memory self-development.

Memory is associative in nature, so storing information related to other information is how the mind organizes memory and manages recall. The more we make a knowledge point emotional and related to the Primal Drives, and past learning, the more it is stored for later recall when needed.

Win the "Why" Positioning

People need to know that a clear end and path exist, and that it is the right end and path. Defining the Why correctly and communicating it effectively are key to people feeling Safety, Hope, potential Self-Interested payback, etc. This unleashes the Primal Drives "animal" in them. Clarity of good ends and the correct path (and roles) increase confidence, commitment, energy, and common-cause teamwork.

In *Smart Thinking*, Dr. Art Markham observed that "Getting answers to *why* questions plays a key role in everyday life...asking *why* allows people to create explanations...*causal reasoning*..."

We also saw earlier that the person who best knows the Why will be the boss. The advantages of Why are many and powerful. The Why factors must integrate, weight, and sequence the key elements of the power forces, changes in the forces, and others' Primal Drives needs—and harness all of these affective factors for success, together.

In his great book *Start with the Why*, author Simon Sinek talks about "the Golden Circle," which starts with the Why. He notes that great leaders have always had this skill more than others, and it is the key to their enduring success. They were always able to motivate others by their Why envisioning and communications.

He also correctly notes that all companies know What they are doing, and How. Positioning the What/How relative to the higher-order, more important Why is the key to differentiated success. Then the What, How, When, Who, and How Much can be correctly defined as well to guide tactics in an optimal-results way. *Primal Leadership* by Goleman et al talks about resonance and meaning being important Why factors.

In Root Cause Analysis (RCA), popularly attributed to Kepner-Tregoe, the "5 Whys" is a good construct to use. The focus is to avoid just flailing at the "smoke" symptoms that would continue to billow as long as the most base-level, causative "fire" still burns.

Very importantly, the Why insights and their communication need to be:

- New and also valuable for *all* parties' self-interests (Primal Drives) to be stimulated
- Credible according to common sense (even if it stretches some) over time
- Sensitive to internal and external power forces that will impact programs and results, and how to harness these for the ends to be achieved
- Well defined and communicated
- Tied to the supporting What, How, When, Who, and How Much elements that will be needed
- Metricized (SMART goals, KPIs, etc.)
- Regularly monitored, measured, and evolved
- Regularly reported
- Rewarded
- Revisited on a scheduled basis

Only after core values and the ability to understand the Primal Drives at work (and how to use them), I believe this native "spatial" skill of Why envisioning is the number-one attribute of a leader. Even a narcissistic "jerk" with the right vision who protects the Safety, Self-Interest, and Hope of subordinates will have zealous followers because the success potential will be worth the negatives (I have personally seen this). In the obverse, a nice person in whom no one has visionary faith will have few followers because the vision does not meet Primal needs of subordinates (Safety, Self-Interest, Hope, Energy and Time Optimization, etc.).

Of course, an envisioning, motivating leader is the best combination (chapters 5, 6, and 7).

Values

Values are significantly learned by life's experience and again are formed on the bedrock of the Primal Drives. The leader's values will be reflected by the organization.

Below are just of few of the key value spectrums for leaders. The underlined ones are what are needed to stoke the Primal Drives in others (chapter 5). The obverse functions are what not to do (chapter 4, "You Can't Manage Others until You First Manage Yourself").

- Honesty or dishonesty?
- Risk taking or risk aversion?
- Brave or cowardly?
- Accepting responsibility or shirking?
- Giving others the credit or taking credit?
- Giving others the rewards or taking the rewards?
- Empathy or insensitivity?
- Teaching or blaming?
- Hard work or laziness?
- Achieving the mission or allowing shortfalls?
- Being of service to others or being a taker?
- Working as a team (or family) member or being a loner?
- Satisfied with the basics or oriented toward material things?
- Role satisfied or dissatisfied?
- Magnanimous or envious?

In their book *Growth Thinking*, Simmons and Crawford listed five key value constructs:

- Creating value for shareholders
- Creating value for employees
- Creating value for the ecosystem
- Creating value for customers
- Creating value for communities

Independently Assess Yourself (Summary Excerpts from Appendix B)
Assessing your self-leadership potential and challenges (a.k.a. opportunities) is critical. Either leveraging or overcoming one's own values and challenges takes total self-awareness, understanding of the need to self-manage, and values. How do we know if we have those values and drives to be a leader, and where the gaps might be so we can tackle them? To do so, we can solicit 360-type feedback with a promise of no retribution (anonymously perhaps). *Primal Leadership* suggested the ECI-360 assessment.

For values insights, let's look at a leadership profile from my favorite psychological battery, the Hartman Values Profile (in which I have no financial interest, but I have found it to be especially insightful, once understood). I have used it since 1987 very effectively for self-analysis, team building, hiring, promoting, and organizing. A better alternative may exist, but I have found nothing else that comes close to getting "between the ears" of the test taker related to true leadership insights (by role) and values—and an online report is ready the next day. It is not expensive, either. As noted, other assessments can be used.

Any assessment must be job specific per profiles, EEOC validated, and just one tool.

The Hartman insights structure is used here just to provide example definitions of the key values needed for leadership. The principles are the important focus.

Below are example Hartman Profiles for a general leadership role, and how I have learned to read them from many experiences (and results, after hiring compared to the scores) related to leadership success. While the technical answers used in the report are broad, use of this battery over the years has resulted in observational views of results as presented below.

The first is the adapted Motivations Page, with example scores for a good leader (and further defined in Appendix B).

Criteria	Excellent	Very Good	Good	Fair	Poor
Being of Service	X				
Mission Achievement	X				
Sense of Belonging	X				
Money, Material Things		X			
Personal Development			X		
Status, Recognition				X	

As Covey noted, the mature leader (all leaders!) need to have a balance of consideration (for others) and courage (to benefit their and the organization's needs).

In this example, this is a leader. He is dedicated to mission achievement, wants the mission to be of service to others, and wants to achieve the mission as a member of a successful team to which he belongs, contributes, and helps. All three are critical success factors for leadership, to energize the team's Primal Drives.

||||||||||||||||||||||||||||||||||||||||||||||||||||||||||||||||||||||||||||||||||||||||||||||||||||||||||||||||||||||||||||

Leapfrog!

(No immodesty intended; just insight.) At one company I was continually promoted to higher positions ahead of strong peers, mostly other MBAs with more seniority. When my first boss, who hired me out of graduate school and was a giver also, and I talked about this (over CC on the rocks and his martini), he observed that not only did I do my work, but I was always helping others just to help. This included helping peers and giving unsolicited ideas to senior execs to help them with their thorny problems. Thus, when a slot would come open, they already knew I could perform it well. Their Safety, Self-Interest, Hope, and other Primal Drives were quietly in play.

||||||||||||||||||||||||||||||||||||||||||||||||||||||||||||||||||||||||||||||||||||||||||||||||||||||||||||||||||||||||||||

Notice that the Giver cluster is well to the left of the Taker cluster here. This is important. It is fair to want reasonable rewards and to personally grow. The key one to be far right is the Status/Recognition need. If it is to the left, the person may tend to take credit and pass blame.

||||||||||||||||||||||||||||||||||||||||||||||||||||||||||||||||||||||||||||||||||||||||||||||||||||||||||||||||||||||||||||

Takers Can Lead

Three situations exist where a Taker will have people follow:

1. When the vision is very powerfully compelling to their Primal Drives (but had better be realized, and quickly)
2. When there is a crisis and control lines have to be very short for survival
3. Just kidding about #3.

Be careful that a Taker does not cause a crisis in order to control. It has happened.

||||||||||||||||||||||||||||||||||||||||||||||||||||||||||||||||||||||||||||||||||||||||||||||||||||||||||||||||||||||||||||

The extraordinary importance of being a Giver as a leader, to stimulate the Primal Drives of followers, is reflected in the following excerpts from the Booz and Company article "Turning the Table on Success" (penned for Booz by Dr. Adam Grant, Wharton University):

(In collaborative teams) Givers...are the teammates who volunteer for unpopular projects, share their knowledge and skills, and help out by arriving early or staying late...takers stick out. They avoid doing unpleasant tasks and responding to requests for help...I've found that changes (in the workplace) have set the stage for takers to flounder and givers to flourish...*recent research has shown that employees with the highest rates of promotion to supervisory and leadership roles exhibit the characteristics of givers*...In fact, when givers become leaders, their groups are better off...*employees work harder and more effectively for leaders who put others' interests first*...this motivates group members to give back to the leader and contribute to the group's interests...*The single strongest predictor of leadership was the amount of compassion that members expressed toward others in need...compassionate people were not only viewed as caring: they were also judged as more knowledgeable and intelligent...*

Thus, Givers energize most or all of the Primal Drives in followers and/or team members. *The beast in others is best unleashed by this process.*

The second (of several) Hartman Profile reports I pay attention to is the "ProForg." An example is below. For six key attributes it simultaneously assesses potential (Capacity) and actual practice ("- -" or "-" or "+" or "+ +") at the time. Varying combinations will exist, and practice scores can change over time with experiences. Profiles will also vary *by position/role type*. A strong, successful leader's profile is below (and further defined in Appendix B).

Criterion	- -	-	Capacity*	+	+ +
Empathy		X	Excellent		
Practical Judgment		X	Excellent		
System Judgment			Excellent	X	
Self-Esteem		X	Excellent		
Role Awareness			Excellent	X	

Criterion	- -	-	Capacity*	+	+ +
Drive			Excellent	X	

* Can be Excellent, Very Good, Good, Fair, or Poor

The center "Capacity" column is for potential, and I have come to believe is a surrogate for IQ. Do they have "gray matter" or not? Can they grow over time or not?

The other four columns are for present-day practice, from very low practice ("- -") to over-practice ("+ +"). These four situational columns can change over time with new experiences. I have not seen the center Capacity potential change much over time, however.

The six criteria in the rows are expansive in defining key values in regard to any job. The mix will vary by job type, so it is important (and EEOC compliant) to effectively profile proven successful people in a role as the basis for evaluating others relative to that role.

Empathy is other directedness. A leader needs to intrinsically be in tune intuitively and attitudinally with the needs, feelings, aspirations, and concerns of those around him, internally and externally. Thus, an Excellent or Very Good Capacity score is essential.

I believe an Excellent Capacity and a "-" score is optimal. The Capacity is there, but the leader will decisively act when needed, even if someone is pained as a result. I call it "constructive toughness," or "fair but firm." In this situation, explain the Whys.

(In my upcoming book *Primordial Marketing and Sales,* we will delve into how to find sales closers versus "professional visitors," or those with high call reluctance. The right profile will differ by selling situation. Matching selling skills to selling needs will be covered. We will also review how to hire a right-brained marketing strategist versus just a good marketing communications person.)

System Judgment may be the most critical for policy-level leaders. From direct observations, I believe it reflects right-brain, spatial, holistic, end-in-mind thinking capability, and its intrinsic use (or non-use) for envisioning. An Excellent Capacity and a "+" are good. If the Capacity is lower the leader had better surround himself with a spatial thinker, and listen to and support that person.

The old saying "Luck is preparation meeting opportunity" is anchored in the ability to correctly and practically envision surrounding contexts and the future, inclusive of all the causal power forces and how they will (always) change the status quo, and to "be there" at the right time with the right program. Once we get those visions right, we then have a chance to figure out what to do to Judo-leverage the coming changes *for* us versus being harmed by them. We can be on the balls of our feet versus others being on their heels, and not vice versa.

The Importance of Luck

Jack Welch has often said he will not hire anyone that is not lucky, reflecting they have this spatial sense of what to do correctly and have proven it. That "Luck is preparation meeting opportunity" reflects that spatial abilities are key to the right preparation ahead of the as-yet undefined, coming opportunities. Envisioning, a spatial skill, is critical to consistent luck. (It is also true that "Even a blind pig can sometimes find an acorn," but that is not dependable enough.)

In summary, from direct observation, this spatially based System Judgment area is where I believe many types of leaders struggle. Covey noted that about 1 percent are spatial. We will cover these areas more in chapters 5, 6, and 7, with some helpful ideas. Leaders need to continually grow in this area.

Drive. Author and speaker Dennis Waitley correctly commented that "Success is almost totally dependent upon drive and persistence. The extra energy required to make another effort or try another approach is the secret of winning."

President Calvin Coolidge wisely stated that "Nothing in this world can take the place of persistence. Talent will not; nothing is more common than unsuccessful people with talent. Genius will not; unrewarded genius is almost a proverb. Education will not; the world is full of educated derelicts. Persistence and determination alone are omnipotent. The slogan 'press on' has solved and always will solve the problems of the human race."

The Drive attribute is about the "need" to achieve goals versus just a "want" to do so. This Drive is where perseverance, zeal, and related attributes exist. Long hours, creative thinking, rule breaking, risk taking, and other success factors are the result. The strength of Drive relates to how strong the Primal Drives are in the aggregate. Any combination of needing (versus just wanting) Safety, Self-Interest, Transcendence, etc., are the sources of Drive energy.

Drive without Wisdom Is a Formula for Disaster

I once saw a cartoon of a Viking ship with the row master rapidly pounding away at the rhythm drum—as they rapidly shot over the 90-degree edge of the flat earth! Drive alone is not enough.

An Excellent Capacity and a "+" practice are optimal. Strong energy will exist, with some balance and perspective. A "++" score can be too strong, with burnout potential eventually.

Overall, the above two Hartman profile graphics generally represent an optimal leadership values and capabilities profile for most businesses. We are all complex beings, and a blending of the key factors will exist. Capacities need to be strong, and System Judgment needs to be strong and well used, with street-savvy common sense applied. The need to achieve the mission by being of service to others and doing so via the team (belonging) is important (aggregating into a "Giver"). Not needing credit is very important, as well as a high Drive capacity that is balanced with surrounding realities. A high Empathy Capacity and the ability to be direct when needed are important to have, together.

Handling Pain and Fear

Another rating by the Hartman Profile is the ability to handle disappointments. Do you absorb them and keep "ice water in the veins" to make good decisions? Or does "your hair get on fire" and cause you to make the wrong decisions and worsen things?

I once had a sales EVP reporting to me who was the latter. He would run in and declare a crisis, with mostly the whites of his eyes showing. I'd say (let's call him Pete here), "Pete, a crisis is a rocket-propelled grenade coming at you. This is just an issue to deal with that we need to determine how to Judo-leverage into an opportunity." He would then smile, calm down, and usually come up with the right answer.

Remember: who gets mad (or scared) last, wins! (In labor negotiations it is often who "blinks" last.)

Again, see Appendix B for many other behavior insights and ideas, especially values and behaviors to flag.

Chapter Four

Unleash The Results *Animal* in You...and in Others

YOU CAN'T MANAGE OTHERS UNTIL YOU FIRST MANAGE YOURSELF

"It's not what you gather but what you scatter that tells what kind of life you have lived!"

—Helen Walton

"Too soon old; too late smart."

—Old Pennsylvania Dutch saying,
often used by my now deceased mentor Dave Davis

"There is nothing to fear but fear itself."

—FDR, in regard to the Great Depression

"Physician, first heal thyself."

—evolved from *Luke 4:23*

"...chronic stress is proposed to induce...impaired spatial memory..."

—*Behavior and NeuralScience Reviews*

We have seen that the Primal Drives are key enabling forces for the brain's core Primordial Drive to optimize the perpetuation of our genes, as identified by Neuroscientists. The Primal Drives are hidden from our conscious mind's eye, have many elements and symptoms as shown in the previous chapter, and are all-controlling in reality. Judo-leveraging them for better results is now the focus... including what *not* to do in this chapter.

There are two key elements to successful, results-driven leadership. One is getting the best performance from others. As leaders our imperative is to achieve results via our people's performance relative to specific goals. That is why they pay us. But before we can get the most from others, we must first master ourselves. Self-management means to at least stay out of the way of others harnessing their own' Primal Drives for the organization's benefit, even if we don't actively foster their Primal Drives. At a minimum we must not be part of the problem. Hopefully we can be part of the solution.

As I often say in seminars, "I've never met a happy taker, or an unhappy giver." Per chapter 3 everyone benefits from a giver, including the giver. The greatest teacher of all time reflected that we should "do unto others as we would have them do unto us." Most of the bosses for whom I have worked the hardest embodied those values. The "takers" were actually fearful men who protected that fear and overcompensated with negative, overpowering styles. Giving takes a level of bravery and ability to absorb pain that is absent in others. For taker leaders the private disdain for them was palpable. The emotional commitments were sub-optimal, and the limited "just dial it in" efforts well concealed. The most damage was to the leader.

Just as respect is earned, true leadership power is earned. If others do not sense opportunity based on their Primal Drives being realized they will be less productive than we need, and perhaps even resistant. Here are the four key elements we as leaders need to earn true leadership power:

1. We must have the insight and vision to correctly determine *what* needs to be done and *Why*; and communicate it (via "communisuasion"-Kotler).
2. We must ensure that others' Primal Drives will be met both by the correct vision, and in how that vision is executed.
3. We must practice the needed Values that serve the Primal Drives in others.
4. We must not get in the way, at the very least.

Thus, we must first be worthy of success as a leader. Vision, smarts, bravery, a giving character, inner confidence, values and drive are all required-- and self-management, to align and maximize the Primal Drives of ourselves and others-- are the combined keys.

With the exception of a powerful, controlling vision, nothing trumps a leader's emotional commitment to harnessing his own Primal Drives to get others to commit so as to realize their Primal Drives—including other important leadership characteristics such as proactiveness, competitive spirit, street sense, risk acceptance, passion, values and charisma. All of those can, and should, also exist. But unless leaders emotionally put their shoulders to the wheel to harness their own and others' Primal Drives, results will not happen as desired. I call such emotional commitment "unleashing the beast." As a matter of fact, if the Primal Drives are energized, then weaknesses in the other leadership areas can be overcome (except for vision quality and values).

Therefore, energizing the Primal Drives in others does require leaders to live and display the many above attributes. If not, the loss of Safety, Self-Interest, Hope, and other Primal Drives will arise in others as barriers to success. We must both talk *and walk* these attributes at our core. They cannot be faked."Communication is 95 percent nonverbal," and "it is not what we say, but what we do that counts," and how we do it. There is no true hiding...for long anyway.

The Absence of Such Self-Management Is Costly

In many (not all) of the companies I have taken over or consulted for, and often re-directed or turned around, some past leadership "flatside" had existed that was holding the organization back. Perhaps external value position envisioning was flawed or inadequate. Or past leaders were insecure and thus over-managed to emotionally feel in control. Or their views and programs were too impractical to be successfully implemented. Or they did not have enough personal drive to *cause* (as an active verb) success when normal obstacles presented themselves. Or it was a "taker" organization unable to generate the internal "racer's edge" motivation to compete well; they were Selfish and caused sub-optimal emotional commitments in the company. Or they were dishonest. Or they were "small ball" thinkers that could not intellectually or emotionally grasp major league performance requirements, and allowed the resulting discomfort of "big ball" thinking to limit needed actions...and results.

||||||||||||||||||||||||||||||||||||||||||||||||||||||||||||||||||||||||||||||||||||||||||||||||||||||||||||||||||||||||||||||||||||||||||||||

Protection from the Leader Should Never Be Needed!

As president of a company, I sometimes found that my key role was to protect the employees from the CEO's angry outbursts, occasional win-lose values, an excessive need for control, sub-optimal envisioning, or other problems.

A symptom was that historical turnover had been very high, and perhaps included the best people. The company would have a heads-down culture with few making an emotional commitment.

In some cases I could coach the CEO, explaining that his style was hurting him, and he would evolve. In other cases I had to use a two-by-four, or get the board to act. Luckily, boards representing investors suffer no fools...for long.

||||||||||||||||||||||||||||||||||||||||||||||||||||||||||||||||||||||||||||||||||||||||||||||||||||||||||||||||||||||||||||||||||||||||||||||

Self-Leadership Insights

A definition of excellent leadership is needed that encompasses all possible situations. After much soul searching, and in light of all of the above, I have concluded that the great leaders are positively compelled by their own Primal Drives, spatial thinking/ envisioning ability, and Values to achieve whatever mission they have in front of them. It is a personal, emotional, self-worth, goals-focused, people improving *compulsion*. Innate leadership drive is a must-do compulsion more than it is a choice.

"Give me the ____ ball!" Or, "I'm on point. Follow me." It is native to most good leaders. Also, it can also be learned by being around great leaders who hate to lose (Safety), want rewards (Self-Interest), have high Hopes and constantly want to improve (Transcend), want to Trust and be trusted, want to continually do more with less Energy use and in less Time, and enjoy Socially working with and through the people around them. They especially enjoy seeing others grow and progress, as a giver.

Also, great leaders get results through the Primal Drives of others, and do not need the limelight. They know that the fewer decisions they have to make, reflecting that a great organization has been built, the better. The organization is executing the vision, and growing also.

Great leaders literally *hate* not achieving the mission, at the emotional level, and no standards are higher than their internal ones. Internally, they hate to lose (but are good at not letting the anger flow "downhill"). They have a clear picture of where they are going and a Primordial-level, uncontrollable compulsion to get there. *Most importantly, great leaders do what they do for others' gains in addition to their own. Without such needs being satisfied, based in the leader's Primal Drives and Values, there is no basis for followers accepting the costs of high energy usage, stress, long hours, career risks, investment risks, and other costs for the endeavor.*

These costs are very real, and they reflect the underlying Drives that must exist for those costs to be incurred, including Safety, Energy use, and others. Thus, Primal Drives–based willfulness must exist for great leadership to overcome the innumerable obstacles and challenges that will be encountered during the mission achievement process. Success must be *caused* to happen, via Primal Drives.

Put A-Players around You

The way to ensure the control of end results is to give up the control of process to the A-players you bring in. However, many weaker leaders hire people they can control emotionally. This leads to the truism that "A-players hire A-players. B-players hire C-players." Hire constructive A-players that push and stay ahead of you. Help set strategy and then evolve to be a servant and monitor. Monitor the vision's requirements, but try to avoid over-control.

An excellent leader must necessarily be a bad loser, but only to himself. Losing *should hurt*, but internally only. It should cause deep, honest evaluation and learning. The good news is that we will learn more from our mistakes, and grow more as a result. This is reflected by the old story about how Tom Watson, the famous CEO of IBM during its heyday, who, when asked by a young salesperson if he was to be fired after losing a $1 million deal (about $10 million in today's dollars), Watson said something to the effect of "_____ no! I just paid a million dollars to educate you!" Allow learning from mistakes, and grow.

Thus a key attribute of excellent leadership is "pain absorption." Feeling the pain is good. Not giving it back, unless it is a purposeful thing to do, is essential. Tremendous levels of self-control are required, no one will be perfect at it, but pain management is a hallmark of an excellent leader. If anger is displayed, it must be by conscious thought, on purpose, and goal focused to energize a purposeful set of Primal Drives-based "will-do" emotions in others, to enable the needed actions.

I also believe that any anger expression must include the leader himself: "*We* screwed up." Or, if the shoe fits, "*I* screwed up."

The Truth Will Set You Free

At an annual meeting of a large outsourced services company, where I was a twenty-nine-year-old general manager of a high profile management services contract, I was tasked to go over the excellent strike plan I had built and implemented when the Teamsters went on strike. My opening comment to all 300 leaders (who managed about 25,000 employees) was not about the strike plan. It was, "I SCREWED UP!" The group went stone-cold silent. "The strike plan should never have been needed! I pushed so hard to right so many bad work rules that had built up before my time that the union had to push back to regain some of its authority and stature, and self-respect. I could have been smarter, and I will be next time."

Top management was dumbfounded, apparently at the admission's suggestion of self-responsibility and inner confidence. I believe, based on a mentor's later statements, that it led to a major promotion shortly thereafter, when I became a young vice president.

What *Not* To Do

There are many things that a great leader does not do. The chart below lists the six key Primal Drives and lists *some* examples of what a leader needs *not* to do to successfully leverage these Primal Drives in others to lead well and relate to other key constituencies. Some of these "not to do's" have negative impacts on multiple Primal Drives.

Safety: What Not to Do
- Be emotionally fearful vs. intellectually careful
- Be negatively feared
- Be immoral or dishonest
- Be reckless or rattled
- Use fear as a motivator

- Not proactively practice good manners; by anyone (not allow complete thoughts)
- Be highly unpredictable in stress situations (vs. "ice water in the veins")
- Be a "small ball" vs. "big ball" thinker, limiting potentials
- Not take calculated risks
- Not correctly deciding what *not* to do, when strong advocates exist*
- Be mercurial, and perhaps volatile, when problems arise
- Be a blame finder
- Allow politics to exist
- Have favorites
- Limit communications
- Limit receptivity to new ideas
- Punish goals-focused challenges and criticisms
- Show fear
- Allow open dissention in the management team
- Not explain "lesser-of-the-evils" reasons why seemingly threatening change is actually the lesser of the evils
- Find the wrong first (contrary to Blanchard's *One Minute Manager*)
- Allow negative politics and unfounded rumors in the organization
- Punish the messenger that brings bad news you need to hear
- Not remember to address others' Safety needs in action plans
- Hire C-grade players because they can be controlled
- Not delegate enough, for control; but reducing others' self-control
- Micromanage when delegating, thus reducing others' control
- Delegating without enough goals structure, and milestones to monitor.

Self-Interest: What Not To Do

- Have consuming selfishness; be a non-rewarding "taker"
- Not care for the self-interests of others
- Be juxtaposed to the self-interests of others
- Take credit; avoid blame
- Not share rewards; not recognize achievements
- Be a "small ball" vs. "big ball" thinker, limiting potentials
- Not take calculated risks
- Not correctly deciding what *not* to do, when strong advocates exist; and incurring unnecessary "opportunity costs"*

- Try to get more than is reasonable ("Pigs get fat, hogs get slaughtered")
- Not mentor and develop high-potential people
- Reward pets vs. achievers
- Protect underachievers
- Be seen as favoring "Yes men"
- Let nepotism override merit
- Let friendship override merit
- Let politics override merit
- Not remember to address others' Self-Interest needs in action plans.

Hope and Transcendence: What Not To Do

- Use "as is" thinking vs. "could be/should be" to drive plans
- Allow "kinetic energy" to control (a body in motion tends to stay in motion; a body at rest tends to stay at rest-Newton)
- Let others see you down
- Let others see management team dissention
- Be satisfied
- Let political turfs control
- Fear change
- Change just for change's sake
- Limit opportunity
- Not have clear, merit-based career criteria
- Not using the career criteria if they exist
- Not incentivize
- Avoid participation
- Avoid constructive, mission-focused disagreement
- Engage in poor bi-directional communications
- Not smartly delegating (and not using the Reagan method of "trust but verify")
- See delegation as an end versus a means
- Not decide what *not* to do*
- In planning, failing to forecast coming external trends in technology, law, competition, and economic conditions, and how they can be leveraged and positioned for
- Not remember to address Hope and Transcendence needs in action plans.

Honesty and Trust: What Not To Do
- Deceive anyone
- Cheat
- Avoid responsibility
- Avoid or delay difficult decisions
- Take credit when not due
- Allow dishonesty at any level
- Allow politics vs. meritocracy
- Not remember to address Honesty and Trust needs in action plans.

Energy and Time Optimization: What Not To Do
- Be perceived as not hardworking
- Be lazy; or be perceived as lazy
- Waste time; not see time as a finite resource within which results should be maximized
- Let others set the timetable
- Not recognize hard, smart work
- Poorly understand the "input-output model" for programs
- Not prioritize
- Not decide what *not* to do when appropriate
- Not get involved with helping others do it easier and faster
- Not setting SMART goals (Specific, Measurable, Action-oriented, Resourced, Time-based)
- Not being dedicated to continuous improvement
- Not remember to address others' Energy and Time Savings needs in action plans.

Sociability: What Not To Do:
- Be personally insecure: Be a cynic, versus a romantic
- Distrust others
- Be insensitive; not care for others
- Be introverted and non-sociable
- Be too friendly
- Be too serious
- Not proactively practice good manners; by anyone
- Stifling humor and fun

- Be too antiseptic, squeezing out emotions
- Be aloof and unapproachable
- Limit information flows
- Use a closed-door style
- Not walk around
- Not play enough
- Put family second
- Not understand that your employees *are* your number-one asset, and they are "80 percent emotional" whose deepest motivations lie in their Primal Drives
- Not remember to address others' Sociability needs in action plans.

* It can be argued that correctly deciding what not to do, and being willing to counter advocating constituencies, is a top task of a leader, behind morality and self-management. (chapters 5 and 6 have some tools to help this process.)

Avoid McGregor's Theory X Views

According to *business dictionary.com:* "Theory X assumptions are: (1) most people dislike work and will avoid it to the extent possible; therefore (2) they must be continually coerced, controlled, and threatened with punishment to get the work done, and (3) they have little or no ambition, prefer to avoid responsibility, and choose security above everything else."

For a vast majority of workers this is no longer true, if it ever was. Thus, the smart leader "needs to focus on the donut, and not the hole" when leading. Also, the Pygmalion effect (the opposite of the Golem effect) will apply. Believe and it will happen. The more you believe, the more it will happen.

The Warlords' Time Has Passed

The "kill or be killed" starkness of the subsistence eras of the Tamerlanes, Attila, and Genghis Khan no longer exist today. Hopefully they never will again. Thus, these negative leadership styles will not prevail today and should not be used.

||||||||||||||||||||||||||||||||||||||||||||||||||||||||||||||||||||||||||||||||||||||||||||||||||||||||||||||||||||||||||||||||||||||||||

Do the Right Thing

An old football coach once said, "When in doubt, hit somebody!"
Good advice for football, but should be "just do it!" for business.

For leaders, when in doubt just lead toward the Primal Drives being realized in yourself and in others. Primordial energy forces result. Pity the to-be-bruised opponent.

||||||||||||||||||||||||||||||||||||||||||||||||||||||||||||||||||||||||||||||||||||||||||||||||||||||||||||||||||||||||||||||||||||

In summary, a leader must have the right Vision, display and practice the right Values, and align his direct Primal Drive needs to others' meeting their own Primal Drive. It is a "give to get" model, by actually *giving-to-give*. Also, for execution, the "angel is in the (delegated) details."

Powerful energies are unleashed as a result. In varying degrees, achieving these self-managing attributes is an "unnatural act," and it is one reason why leaders are a small percent of the overall population. It is reverse psychology in action, plus values and rare right-brained spatial thinking.

Always being part of the solution and not part of the problem is a major self-management challenge. The right actions are often counter-intuitive and can be downright uncomfortable. If so, "play with pain," and lead correctly.

Assessing Your Self-Leadership Potential and Challenges (aka Opportunities)

Overcoming one's own drives and challenges, especially fear, takes total self-awareness, an understanding of the need to self-manage, and values. How do we know if we have the values and drives to be a giving (not a taking) leader, and where the gaps might be so we can tackle them? Assess yourself, using whatever objective battery you choose. If it is the Hartman Values Profile, compare with these reports, explained in chapter 3 and more fully so in Appendix B.

Below is the adapted Motivations Page, with example scores for a good leader.

Criteria	Excellent	Very Good	Good	Fair	Poor
Being of Service	X				
Mission Achievement	X				
Sense of Belonging	X				
Money, Material Things		X			

Criteria	Excellent	Very Good	Good	Fair	Poor
Personal Development			X		
Status, Recognition				X	

As also noted earlier, the second (of several) Hartman Profile reports I pay attention to is the *"ProForg."*

Criterion	"- -"	"-"	Capacity*	"+"	"+ +"
Empathy		X	Excellent		
Practical Judgment		X	Excellent		
System Judgment			Excellent	X	
Self Esteem		X	Excellent		
Role Awareness			Excellent	X	
Drive			Excellent	X	

* Can be Excellent, Very Good, Good, Fair, or Poor

In addition to being Mission committed, getting there by teamwork and being of Service in doing so, *System Judgment* may be the most critical for policy-level leaders. Spatial skills resulting from System Judgment, for envisioning, are important for followers' support.

Since change is the only constant, the key is to always be envisioning new potentials, driven by any combination of increased Safety, Self-Interest rewards, Hope and Transcendence, and other Primal Drives.

We will cover these areas more in chapters 4 and 5, with some helpful ideas.

Summary

In leadership, Pogo is too often right: "We have met the enemy and he is us." Many leaders cannot get out of their own way, and in such cases "the fish stinks from the head." The one that gets most damage from this is the taker leader himself.

The Primal Drives provide an excellent self-management construct to understand and use. A starting point is knowing what *not* to do.

Proven self-assessment tools can be used individually and with the leadership team to be the basis of further leadership improvement. This includes self-assessment and team assessments. It can be used for hiring and promotions also, *as one tool only.*

Right-brained System Judgment and the resulting envisioning capability, plus Values and triggering others' Primal Drives are key success factors for all leaders.

Chapter Five

Unleash The Results *Animal* in You...and in Others

EFFECTIVE
PRIMORDIAL LEADERSHIP

"The greatest leader is not necessarily the one who does the greatest things. He is the one that gets the people to do the greatest things."

—Ronald Reagan

"Do you want to know who you are? Don't ask. Act! Action will delineate and define you."

—Thomas Jefferson

There are enough management, leadership, and entrepreneurism books to fill a good-sized room. And all of them provide value. However, they mostly deal with the impacts or symptoms of the Primal Drives, rather than the underlying causes themselves, which are less directly observable. Defining the underlying Why's gives us a better understanding of the "fire" vs. the "smoke," and a more consistent and powerful structure to differentiate leadership quality. Per an earlier quote, understanding the Why's provides differentiating power versus other typical observations that just see the What and How elements.

The very good news, based on years of direct experience (and not just indirect theory), is that leveraging the Why Primal Drives as a construct is much simpler, and provides more consistent and powerful results, than the many What and How bromides we read that deal with the symptoms of the Primal Drives only. While in these cases specific leadership values and cognitive envisioning factors must be considered for each individual situation, the Primal Drives are consistent for all people. There will be a "marbling" of the Primal Drives for each situation, with different weightings of the Drives. This needs to be considered, but always from a consistent starting point of the six universal Primal Drives that enable the genes perpetuating Primordial Drive, per the earlier "iceberg" graphic:

1. **Safety**
2. **Self-Interest (including Greed)**
3. **Hope and Transcendence**
4. **Honesty and Trust**
5. **Energy Surplus and Time Optimization**
6. **Sociability (including Altruism)**

With economic times continually improving (and thus the resulting Safety), the people we deal with will have many more alternatives, will be more confident of taking an action, and will be much less controllable than in the past. It's a good problem to have, and as always is really an opportunity. What we're seeing in leading Millennials and Gen Xers is just the beginning. We haven't seen anything yet. There is no way out, so we must go further in.

Therefore, consistent with the principles of Judo, where we redirect the power of a force to our advantage (versus it harming us!), we *must* leverage these evolutions in expectations using the Primal Drives. Further leadership details about how to do so are in the below "To Do's" table. The objective, clearly stated, is to Judo-leverage others' Primal Drives *for your benefit*.

Applying the truisms will vary by situation and need. Purposeful artful thinking and actions will be needed. But, that is the pathway to what we are paid to do: *deliver results*.

Some Proven, Primordial Leadership To Do's

Once again, refer to the self-assessment tables in chapters 3 and 4 and Appendix A for personal reference. The below table summarizes the actual To Do's for each Primal Drive to be Judo-leveraged in others (for your benefit). These To Do's correspond very well to the bromides of Maslow, Herzberg and McGregor, and others. Organizing the To Do's according the six Primal Drives reveals the important, underlying, DNA-level Why's behind the authors' truisms. This helps to fortify the value of those leadership bromides by verifying that they are not whims of mere observers but actually reflect deeper, core Drivers in all humans, as increasingly discovered by neuroscientists and sociobiologists. Also, as noted, the six Primal Drives provide a consistent, least-common-denominator construct for leadership action, strategically and tactically. These can be contrasted with the No To Do's in chapter 4. Overlaps exist.

Safety/Risk Aversion

- Be emotionally strong and confident, "charismatic"
- Be moral and honest, no matter the costs
- Proactively practice good manners; insist on it for all
- Be brave and see fear conquering by the company as a possible differentiator[3]
- Be respected but not feared
- Be steady, and absorb pain
- Use insight, vision, and fairness as motivators
- Be a "big ball" vs. "small ball" thinker, optimizing potentials
- Correctly decide what *not* to do, even if strong advocates exist; avoid "opportunity costs"
- Take calculated risks, even if failure is a possibility (as it always is)
- Protect and reward the messenger; especially for early bad news
- Be a blame acceptor as applicable
- Be highly predictable in stress situations (have "ice water in the veins")
- Do not allow politics to exist
- View all as favorites
- Communicate well

---

3   Welcome challenges, as reflected by Thomas Paine: "If there must be trouble, let it be in my day, that my child may have peace." Ride to the sound of guns…with better guns.

- Reward ideas
- Explain the "lesser-of-the-evils" reasons why an action is the best way forward
- Reward goals-focused challenges and criticisms
- Choose A-players with whom you have to run to catch up
- Delegate smartly, assuring results control but also giving the subordinate some autonomy-based control
- Remember to address Safety in action plans.

Self-Interest
- Be a "giver;" NEVER BE A TAKER
- Find the right first (per Blanchard)
- Proactively care for the self-interests of others
- Proactively be positioned for the self-interests of others
- Be a "big ball" vs. "small ball" thinker, optimizing potentials
- Take calculated risks, even if failure is a possibility (as it always is)
- Correctly decide what *not* to do, even if strong advocates exist; avoid "opportunity costs"
- Use fair, objective rewards, promotion and discipline criteria; and apply them
- Don't take credit; accept blame
- Proactively share rewards; recognize and celebrate achievements
- Mentor and develop high-potential people
- Practice using zeal
- Remember to use Self-interests in action plans.

Hope and Transcendence
- Use "could/should be" to drive plans; do not allow "kinetic energy" to control plans (a body in motion tends to stay in motion; a body at rest tends to stay at rest)
- Find and define the higher meanings (resonance) of the plans
- Never let others see you down
- Be charismatic in style; be uplifting; have "presence"
- Never let others see management team dissention
- Be "constructively dissatisfied" at all times; manage "simultaneous tight and loose properties"
- Do not let political turfs control results and rewards

- Embrace smart, reasoned, goals-focused change
- Practice urgency
- Make no change just for change's sake
- Provide unlimited merit-based opportunity
- Accurately incentivize and enforce the criteria
- Facilitate participation
- Foster strong bidirectional communications
- Smartly delegating (using the Reagan method of "trust but verify")
- See delegation as a means versus an end
- Purposely decide what not to do, and communicate why
- In planning, forecast coming external trends in technology, law, competition, and economic conditions, and how they can be leveraged and positioned for
- Remember to use Hope and Transcendence in action plans.

Honesty and Trust

- NEVER deceive anyone
- NEVER cheat
- Take responsibility
- Give credit when due
- NEVER allow dishonesty
- Reward honesty visibly
- NEVER allow politics
- Require the above in all leaders, all the time
- Remember to use Honesty and Trust in action plans.

Energy and Time Optimization

- Be seen as hardworking
- Be energetic; set the pace
- Lead from the front
- Optimize time; see time as a finite resource within which results should be maximized
- Watch out for the cost of that last "5%"
- Continually try to improve processes to make them faster and/or easier
- Set the timetable
- Reward hard, smart work

- Understand the "input-output model" for programs
- Prioritize
- Decide what not to do; or not to do yet
- Get involved with helping others do it easier and faster
- Set and track SMART goals
- Remember to use Energy and Time Optimization in action plans.

Sociability

- Be personally secure: Be a romantic, versus a cynic
- Trust others
- Be sensitive
- Be sociable
- Proactively practice good manners; insist on it for all
- Use humor
- Foster fun and play ("a family that plays together stays together")
- Be friendly, but not too much so
- Be focused and determined, but not too serious; be uplifting
- Be antiseptic, but not insensitive
- Be approachable
- Foster information flows
- Use an open-door style
- Walk around; talk to all and listen openly
- Make sure any needed discipline is applied, fairly (people are watching)
- Put the family first and you second
- Put the employees first and you second
- Understand that your employees are your number-one asset, and they are "80 percent emotional"
- One key concept for all of the above is to "build heroes!"
- Remember to use Sociability in action plans.

Both Self-Manage and Lead: 1 x 1 = 4

To repeat, self-management means Judo-leveraging the Primal Drives of others, even when counterintuitive. If we listen to Jesus and choose to be a servant first as a leader, versus being foolishly selfish, then all things are possible.

By avoiding the chapter 4 Not To Do's and practicing these To Do's, the best self-motivations in people can occur. Unleashing the beast(s) will occur. You will come the closest to bringing out the results of "Outliers" (per Malcolm Gladwell), even if you did not get raised in the special ways cited in the book. Doing so will result in more "go to" players on the team. Your job then is to lead the envisioning process, assure the right Values, monitor the planning, monitor that value-giving purposes exist, be there to coach, monitor in regard to results per plan, and stay the _____ out of the way of the star performers.

The below table is easy to reconstruct and use for each planning or action situation, including for leading employees' motivation, partnering, program management, marketing, selling, securing funds, and more. For marketing and selling, both absolute value and relative value (to others) must be addressed together. See chapter 6 for more tools.

Program/Audience Focus:		
Date:	By:	
To Do's	Primal Drives To Leverage	Not To Do's
	Safety	
	Self-Interest	
	Hope and Transcendence	
	Honesty and Trust	
	Energy/Time Optimization	
	Sociability	

Now that we've established how to Judo-leverage the Primal Drives through specific To Do's and Not To Do's, we're going to cover some specific attributes of Primordial Leadership, in light of the Primal Drives.

Understand the Nature of Power and Its Use (and Non-Use)

Strong leaders develop merit-based power, which is given to them by others when it is earned. As noted, the first three Primal Drives are the most pervasive and affective. These three combine with the Energy and Time Optimization

Drive to mostly form the derived drive for power. Power helps to facilitate and implement the Primal Drives. Safety results from well-used power. Selfish gains result from power. Hope and Transcendence are aided by power. Also, people are likely to be less dishonest around positive power. Saving Energy and Time can be enabled by power. And powerful people draw out Sociability. Power begets power.

Everything in moderation is a good axiom for life, and for seeking and using power. Power for its own sake is dangerous and can easily let ends and means become inverted, detrimentally. Doing so will often threaten the Primal Drives of people you are trying to lead and will diminish leadership efficacy and results (and rewards for the leader). They may even resist and undercut the leader if it serves their Primal Drive needs. Thus, make sure you have "a driving ego and not a consuming one." If so, the horse (leading to trigger the positive Primal Drives of others) and cart (the results of their positive Primal Drives) will stay in the proper positions and roles. Getting the "cart before the horse" will have questionable, and perhaps even destructive, consequences.

Envisioning Is Critical! It Is The Source of Defining The All-important WHY

"Who wins the Why battles wins the results war!"

—The Author

Envisioning quality is the top power force. It can overcome other shortfalls.

As mentioned previously, great athletes envision success then execute to the vision. Creative people, like architects, composers, and others, envision the result *before* they start. They also envision Why the vision has a value-add externally (purpose). *A leader must do the same—continually.* A literal back-to-front "roadmap" in the mind is needed. "Fit" with external needs, present and/or coming, is important to perceived value.

Yogi was right about being able to "see 'em" first. If you have a great vision that adds valued value, well communicated, people will literally follow you to _____ and back, barefoot and over fire coals. It will overcome other concerns virtually every time because their Hope, Safety (in success), Self-Interest, and other Primal Drives will be triggered.

Native Americans Depended on Visions

Native Americans, even though vastly outnumbered and resourced (and could not sustain themselves as a result), were remarkably effective in defending their territories and lifestyle from encroachment. Leaders would go off and fast, pray, self-flagellate, and more to be able to see a vision for their people. Tatanka Iyotanka (Sitting Bull) needed a vision, went into seclusion, called for a Sun Dance, allowed himself to be cut many times, prayed, "and his vision came. He saw many, many bluecoats (white soldiers who had been sent to protect the gold prospectors) attacking the encampment." (Source: manataka. org.) He prepared his tribe for this vision and recruited others. The 7th Cavalry attacked two weeks later. The Native Americans were obviously ready due to the communicated vision.

Developing a correct and compelling vision has many components:

- Being comfortable with peering into the very uncertain fog of the future
- Constant external and internal awareness of events and power forces and megatrends, pro and con (find the waves to ride, or the waves to circumvent)
- Understanding and incorporating the "R^2" (Coefficient of Causation) impacts of surrounding power forces, megatrends, internal factors, etc., to then be able to Judo-leverage them
- Setting the corporate ends-in-mind before starting actual planning (e.g., increasing shareholder value and liquidity, employees' gains, societal value)
- Purposely intending to provide higher-level meaning and benefits to others via your vision (being part of the future good, macro and micro)
- Define your "Driving Force" (see chapter 7)
- Forecasting the projected changes in the forces over time
- Setting an initial, unique value-add vision as a guideline
- Using the multilevel planning processes in chapter 6, including competitive analysis
- Personalize and live out the higher values, end objectives, and plans (nothing is more powerful than a convicted, goals-focused, willful person)

- Constantly communicate and document the higher meanings of the vision and plans
- Constantly communicate and document the results of your vision and plans
- Monitor progress and correct and update as needed.

The specifics of doing this will vary for a government entity, a telecom company, a retail company, a software company, a services company, a manufacturing company, and so on.

Being able to discern the forest from the trees is important to good envisioning. Relative to the highest meanings and the major power forces, also, metaphorically, look beyond the forest to the county, then the state, then the country, then the planet, and then the universe. These higher contexts are important for optimal "fit."

If You Don't Have Spatial Envisioning, Then Get It

Attaining personal spatial/envisioning capabilities for the first time may or may not be possible. If not, how do you get your organization more visionary, pace setting, change oriented, and successful?

Answer: Buy it or rent it, and then nurture and protect it (even if it drives you crazy). Covey's one percent may be low, but the crop from which to choose visionaries is not large, and errors are easy to make. The Hartman Values Profile for System Judgment (overviewed more fully in Appendix B) and other such tools can help. Experience is a key barometer, as well as a strong track record of success. The leader's spatial/envisioning capability can grow also, with purposeful practice. This book's processes help also.

More and more companies are adding a Chief Strategy Officer (CSO) to help with all of the visioning, planning, and execution to the vision.

Listen to the Board!

In a turnaround situation, the board got impatient with the agreed-on redirection gestation period and ordered it shortened by six months. The efforts were difficult but the results were optimal for shareholders. Leaders, no matter how self-managing, can get too close to things. Outside pressures are to be appreciated and harnessed. That pressure provided me with many new action powers to use to better drive results, and I did.

The entrepreneurial leader must avoid "founderitis," which is the need for emotional control far too long. In technical or financial companies often started by smart, detail-oriented people, sometimes they are outgrown (of course there are many exceptions, such as Bill Gates). The unsettling "gray" realities overpower the more definable and comfortable "black and white." A spatial person sees and welcomes the change as a way to outstrip competitors moving more slowly due to less vision-based foresight and resulting action.

The comfort with grayness is disconcerting to some, and it can out itself in subtle but costly ways.

Also, for the company that brings in a more spatially oriented leader, the founder's ability to emotionally absorb the highly certain uncertainty is *the* key success factor. That acceptance is 50/50 probably. Where a strong board exists, it may work itself out if there is a conflict. If not, or if there are other problems, then usually the visionary will leave due to too little Hope. Doing so will hurt the organization in many ways.

Offset a Dreamer with a Doer

Per Patton, "A good plan violently executed now is better than a perfect plan next week." Getting the enterprise "plane" landed is key to success. A dream that remains just a dream, or tries to be too perfect, is majorly frustrating to all. The philosopher Voltaire stated that "Perfect is the enemy of good."

The dreamer needs to appreciate the value of the landing, especially before the fuel expires, versus the experience of the flight; and appreciate the skilled person that does the landing. Making sure this talent exists to augment the dreamer is critical. This will be hard on both entities to co-manage, but mutual appreciation, sensitivity and cooperation is essential.

The organization will always be watching these different skills and personality dynamics. Thus, the emotionally "big" leader will work hard to both foster and project cooperation and appreciation. Any disagreements are to be fully behind closed doors or offsite. When resolved, both need to present a common, friendly, positive (Hopeful) face.

Often dreamers will be uncomfortable if the new dream is not being quickly acted on, while the doer is absorbed with getting the last dream landed. Both dynamics need to be managed.

Effective "communisuasion" (communicating to persuade and not just inform, from Philip Kotler) will be needed, often needing "avoids" positioning, to avoid bad things from happening.

In both cases the position "give" will have to be negotiated, which will be emotionally difficult. True emotional "bigness" will be needed by both. Good luck. The pain will probably be worth the gain, but the pain will be high. The major responsibility for interpersonal success lies with the CEO, whether a visionary or not.

Win the Pecking Order

Whether you have native envisioning ability or you hire it, the one who best exhibits it, directly or indirectly, will be at the top of the pecking order. Metaphorically, in a sled dog team the leader's view is much more rewarding than those following. Think about it.

Evaluate, and Be Open To, the Road Less Traveled

It is possibly less traveled because it embodies discomforts of multiple possible types. Others fall away. The quote that "success is doing what others are not willing or able to do" may apply. The higher returns are linked to some combination of the higher risk or higher effort, where many fall by the wayside. Careful gain versus pain calculation is needed, but be open to more risk or more effort—or both. You may laugh all the way to the bank. As Chief Justice Warren Burger stated, "Calculated risks of abuse are taken in order to preserve higher values." Or achieve outlier-type goals (per Gladwell).

Delegate Well

The extremes of no delegation/micro-management and "fire and forget" are equally bad. Proper delegation includes all of the following:

- Vision/purpose
- SMART goals
- What is *not* to happen
- Key success factors
- Timelines (with milestones to monitor against)
- Get inputs and listen; adjust as needed (including to get buy-in)
- Resources
- Reactive support
- Providing coaching as needed, but protecting their autonomy as much as possible within the above constraints
- Regular monitoring of agreed on milestones
- Recalibration as needed

- Recognition
- Rewards (or sanctions if needed).

||||||||||||||||||||||||||||||||||||||||||||||||||||||||||||||||||||||||||||||||||||||||||||||||||||||||||||||||||||||||||||||||||||||||||

Where is the Monkey?

It is a human reality that some do not like the risks that come with delegation to them. A punitive environment makes this especially so.

In such situations they can be very crafty in putting the "monkey" of decision making, and related responsibility, on the leader's back. Always decide where the monkey should be and act accordingly, per this book's principles.

||||||||||||||||||||||||||||||||||||||||||||||||||||||||||||||||||||||||||||||||||||||||||||||||||||||||||||||||||||||||||||||||||||||||||

Character Is Critical!

Character is critical for unleashing the Primal Drives of subordinates. The lack thereof will show quickly, and badly.

Character is doing the right things even when it hurts, and when no one is watching. Having character is a great gift, and one should kiss his parents because it is heavily nurture based. The others are victims to be sorry for, but only so much. They must find a way to manage that ascribed or acquired flaw. We all have crosses to bear, so we must learn to bear them. It's especially what leaders do.

Relatedly, Professor James Miles of Purdue University stated that "You can easily judge the character of others by how they treat those who they think can do nothing for them." It's not about giving to get, but *giving to give*. Caring equally for the janitor as well as the EVP is a good sign. More walk-the-talk character signs are needed.

The quality of an organization's character starts at the top. All will emulate it. It's all on you, the leader. Relative to the Primal Drives, character is a key energy source for realizing the Primal Drives of all. Especially for the leader.

Relative to employees, Sun Tzu advises us to "Regard your soldiers as your children, and they will follow you into the deepest valleys. Look on them as your own beloved sons, and they will stand by you even unto death!" They, like customers, want their Primal Drives protected and enhanced. This takes character, because they, as humans, will be imperfect in many ways. The one who handles the annoying human variances with character has a chance for success. At least figuratively avoiding strangling them is a good start. Absorb the disappointments and pains, and move forward. See them as "teaching moments" where possible—which takes character. It is true that "Running a company would be easy if not for employees." Grow to it.

Also, Dale Carnegie had it right when he opined that "Any fool can criticize, condemn, and complain, but it takes character and self-control to be understanding and forgiving."

Character and ethics are "auto-correlative." Character and ethics continually and iteratively affect each other. Character cannot exist without ethics, and ethics cannot exist without character. Ensure your character! Fix askew ethics.

Einstein tied character and attitude together. They are auto-correlative also; one needs the other to exist, and they continually affect each other. Manage attitudes!

Lincoln observed that character, or not, really shows when a person has power.

Courage Is Vital to Character (and Confidence)

Character needs courage as an engine. Courage and confidence are dually dependent. They must co-exist. There is no alternative. Courage is intangible, and it can come from any combination of birth, parental nurturing, facing the beast then growing, or some combination. A key is having the confidence to fail. The confidence to fail is also courage based.

Fear is an opportunity. There can be no courage until there is fear first.

Courage is needed for handling tough trade-offs like below. As perhaps the most courageous person of the twentieth century, Winston Churchill noted, "Courage is the first of the human qualities because it is the quality which guarantees all the others...Without courage, all other virtues lose their meaning."

Homer observed that "A decent boldness ever meets with friends." U.S. Grant summed up the application of leadership courage very well: "In every battle there comes a time when both sides consider themselves beaten; then he who continues the attack wins."

||||||||||||||||||||||||||||||||||||||||||||||||||||||||||||||||||||||||||||||||||||||||||||||||||||||||||||||||||||||||||||||||||||||||||||||||

Hire a Vet!

Eleanor Roosevelt once noted that confidence is built on experiencing horrors and moving forward. Combat vets have "seen the beast." There is no horror in business that can compare. They will stay in the foxhole and fight, and not run.

||||||||||||||||||||||||||||||||||||||||||||||||||||||||||||||||||||||||||||||||||||||||||||||||||||||||||||||||||||||||||||||||||||||||||||||||

Australian author and speaker Margie Warrell (*Stop Playing Safe*) notes that a leaders (male and female) need to "Live and lead with courage...(the) courage to challenge what is possible...(the) courage to speak up and make a stand...(the) courage to risk failing and look foolish...(the) courage to dare to do more, care more and become more."

There can be no true passion without courage and confidence-based conviction.

It is also true that "Running a company would be easy if not for customers." Customers and stakeholders require a high-character company with which to work. Their Primal Drives (Honesty/Trust, Safety, Self-Interest, Sociability, Ease/Flexibility/Speed, etc.) are vital to them, so the providing company must be adaptive to them, which takes character. Versus the company's structure, processes, and policies for their solution, the customers will often be messy, demanding, varying, sometimes narcissistic, and sometimes unfair—and present other challenges. Company character is needed to adapt and leverage, and thus maintain, long-term relationships. These relationships are important and valuable. *Inc.* magazine once noted that selling to a new customer is thirty-two times more expensive than selling to an existing customer.

"Find the right first." This bromide from Blanchard's *One Minute Manager* is powerful, and true. When bleep happens it is easy to fly off. Find some right to say first if possible. Start with a positive. Then zero in on a problem and its solution.

"Just Don't Scratch My Desk"

I tell my team, and employees, that they do not have the right to criticize related to the mission—they have the *obligation* to do so. Also, if they are going to get on my desk to do so, just let me put down some paper so the desk does not get scratched.

Then I openly reward the criticism if it helps. If it does not help, I patiently and positively explain how it does not help, and why.

Make sure you *never* attack the messenger bringing you *any kind of news*, especially negative. If you do, you won't have the problem again, because you will get no more news—from anyone!

Also, avoid the self-limiting "He is agreeable who agrees with me" approach, rooted in a dangerous need for comfort. As long as it is mission/goals focused, *seek* (and celebrate) alternative views, intellectually and emotionally. Even if not used, appreciate and recognize the views. If they are not used, explain why. Through this character-based process, the best ideas can be used. Such "ideation" is critical to have and use.

In situations where there is not enough passion, inject it. Where there is too much passion, and even anger, quell it. You need to bring out ideas and commitments from the deep Primal Drives versus just Cognition. Doing so requires just the right amount of passion and emotion.

While tact is not unimportant, be courageous in saying what needs to be said. Be constructively candid.

In closing on character—on which much more could be written—carefully control yourself!

Confidence (but not Hubris) Is Vital

Once again, courage is critical to confidence. They are co-dependent. Confidence supports character.

If you do not believe in yourself, who will? One must emotionally be willing to lose and have strong self-belief. Murphy is always lurking, and knows when to strike the hardest. Setbacks will happen. How quickly and well we get up, dust ourselves off, and press on are critical. Perseverance results in success potential, per the earlier Calvin Coolidge quote.

The *Dictionary.com* definition is instructive:

> **con·fi·dence** *noun* 1. full trust; belief in the powers, trustworthiness, or reliability of a person or thing: *We have every confidence in their ability to succeed.*
> 2. belief in oneself and one's powers or abilities; self-confidence; self-reliance; assurance: *His lack of confidence defeated him.*
> 3. certitude; assurance: He described the situation with such confidence that the audience believed him completely.

The importance of confidence is less about our body English and nonverbal cues affecting others, and more about the inner, core, intestinal fortitude (aka "guts") to push through inevitable barriers—*which results in strong nonverbal cues!*

||||||||||||||||||||||||||||||||||||||||||||||||||||||||||||||||||||||||||||||||||||||||||||||||||||||||||||||||||||||||||||||||||

Confidence Will Carry the Day!

When pitching to a large Fortune 50 company "Mahogany Row" executive team to OEM (Original Equipment Manufacturer) our products, competing against a strong internal group, it came to the point of us saying, with conviction, "We'd love to work with you, versus us having to beat you in the marketplace, which we would do if necessary, but hopefully not." The room fell deadly silent for long seconds. My Operations VP went ghostly white as the blood drained in fear. Then the Division EVP turned to his program manager and said, "I think he is right. Let's do this deal." We did, very successfully. Nothing ventured, nothing gained. No guts, no glory. The key was that they would benefit. They did benefit as well.

||||||||||||||||||||||||||||||||||||||||||||||||||||||||||||||||||||||||||||||||||||||||||||||||||||||||||||||||||||||||||||||||||

In his 1994 inaugural speech, after being imprisoned for over twenty years, Nelson Mandela, a study in goodness and confidence if there ever was one, observed that: "You are a child of God. Your playing small does not serve the world. There is nothing enlightened about shrinking so that people won't feel insecure around you. We were born to make manifest the glory of God that is within us. It's not just in some of us; it's in all of us. And when we let our own light shine, we unconsciously give other people permission to do the same. As we are liberated from our own fear, our presence automatically liberates others."

A real, unspoken, powerful energy behind strong confidence is the desire to give value to others. There is no better calling, or energy.

Fear is a Safety-based Primal Drive in humans, and judgment must be made when to push past it, to realize other Primal Drives. Bravery cannot exist unless there is fear first. As FDR once noted, "There is nothing to fear but fear itself."

That great sage Dr. Seuss said, "Be who you are and say what you feel because those who mind don't matter, and those who matter don't mind."

Confidence is key to correctly "know when to hold them (go forward) and when to fold them (cease and desist)." Intellectual carefulness is important, but not taking "counsel of your (emotional) fears" is also. There is no shame in walking away from a bad business outcome to live to fight another day. It just needs to be a calculated decision versus knee-jerk or fear based.

||||||||||||||||||||||||||||||||||||||||||||||||||||||||||||||||||||||||||||||||||||||||||||||||||||||||||||||||||||||

Four Poker Rules

I often played poker in college to get money to take my girlfriend (later wife) to dinner at nice places. We ate well for college kids because I learned and applied five rules:

- Learn the idiosyncrasies of the other players.
- Know the odds.
- Play your cards and not your money.
- If bad odds, get out as close to the ante as possible vs. emotionally staying in and hoping…and probably losing.
- If the seventh hand you win is more than you lose in the other six, your net winnings let you dine well that night.

Be confident and courageous; and a good loser if that occurs. Also, a good winner.

||||||||||||||||||||||||||||||||||||||||||||||||||||||||||||||||||||||||||||||||||||||||||||||||||||||||||||||||||||||

Someone once noted that even more important than the leader having confidence is that the team has confidence. They will do the heavy lifting. As always, confidence infectiously starts from the top.

Hubris is bad! It is just an over-compensation for fear and character weakness, and others know it. It really only harms the leader. In the same inaugural speech cited above, Nelson Mandela also noted that "Our deepest fear is not that we are inadequate. Our deepest fear is that we are powerful beyond measure. It is our light, not our darkness, that frightens us most. We ask ourselves, 'Who am I to be brilliant, gorgeous, talented, and famous?' Actually, who are you *not* to be?"

Leaders will encounter many painful tradeoffs. Character, with underlying Courage and Confidence, will be the determinant of action success or failure. Some examples of what to do can be found in the following table.

Challenge	Character-Based Action
The best salesperson, who has saved many quarterly results, sexually harassed another.	Terminate. Assure the harassed person, and all, that such actions will not be tolerated. Period.

Challenge	Character-Based Action
An EEOC-protected employee repeatedly fails a valid due process and will certainly file complaints and possibly even a lawsuit.	Terminate fairly, or let them resign. Get the lawyers ready. If it is just a competence issue, see if a less rigorous (probably lower paying) job might work, under agreed-on probation.
A customer commitment turns out to be much more expensive than projected, and will even incur losses.	Try to renegotiate. If not possible, meet the commitment. Learn.
A board member wants a less qualified relative to be hired or promoted.	Hire or promote the best. Always.
A to-be-hired superstar wants more options than are in the shareholder-approved pool, and the annual shareholders meeting is nine months off.	If he is worth it share enough of your options to make up the gap. Trust the board and shareholders to later support you.
You are experiencing heavy turnover of good people.	Fix yourself! It is on you to resolve.
The recession means cost cuttings, including personnel costs.	Go for salary/pay reductions vs. layoffs, usually. Harder to sell perhaps, but better. Execs take the largest "haircut." You take a larger "buzz cut."
There is pressure to change the revenues recognition policies to protect quarterly results and stock price.	Don't. Period. Take the pain. Make it up next quarter, and more.
Your company has violated a bank loan covenant.	Notify the bank, and let them know the cure plan. (Also, the worst thing is to let them find it.)
A judgment mistake is made.	Be the first to surface it. Admit it. Then fix it.
A prospect or customer is openly abusive and will not relent.	Fire the prospect or customer if they do not relent no matter the efforts.

Challenge	Character-Based Action
A major failure occurs.	Take your part of the blame, openly. Set it up as a teaching moment. You might use an office wall quote I saw: "Ah, I see the screw-up gnome has visited us again!" Use humor. Relax the folks so they can think straight and fix the problem versus knee-jerking and causing other problems.

Listening Requires Character, Courage, and Confidence

As will be further reviewed in chapters 6 and 7, getting internal inputs (what I term "in-crowdsourcing") is vital to a leader. Time and energy need to be allocated. This needs to be done both formally and informally, and regularly.

Informally, the best way is to apply MBWA, (Management By Walking Around), a term and concept coined by Tom Peters in the 1980s in his book *In Search of Excellence*. Dropping in on employees at all levels, asking them their ideas and concerns, and imparting your views, has many benefits. The Hawthorne studies reflected the employees' appreciation of attention. The leader must be careful to absorb any criticism, including nonverbal cues, and to even appreciate them. Otherwise upward information flow will stop.

As touched on earlier, losing this upward information flow is one of the most common mistakes leaders make. People's Safety Primal Drive will assess the merits versus the risks of providing candid information. Many will think, *Will the messenger be killed?* Being able to identify a problem when it is just a spark—versus allowing a later forest fire—is vital.

Celebrate "Firemen"

At one company we would annually award a fireman's hat to the best customer problem solver. It was coveted, and it was always displayed in offices. Getting a problem redirected, then solved, was an important, respected skill.

This internal openness, listening, and appreciation will have many benefits:

- Important information can be gleaned—hopefully early;
- Results potential can be enhanced.

Proactive external information gathering is always important, especially for prospects, customers, and partners; and perhaps regulators. Frequent calls and visits are good. Handwritten notes with question forms, for handwritten feedback, are creative and personal (with a hand-addressed return envelope to you). A systematic, simple feedback system is a good idea, so the entire organization can see the issues.

Go into the "lion's den" to directly solve a problem if there is a material problem—as early as possible. When the problem is on them, identify it. Often times the vendor has to protect the customer from the customer. Right should make might. If not, take action. Per the above, "know when to fold."

Be Honest With Customers

Six months after I left my acquired company, the acquiring CEO called to see if I could help solve a major customer problem (it was our customer originally, and the relationships were very strong). Upon research, I discovered the problem was on the customer's end. I visited the key C-executive, and constructively presented documented facts that the issue was his. He agreed, fixed it and the relationship was refreshed.

Set up legal competitive information gathering. As Sun Tzu advises, attack their strategy.

Drive Is Needed

An insatiable *need* to achieve (versus just a want) is critical for a leader to successfully deliver results. It is not a matter of if, but how. It is an involuntary force, not a voluntary force. Hopefully it is directed to giving value versus receiving value. It needs to be a self-worth and self-actualization need (Maslow's highest "Needs" level). It needs to be who you are at the core. Medal of Honor winners all have it. Putting themselves on death's door to take out a machine gun nest or carry wounded to safety under fire, and many more such "above and beyond the call of duty" actions, emanate from the involuntary drive to do the right thing regardless of the possible consequences, even death.

One aspect is the truism that enterprise products and services are not bought—they are *sold* (active verb). For that active verb to exist Drive must exist. Barriers need to be pushed through, climbed over, or gone around. Without Drive wilting will occur. Again, it is not if, but how?

As Jack Welch noted, drive is key to vision achievement: "Good business leaders create a vision, articulate the vision, passionately own the vision, and relentlessly *drive* it to completion." Tom Peters, in *In Search of Excellence,* recommended having a "bias toward action." A key aspect of this is keeping negative forces on their "heels," backing up, while you are on the balls of your feet moving forward. Like in boxing, if you are hitting them they are not hitting you. The former is better, trust me!

Motivational speaker Denis Waitley rightly observed that "Success is almost totally dependent upon drive and persistence. The extra energy required to make another effort or try another approach is the secret of winning."

If you don't have native drive, hire someone who does, and hold on for a great ride! Put up with them and support them. However, this should not be an "axe man." It should be a builder... a giver. A giving (versus taking) spirit is the most powerful basis of drive a leader can have.

A way to differentiate is to "ride to the sound of guns" (to where the thorny problems are). Most will not. Look for thorny problems that will be valuable to fix. Make sure it is possible, then execute. Success will stand out. Failure will often be judged as trying to do the impossible, so less negatives exist. Take smart initiative.

Remember that in all things, "the angel is in the details." This assumes the vision, motives and strategy are correct, of course. If so, detailed execution will be critical to results.

Zeal Is Drive On Steroids!

Zeal is un-stoppable and powerful. It has many faces, but must be, along with complementary *urgency*, a energy source used by leaders.

‖‖

Be in the Zone

When playing football, I noticed how the best players would, in practice and in games, go into a trance-like zone. They got that far away, glazed look in their eyes. They were in a special psychological place, somewhere around Pluto. Somebody on the other team, or in practice, was in deep trouble! That was a learning experience.

‖‖

Smaller companies have more built-in zeal and urgency because survival (Safety, Self-Interest, Hope, etc.) is literally at stake. It is a natural fear-avoiding dynamic, and the key to competitive success against larger players. It takes Energy and Time, but the alternative is very bad.

In sports, the team that "wants it" more (zeal) usually prevails. Their tempo will be faster, and they will be more on offense. The other team is then put on the defensive, just reacting. History is replete with teams trying to sit on a lead, but being overtaken by a zealous competitor that "keeps on truckin'" with zeal and urgency. Momentum is handed over.

In *In Search of Excellence* Tom Peters fostered a "sense of urgency." He was right, again.

Larger companies have the most zeal challenge for several reasons. They generally feel safer due to size. The employees are more removed from disaster due to aggregate resources and organization layers; a loss can be absorbed. There are more action slowing politics, including turf protection. Procedures in the bureaucracy impact zeal and urgency. Comfort zones based "Rusting on our laurels" is a major challenge.

The large company's "soft underbelly" is smaller, fleet, zealous competitors. Because they have to, the latter will work faster, more creatively and more diligently to outpoint "the big guys." This often enables perceived value to overcome size safety in many buyers' eyes. Zealous smaller companies will often be better at forming service-based personal relationships as a competitive weapon.

Whether large or small, how does a leader assure zeal and urgency?

- First, live it and lead with it. The ambiance is infectious. The buzzards' "Patience my __, I'm going to kill something" is a good metaphor. Or, "No prisoners!"

- Personally practice zeal and urgency in everything you do (without unduly sacrificing quality). Remember that the last 5 percent is the most costly. Perfect can be costly. Practice and preach optimality (any more or less will be sub-optimal; follow-up actions can fill any non-lethal holes).
- Constantly talk about the vital need for zeal and urgency.
- Continually ask how more zeal and urgency can be infused. Act on the ideas, visibly.
- Reward zeal and urgency champions and achievers, visibly.
- Identify and fight bureaucratic limitations, with a vengeance. The enemy of zeal and urgency is always within. Fear it. It can be controlled with purposeful efforts.
- Smaller business units, project teams, etc. put the people closer to the edge. Being at the edge is automatically self-energizing. Politics and procedures limitations are automatically reduced as well. "Intrapreneurship" is an aspect of this. Develop and nurture many "P&L" centers, with related results rewards.
- Understand and communicate, and support, the power of being "the first mover" in many situations. Get others responding TO YOU AND TO YOUR COMPANY. (BUT, you must stay ahead and not rust.)

Enthusiasm is key to drive, as verified by the observation of famed motivational speaker and author Norman Vincent Peale: "Enthusiasm releases the drive to carry over obstacles and adds significance to all that you do." Enthusiasm breeds willfulness. Be enthusiastic and your glass will always be full.

When we won a major Department of Defense (DoD) contract re-bid, zeal and urgency were rampant. We understood the ramifications of not winning. It was scary, and energizing. It allowed us to quickly learn what to do, then quickly, and well, do it. A much larger competitor that had the original bid was defeated. (The competitor CEO even called to congratulate us on the surprise win, through his tears I believe. We later acquired them at a very good equity price for us, largely due to the DoD competitive win.)

Be zealous and urgent at all times! Be enthusiastic.

"Creativeship" (per Bob Kelleher) Is Important!

In this book we have repeatedly noted, on purpose, the inevitability of change, and the need to be proactively adapting. We have also seen that being proactive is better than being reactive. Thus, creativity and innovation are essential for sustained business success. Product and services lifecycles are getting shorter and shorter, and this will continue. We have to Judo-leverage that truism for our benefit, to avoid getting harmed (aka hammered). It is a basic either-or tyranny (per Jim Collins) to be avoided.

Innovation (a wholly new idea) or evolution (an improvement) are both functions of creativity. They are a "further in" answer to the "no way out" of change dangers and opportunities.

The very good news is that "We is greater than me," and it applies to creativity also. Unleashing the creativity beast is a leader's job. The specifics will vary by business type (manufacturing versus services versus retail, and so on). But the overarching principles and methods can include any combination of:

- Rich rewards system to harness Self-Interest
- A type of job protection for innovators where the change could be negatively impactful (Safety)
- Constantly support "ideation" (Bill Gates) and "Imagineering" (Walt Disney)
- Encouraging "coloring outside the lines"
- Effective disrupters protection
- Reserve for some breakage and failure costs as "a cost of doing business"
- Introducing and using in-crowdsourcing systems and processes (with recognitions).
- Using external crowdsourcing
- Cultural change seeking versus the more typical change resistance (especially for middle management—"the muddy (or "frozen") middle")
- Time being set aside for innovation thinking and effort
- Experimenting resources be made available
- Tiger teams
- "Skunk works," answerable only to the CEO (some with directed focus, some with no specific focus)
- A business case development system and process for evaluating new ideas (do not rigidly use pre-set guidelines, since they may kill totally out-of-the-box ideas that result in a completely new, more successful company or division as a result). Ideas need to be unique and valuable, as we'll cover in more detail in chapter 7's planning section.

- Processes to tie approved innovations to be incorporated into the strategic plan (which may change as a result)
- Implementation teams, to implement the "red meat" ideas literally "thrown over the wall."

Note: This entire process is incessant, and a CEO-level priority, with regular board exposure.

||||||||||||||||||||||||||||||||||||||||||||||||||||||||||||||||||||||||||||||||||||||||||||||||||||||||||||||||||||||||||||||||||||||||||||||||||||||||||||

Be (or Foster) a "Captain Kirk"

In the Star Trek TV saga Captain James Kirk is depicted as the only cadet to solve the unsolvable Kobayashi Maru test, by creatively reprogramming the computer to make it a solvable problem. He "colored outside the lines."

||||||||||||||||||||||||||||||||||||||||||||||||||||||||||||||||||||||||||||||||||||||||||||||||||||||||||||||||||||||||||||||||||||||||||||||||||||||||||||

Creativeship is pure Darwinism in action! Pity the less proactively creative competitors. They will always lose what Trout and Reis call "Flanking Warfare" (in *Marketing Warfare).*

Judgment Is a Key Attribute

Making decisions is a leader's job. If done right, they will be few because they were correctly made below by competent, goals-focused, common sense, giving, mature leaders. But when decisions do get to the C-leader, they are thorny and each option has major negatives. The path chosen will have major negatives, along with the positives.

Thus, judgment is needed. Dr. Edward de Bono said it best: "An expert is someone who has succeeded in making decisions and judgments simpler through knowing what to pay attention to and what to ignore."

Famed astrophysicist Dr. Carl Sagan observed that "Knowing a great deal is not the same as being smart; intelligence is not information alone but also judgment, the manner in which information is collected and used."

Psychologist Dr. William James observed that "Being wise is the art of knowing what to overlook."

Good judgment requires all of the following: values, knowledge, common sense, a goals focus, prioritization, character, courage, confidence and envisioning. Decisions need to help attain goals ("results," per Drucker). Street smarts need to be applied. The result of the judgment will be felt in the future, so future vision is key. The judgment will have many negatives, and perhaps dangers, so courage is needed ("icewater in veins," but not insensitivity). The judgment will have impacts on others, so character is needed to harness their Primal Drives. Everything can never be done, so apply priorities to judgments. Decide what *not* to do as well.

Judgment needs to be selfless and kept a simple as possible. KISS is a good guideline. Throw out the extraneous and mainly emotional elements. Do not accept the options on face value as defined. See if they can be parsed, and key parts addressed. Change the rules, perhaps. Change the "playing field."

THINK in multiple dimensions, and per these guidelines (from a wall poster):

T—is it True?

H—is it Helpful?

I—is it Inspiring?

N—is it Necessary?

K—is it Kind?

Goals Versus Process Focus

This book is full of references to results goals. chapters 6 and 7 provide some goals-oriented processes.

Having a goals versus process focus is vital. As Lawrence J. Peter, author of *The Peter Principle*, noted: "If you don't know where you are going, you will probably end up somewhere else." Relatedly, I have seen many companies that are weak in this area, and the results reflect it. Several aspects of a goals-versus-process focus are:

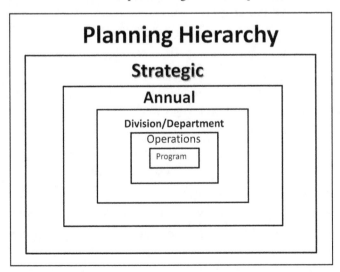

- Goals are where the results reside. Process is where the costs reside. I like the former better. It is unreasonable to expect results with zero process (costs), but it is a nice dream. It's is like someone handing you money with no effort required.
- Per Jack Welch, "What gets measured gets achieved." The visibility of goals, related accountability, and potential Self-Interest reward fuel the Primal Drives of Safety (i.e., don't get caught failing), Self-Interest (rewards) and Hope (for future continued success). Goals unleash the deep mind "iceberg" below the surface.
- Top to bottom goals alignment is needed, from shareholders' needs down to each department' results, and to each major process and person. For example, for a public company, how do departments' results affect Earnings Per Share (EPS) and the psychological Price/Earnings multiple (P/E)? For private companies, how do departments' results help with positioning for an IPO (Initial Public Offering) or being acquired for a good multiple of revenues or EBITDA?
- The value of goals is critical for optimal resource allocations (input/output) in planning and budgeting.
- Goals help to rationalize trade-off decisions (both the greater good and the lesser of the evils) that will regularly occur.
- Good goals setting leads to smarter-not-harder work. Decisions become more automatic. Management needs to be less involved, and more delegation with Safety can occur.
- Goals-focused people grow more. Future promotions using past successful results is not only safer, but less EEOC risky due to documented business requirements.

BHAG (Big Hairy Audacious Goals) focuses can be good, or bad. It is very good to stretch out of natural comfort zones that *always* form.

As wonderful writer Louisa May Alcott advised, "Far away there in the sunshine are my highest aspirations. I may not reach them, but I can look up and see their beauty, believe in them, and try to follow where they lead."

But "breaking the rubber band" in the process is stupid. Common-sense judgment is needed. The goals need to be motivating, not "Oh bleep! We are doomed to failure from the start." If the latter, your people will, quietly, not put Energy in because they know there is no Hope of Selfish reward, and there may be a Safety problem. Resumes may start to fly. Failure becomes a self-fulfilling prophesy. If so, the leader will pay the biggest cost, including common-sense respect being lost. Also, the leader may be seen as just an unreasonable, taking maniac. Not good.

You can get away with stretch goals if:

- The rewards are large.
- Curvilinear rewards are set (e.g., 90 percent =75 percent bonus; 80 percent=50 percent bonus).
- Job safety is reasonably assured if the BHAG goals are not met.
- You make sure that every tangible and intangible resource need is predetermined and provided for.
- List the assumptions about uncontrollable external forces. If these materially change, then re-planning is needed.
- Coaching occurs.
- Regular monitoring occurs.
- Past BHAG achievers have received visible rewards and promotions.

The importance and the nature of SMART goals are covered in several places in this book (and outside it). Use that construct. Doing so may be hard versus just some process statement, but that is one of the reasons they pay you, or will pay you, the big bucks.

Use Teams

This is increasingly important. Multiple disciplines are brought to bear, and subsequent implementations by these participants will go better as a result. The plans will be better, and the buy-in stronger. "We is truly greater than me."

There are many ways to set up and manage teams, and numerous books exist. I have a bias toward setting goals, process milestones and timetable, and using a skilled facilitator with access to needed resources, including information. This process allows leaders to emerge naturally, for future promotion reference. The increased team autonomy better taps the Primal Drives as well.

"Skunk works" creativity teams need to have more autonomy. If goals are set, they need to be broad. Pure "bottom up" teams do not need goals, just a "greenfield" mandate.

Introduce and Use Leadership Development Programs

The Preface talks about leaders being the backbone of the economy. Likewise, leaders are the backbone of the organization, and need to be proactively nurtured as a key asset.

Doing so can include many elements, including any or all of:

- On the job training
- College programs, funded
- Mentoring
- Internal leadership programs
- External leadership programs
- Teams participation
- Self-learning
- Formal evaluations.

The below "C's" are good criteria to use. They will engender respect and foster results.

||||||||||||||||||||||||||||||||||||||||||||||||||||||||||||||||||||||||||||||||||||||||||||||||||||||||||||||||||||||||||||||||||||||||||

The "C's" Rule!

Character
Courage
Conscientiousness
Confidence
Conceptualization
Competitiveness
Conviction
Conviviality
Commitment

||||||||||||||||||||||||||||||||||||||||||||||||||||||||||||||||||||||||||||||||||||||||||||||||||||||||||||||||||||||||||||||||||||||||||

Respect Is the Must Have Culmination

Do worry about being respected. All of the above attributes will be needed to be respected. Practice all of the "C's." Respect is the single, cumulative vehicle for others feeling their Primal Drives will be served. Respect is more important than being liked, but being liked is icing. Just don't put likeability before respect.

Remember, "the hard way is the easy way, and the easy way is the hard way." Do the right things, even if they're harder. Just win the Why positioning. This will trigger the Primal Drives of others, and the beast of personal commitment to the mission will be unleashed. Lead from the front and walk your talk. Keep your word. That you will reap what you sow is an immutable law of nature (like the Primal Drives are as well).

Summary

In just a little over fifty years, leadership success practices have dramatically evolved—and will continue to do so. The cultural, economic, technological, and political contexts will also continue to change. But our core Primal Drives will not. However, they just have to be connected to the surrounding contexts by smart, savvy, results-focused leaders who strongly serve the Primal Drives of followers. Many To Do's exist—which contrast sharply with the chapter 4 Not To Do's.

Vision, character, confidence, courage, correctly used power and drive are all needed to achieve results in an ever more challenging world. That's your job. Go for the gold—intelligently, with common sense, a giving purpose and vision, attitude, judgment, and ethics. Bring out the Primal Drives in your people by practicing the To Do elements for each Primal Drive.

Effective listening is important. Having a bias for action is an attribute. "Creativeship" to foster new ideas innovation and evolution are Darwinism personified.

Good judgment is an attribute to have and foster.

Proper goal setting is vital for results Safety and other Primal Drives to be realized.

Use teams and proactively develop leaders.

The culmination is earning all important RESPECT!

Chapter Six

Unleash The Results *Animal* in You...and in Others

SOME PRIMORDIAL LEADERSHIP METHODS AND TOOLS

U p to now, we have covered the Why and the What of Primordial Leadership. This chapter will mostly cover some How elements.

While the envisioning, people leading, and people motivating roles are the most critical elements of leadership, surrounding processes, pressures, and expectations contexts also exist that need to be addressed and also leveraged. Managers need these as well.

Foremost among these are:

- A focus on financial success results, to fully realize stakeholder value
- Constant, change-based, multi-level planning
- Value positioning
- Learning imperatives
- Managing change
- Time use
- Go-to-Market competitive success

- Customer support
- People resources development and support.

Each will be briefly addressed.

Leaders vs. Managers

> "A manager does things right, a leader does the right things"
> —Dr. Peter Drucker

A leader can be also be a manager, but a manager is not necessarily a leader.

We can distinguish a leader from a manager in the following ways. A leader:

- Is more envisioning
- Has a stronger "spatial" mind
- Is more intuitive
- Is more Why focused vs. What and How
- Is more ends vs. means focused, and goals vs. process focused
- Is more focused on longer-range thinking
- Is timing sensitive
- Is more aware of affective intangibles (values, principles, megatrends, change vectorings, the Primal Drives, etc.) and thus is more apt to harness them
- Is more comfortable with change (and thus better seeks it out)
- Is more comfortable with risk
- Plans, plans, plans
- Understands that financial results are the key focus
- Is less naturally comfortable/skilled with details (which can be delegated).

Financial Success

In commercial companies, financial success is the ultimate yardstick for measuring leadership success (other factors exist in government entities, as discussed in chapter 8). The role of the Primal Drives is to help optimize financial success. All private companies, public companies, non-profits, and government entities must achieve financial success to be sustained over time. Resources are allocated by others (e.g., venture capitalists, stockholders, boards, donors, politicians), as long as their own

Self-Interest, Safety, and Hope are served. Thus, financial success is a barometer for leadership efficacy, and it has its own aspects.

The financial success requirement is strongest in commercial companies, public or private. The principal focus here will be on stakeholder value being specifically delivered by the leader. (For technical details the reader is pointed to the many books, such as *Finance for the Non-Financial Manager,* by Gene Siciliano.)(The upcoming book *Primordial Marketing and Sales* will focus on revenue generation success.) This section will cover increased shareholder value and liquidity. Non-liquid value has little true value.

Private Companies

For stakeholders, it's all about attaining balance sheet wealth, not just income statement wealth! The former occurs when there is a high-value liquidity event or status. The latter occurs when comfort zones cause us to think that operating a business perpetually is successful leadership, which may be true in only one situation: a family business to be handed down to progeny (perhaps the most challenging type of business to run and sustain if multiple siblings exist).

Seeking balance sheet wealth via a high-value exit or stock price growth is an imperative for several reasons:

- It provides Safety to shareholders: a bird in the hand is worth n in the bush.
- It mitigates risk via diversity.
- It earns money itself.
- It provides more self-control of investments by shareholders.
- It avoids costly and dangerous debt (e.g., for cars, homes, college, etc.).
- New, potentially profitable enterprises can be considered due to the safety and resources base, reflecting the truism, "it takes money to make money."
- Our progeny will best benefit, and potentially have a life even better than we had—a high priority for a parent.

While running a lifestyle or family business has value, I generally tend to agree with the statement once heard that "A true entrepreneur either has sold a company, or will." But how do we do it?

First, Covey's "Begin with the end in mind" is key. While the below exit criteria should not cause poor or poorly timed operating decisions, all operating programs need to consciously enforce these below Exit Criteria truisms over time, in approximate order:

- A combination of the below elements
- Being a defacto leader in a valued space, with strong market share
- Differentiated and valuable products or services
- A leveragable value chain of partners
- Domain expertise that can be leveraged.
- Strong top-line revenues growth
- Strong, accretive EBITDA (Earnings Before Interest, Taxes, Depreciation and Amortization) and cash growth

Obviously, the combination is the best value platform to have.

Defacto market leadership has several inherent values:

1. Acquirer deal payback Safety, since it is hard to dethrone the leader (*Marketing Warfare* by Trout and Reis provide some ideas for the smaller competitors, and I have used them to win against one-time leaders.) Leadership Safety reduces the risk discount in the offer (or the Price/Earnings [P/E] multiple for public companies).
2. For feeding Self-Interest, the acquirer can also better sell its products/services to the new customer base, perhaps via the partners, providing new value (that the seller should get some credit for in the negotiation by forecasting the new potentials).

Strong financial growths are self-defining. Being able to project these out three to five years with credibility will provide a present value basis for the acquisition price and terms. Value positioning and strong go-to-market programs will be needed, based on strategic planning so that inevitable change can be harnessed versus being abusive. These are covered in more detail below. Tangible and off-balance sheet assets and liabilities will also be important to valuation. The customer base is often the most valuable intangible asset. Patents can have safety value. Partners also.

The "deal currency" is an important consideration. If it includes non-cash elements (e.g., stock, options, warrants, debt, assets), then bidirectional valuations and protections are needed in the purchase agreement (PA). The same protections are reciprocally needed. This includes Reps (Representations) and Warrantees, escrow protections, value protections, earnouts, etc. Buyer reps and warrantees are also provided.

Be careful about "earnouts," however. These are increasingly used as a key Safety factor for the acquirer. Negotiate that if carefully defined assumptions, priorities, resources, leadership, organization (e.g., the sales force's role), or control factors change—then the outstanding, contingency-based payments are due immediately. Carefully and completely define what the present and agreed-on criteria are, and how change impacts will be handled. Without these metrics and what-if agreements, any changes will be hard to clearly identify in terms of results and can end in an expensive, risky, delayed legal process. With clear, unequivocal metrics and what-if criteria, an expensive dispute is less likely.

Any "escrows," or conditional holdbacks for a period, often a year, need to be carefully defined and managed. The protection is purely for the acquirer if certain agreed-to possible or unforeseen varying events occur. Some escrow elements could be:

- Five percent or less of the deal value escrow is not uncommon, with 10 percent an occasional amount.
- A "bucket" of a certain value variance size has to be exceeded before escrows are accessible.
- Release criteria, including for "force majeure" events or acquirer actions that are not the seller's responsibility.
- Subsections of the deal might be all that are required.

The PA should allow the escrowed amounts to be properly invested and the interest accrue to the acquired—perhaps with any interest on recaptured amounts to go to the acquirer.

Make the reps and warrantees in the purchase agreement (PA) as detailed and disclosing as possible initially. Get the problems out early in related schedules and accepted as part of the deal, or there *will* be disputes later.

Where "to the best of our knowledge" representations are allowed, make sure a variance's newness can be factually supported later if a variance arises that was unanticipated and not identified in schedules, thus becoming a risk/cost for the acquirer only, as a "cost of doing business."

If non-cash stock or assets, etc., are part of the escrow, then the acquirer needs to hold the acquired harmless for any loss of value or restriction due to actions by the acquirer that had no involvement by the acquired.

Make sure the escrow agreement is tight as to exactly what (and only) is allowed to trigger a "clawback," with metrics, for the release of the escrow to either party.

Make sure the PA says no other variances by the acquirer are permitted for triggering the escrow clawback.

Ensure that the escrow agent is reputable, independent, and well compensated by the acquirer. This includes for legal protection for the escrow agent. Such compensation should have no effect on the escrow release terms. The escrow release criteria need to be very specific and directly relate to the reps and warrantees.

Arbitration is often an option, binding or not.

Legal fees awarded to the prevailing party in a dispute are often included.

Management and non-compete agreements need to be tightly negotiated and adhered to by the parties. Note that these agreements often have special tax treatments for both parties.

ESOPs (Employee Stock Ownership Plans) are still used, but relatively less so today. The IRS and other governments' rules are very tight in this area to protect employees, who usually are not "qualified investors" (do not have over $1 million in net assets each), who have more legal protection and resulting increased "caveat emptor" protections. The extra paperwork, legal expenses, and governmental scrutiny over time, and stiff legal sanctions for fraud, make this an extra challenging liquidity path.

Public Companies

Public company leaders are intimately familiar with elements such as quarterly EPS (Earnings Per Share), the P/E ratio (price-to-earnings multiples), managing analysts' expectations (including the "whisper" expectations), Sarbanes-Oxley (SOX) requirements, and many(!) other SEC and federal rules and procedures put in place to protect present and potential stockholders from many possible abuses. Practicing such abuses has now become criminally liable and not just civil as in the past. Say Enron and Worldcom.

A key leadership role is how to both grow EPS and gain a higher P/E multiple than competitors in the sector. First, each sector has a range of possible P/E ratios associated with it. How one achieves and retains a higher P/E than competitors is a leadership challenge—and opportunity. Changing sectors with Wall Street analysts is one option for attaining a higher P/E ratio.

Geoffrey Moore, in *The Gorilla Game*, well addressed the competitive advantage issue when he described the Competitive Advantage Period (CAP) concept for achieving a better P/E. While it is well known that the weighted P/E multiple is psychological in nature based on Safety, Self-Interest, and Hope expectations, having a valued differentiated advantage is the key focus. Those with this kind of differentiated advantage were seen to be relatively Safer and there was higher Hope that economic gains (Self-Interest) could be better realized. Thus, the stock was worth more, even if the EPS is the same.

The differentiation(s) need to be real and valued by Wall Street. The differentiations provide added Safety, Self-Interest-based outsize gains potentials, and Hope for future results. The weighted differentiation factors vary by industry, but could include:

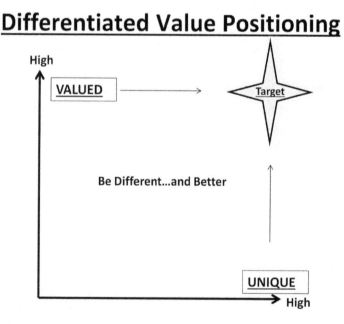

Differentiated Value Positioning

- Efficiency or operating ratios in banking and insurance respectively. These evaluate the underlying use of operating costs to produce fees and net interest income revenue results. Companies continually strive to have these ratios as the best. Financial analysts reward that.
- The best balance sheets, with acceptable debt leverage

- Technology advantages, including patents. This is especially true in technology, pharmaceuticals, manufacturing, and more.
- Advantageous labor contracts, including costs and work rules minimization
- Partners' quality and dependability
- Value chain quality and control (a key for Walmart, for example)
- International footprint, for diversity
- R&D investment and proven results (e.g., Verizon and its continual innovation in "xG" cell speeds for data)
- Automation levels
- Government contracts, which are less likely to terminate in general
- Market share.

Different industries have different core differentiations that must be understood and leveraged.

Achieving the valued positioning among competitors is a function of excellent leadership, including future change forecasting and leveraging, value positioning, go-to-market excellence, operating excellence and some sort of special differentiation power.

Government Entities

Since all budgets must go through a political review process, actually and perceptually providing great services to the public being served, resulting in political support, is the key. The feedback from public stakeholders will affect valuation and subsequent resource allocations among many government agencies by politicians. (This allocation justification may well become ever more important in the future, as government expenditures are reduced per capita after decades of increasing.)

Proactive open disclosure of results is important, especially to constituents of the political leaders on which your entity depends. This is a "pull" strategy. Politicians cannot get surprised by announcements, and should get the credit, but you need to get to their constituency with the value message. The media is a key to this process.

Non-Profits

The stakeholders' needs being well met will provide the feedback and market valuation needed to sustain revenues and critical cash flow. As was noted in chapter 2 in regard to altruism's limitations, creative ways need to be found to go beyond pure altruism as the only value basis. As with government entities, having the end constituents perceiving direct value is the key to support. Chapter 8 has more insights.

Value Positioning

When seeking funding from venture capitalists (VCs), private equity firms or "angels," and when preparing to go public (much more difficult and rare after the Sarbanes-Oxley law), and if a public company already, several key criteria are required, as reflected below.

Such investors begin with a position of risk (aka Safety Primal Drive), so will actively seek Safety via the company's standing on these and other criteria. Self-Interest-based payoff potentials are less of a motivator if survival Safety is not highly probable. They want a highly certain, high value "out" potential down the road, to provide earnings growth for their limited partners' investments of principle.

For VC and private equity investors, and angels, a 10x+ return is the target, knowing that some will fail but others will carry those with strong returns. Thus, VCs et al definitely operate by the Primal Drives of Safety, Hope, and Self-Interest. They expect Honesty. They want to be Sociable—if you succeed. If not, they will, and should, replace you if they have a majority share.

Key Investment Criteria

- The company has truly "disruptive," rule-changing, *differentiated* solutions that are *materially unique,* and *the differences are valued.*
- High ROI and/or compelling needs value exist that <u>drive</u> "best-of-class" purchasing energy and speed, and permits high margin value pricing ("sell to pain"). (For a small company, it must overcome the perception of small company risk to buyers by having compelling, unique solutions.)
- No major, uncontrollable success risks exist.
- The management team has strong domain expertise, technical and growth experience, skills, depth, a winning track record, and sustainability over several growth stages over time.
- Management team has expertise and track record in high value exits. (Investors eventually want a good value liquidity event. Banks and mezzanine financiers safely want their money back plus interest.)
- The company has a large market that can sustain steady revenue growth, good profit growth, good cash growth, and ability to pay the debt.

- The market is not owned by others, or deep-pocket competitors do not exist; there are no or low entry barriers.
- There is good potential for partners, especially on the "sell-side" (and who are also good exit potentials).
- Barriers to entry can be raised, especially by being the defacto leader in one or more segments. Patents and partners help.
- Fast, sustainable revenue and EBITDA growths are projectable with credibility.
- A solid business marketing, sales, and financial plan exists, including how funds are to be used. With Good, Base and Bad Case versions.
- There are sufficient funds to reach a critical mass of positive net cash flow, even under a bad case scenario (the times-interest-earned ratio will be critical to banks, as well as collateral and guarantees).
- There is a strong exit potential and likelihood, at a strong multiple (includes other deals in the space, and multiples).
- The "space" generally feels active and of interest to investors.

Likewise, the success of both IPOs (initial public offerings) and "secondary offerings" for public companies will depend on the quality of the Safety and Self-Interest returns issues. The "road show" must evoke why both will be strong and can be relied on. Stocks are purchased based on "expectations." The market price will reflect the risk-adjusted present value of future expectations. Wall Street analysts are key to this perception. The investment banker will protect the positioning's veracity, because it cares more about long term relationships with investors being protected than about you as a one-off.

Value positioning for markets has its own dynamics and will vary by market segment. Both absolute value and value relative to alternatives must be defined. Valued differentiations are critical to achieve, and such

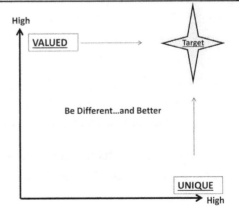

Differentiated Value Positioning

High

VALUED ────────▶ Target

Be Different...and Better

UNIQUE

High

innovations can be rules-changing. Jack Trout's *Differentiate or Die* book reflects the prime importance of differentiated value positioning.

Go-To-Market Success

This will be covered in the coming *Primordial Marketing and Sales* book.

Planning, Planning, Planning!

> "The battle is won or lost long before the first clash of steel."
> —Sun Tzu, The Art of War

Just as "location, location, and location" are the three legs of real estate value and success, strategic, annual, and operational planning (including CPI, or Continuous Process Improvement, Lean, and Six Sigma) are keys for business success. (chapter 7 provides more planning methodologies.)

The importance of this view is contained in these definitions of leadership activity:

- Reactive: Self-defining, and the least strong, but it is sometimes the only option.
- Active: Sees what is to come and prepares for it to be most advantageous.
- Proactive: Determines what will happen, <u>for all to react to</u>.

Obviously the last two are the most desirable, especially the third. Keep competitors on their heels. Planning is the tonic for doing so.

Yet planning often is the weakest leadership area in terms of purposeful, proactive efforts. Thus it is a great opportunity to differentiate from competitors, because they have the same lethargy also. As someone once said, "Who gets there the firstest with the mostest or bestest wins." Figuring out how to continually do that is the purpose of regular planning.

‖‖

Being the First with New Technologies Won Us the Worldwide and Government Business

Our semi-annual strategic planning foresaw that data communications would evolve to TCP/IP, open systems, and later to the Internet (we even predicted a common interface, based on the Primal Drives, much later called a "browser" by Netscape).

When UNiSYS later approached us to do an at-cost TCP/IP "stack," we said yes, where our larger competitor had said no first because it did not have a proactive change vision. We had better foreseen the coming needs and they had not. Game over. We leveraged that and other vision-based innovations to win all the business, worldwide, by entering into a strategic business alliance.

When a large, Department of Defense (DoD)-wide contract for technology was to be re-bid, we went to the controlling military base, learned future needs, and educated them on other ideas, that they liked. Four months later we returned with 201 criteria and a demonstration of all of them. The last criterion was that all features had to be in commercial operation BEFORE the re-bid RFP was published, to avoid "we will be able to do that too" by scrambling competitors. Nine of nine "prime" contractors had to bid our products, as the only complying ones. Very lucrative. Later, having all of DoD as a customer was a major company purchase factor by a large public company. The shareholders did very well.

||||||||||||||||||||||||||||||||||||||||||||||||||||||||||||||||||||||||||||||||||||||||||||||||||||||||||||||||||||||||||||||||||||||||||||||||||||

Win the sales war by winning the criteria battle…via planning.

Why is proactive planning so underutilized? Eight possible answers are:

- Everyone is heads-down, putting out fires, with no time for planning (a self-fulfilling prophesy!). This is an alligator-swamp conundrum.
- Some leaders simply do not value longer term planning versus the time "opportunity" costs.
- Looking into the future fog is very uncertain and emotionally challenging.
- Doing so may change things too much.
- Some feel comfortable with how to successfully do it.
- Some fear it might upset the current "turfs," and be a career risk.
- Some just like "seat-of-the-pants" decision making, driving with their eyes on the hood ornament versus the horizon.

- Some do not have the needed "temporal focus." "A secretary thinks about today. A supervisor a week. A director a month. A vice president a quarter. A president a year. The CEO three years. The Chairman ten years."(Source: A former mentor.)

Some report that Japanese companies are out to fifty years in their planning, the value of which is debatable. I believe three years is the minimum time for most and it may be five to ten years for companies whose production and other processes are time consuming and very costly to implement (e.g., heavy manufacturing). For the 90 percent of companies that are small to medium-sized business, three years is a good starting point. But do five years or more if long launch cycles are required. Update at least annually, if not semi-annually.

This plan then needs to be supported by annual plans that are successful themselves and contribute to the strategic plan.

Operational plans, often by division and/or department, support the annual plan. Goals, resources, authority, rewards, and accountability (aka RARA) need to be cascaded. Since CPI (Continuous Process Improvement) is usually for a specific function, it often resides as a program plan. Lean and Six Sigma programs may rise to operational planning levels, as demonstrated by Motorola, GE, Seagate, and others.

Allocating resources for these planning endeavors, including executives managing day-to-day requirements, is a critical resourcing decision. In the input-output model, if the inputs are weak, the outputs will be weak. Some leaders set aside two p.m. to six p.m. three days a week for a month to conduct this process, with staff or consultant personnel providing the underlying information. Often offsite forums are helpful, with phones off except at lunch. Facilitators may need to be resourced to assure:

- Proper, proven processes are used.
- The tangible and intangible impacts of turfs protection on plans objectivity are mitigated.
- Strategic, annual, and operational plans are truly aligned, and cascaded.

Strategic, annual, operational/departmental and project planning processes are all critical to success. The specific processes are presented in chapter 7.

Operational Execution

Within the annual plan, the operational plans will be prepared that roll up to the support annual plan.

At this level, versus typical job descriptions for personnel, a critical element is using Key Results Descriptions (KRD) for managers versus the normal non-metrical job descriptions (from a Dale Carnegie Basic Management Course I once used to help train the many new managers who were promoted from within). This provides SMART (Specific, Measurable, Action-focused, Resourced, and Time-based) plan support for each role. An example is below.

Operations Director Key Results Description (KRD)

- The budget will be realized with a +/- 2 percent variance, unless varied with or by management.
- Waste will not be below Six Sigma levels (99.9997 successful).
- All production goals will be met or exceeded.
- Voluntary turnover will not exceed 4 percent annually.
- 100 percent of employees will successfully complete assigned training requirements.
- Zero valid EEOC complaints.
- Zero lost time safety events.
- At least two innovations will be either submitted or implemented that improve results at least 5 percent each.
- At least four improved process ideas will be submitted.
- At least three subordinates will be mentored and prepared for promotion.
- Any union grievances submitted will be winnable by management.
- At least two community activities will be participated in.

With such numerical goals, usually segmented into quarters, clear "end-in-mind," measurable actions can occur. This helps ensure the alignment of the self-interests of the subordinates with those of the company. Thus not much "management" is needed; mostly just monitoring, fine tuning, and supporting. If annual and/or operational plans change, new KRDs are developed on an agreed-on basis.

The above allows for a type of Management by Objectives (MBO) program to be implemented. However, care must be taken that the MBO program remains a "means" and not an "end." If a central HR system is not in place, one method to manage this is to use the Milestones Achievement Progress (MAP) scoring system (first introduced to me at a Northeastern University Executive Management seminar).

||||||||||||||||||||||||||||||||||||||||||||||||||||||||||||||||||||||||||||||||||||||||||||||||||||||||||||||||||||||||||||||||||||||||||||

MAP

MAP goals are set at least quarterly in six to eight key areas, with as many numerical goals as possible. They should tie to and enforce the manager's KRD. Key resourcing assumptions or dependencies on others are also noted, to protect the manager from uncontrollable dependencies variances (including when other departments drop the ball).

||||||||||||||||||||||||||||||||||||||||||||||||||||||||||||||||||||||||||||||||||||||||||||||||||||||||||||||||||||||||||||||||||||||||||||

MILESTONES ACHIEVEMENT PROGRESS (M.A.P.) PLAN			FOR: FOR MONTH: DATE:		"What gets measured gets achieved."–Jack Welch			
TASK NAME	OBJECTIVE (S.M.A.R.T. #)	TASK WEIGHT (1-5)	RESOURCE NEEDS	END RESULTS ACHIEVED	COMMENTS	SCORE (5,4,3,2,1,0)	WEIGHTED SCORE	OTHER NOTES
		1				0	0	
		1				0	0	
		1				0	0	
		1				0	0	
		1				0	0	
		1				0	0	
		1				0	0	
		1				0	0	(SCORES WEIGHTS)
		8 WGT. TOTAL	(DELETE EMPTY ROWS WEIGHTS)		TOTAL SCORE	0	0	
2.5 = Goal achievement score								
COMMENTS:					AVG. SCORE	0	0	
					VAR. FROM 2.5 TARGET	-2.5	-2.5	-100.00%

Thus, inter-department dependencies are important to define if they exist.

Scoring is done mutually by manager and subordinate, with constructive and defendable objectivity, and with a 0–5 score range for each goal. A score of 2.5 is goal attainment as planned. A 1 or 2 score means underachievement, and a possible 0 means no effort at all. A 3, 4, or 5 score means the goal was exceeded. The high scores needs to be calibrated to avoid "inflation." And a 4 or 5 might be reviewed at one level higher. A perceived unfair score should be challengeable. Honest accuracy is the underlying purpose, fostering both goals focus, fairness and trust.

In the event that stated dependencies did not occur, then that goal should not be scored, since the results were beyond the manager's control.

A 2.75 average is often the quarterly and annual target, for bonus and year-end performance reviews. The inherent result is a set of reasonable "stretch" goals. Employees are paid a wage or salary, so reasonable average results are already being paid for. If the average results are exceeded, then a reward can be justified. This principle needs to be established early and followed by all. A review policy for averages >2.65 or < 2.35 can be used to assure that objectivity prevails.

The last two columns are for variance explanations (plus or minus), and possible remedial or acceleration ideas.

After scoring, a new MAP program can be mutually prepared for the next quarter. The scored MAP is filed for use at annual performance review time.

Scores can be used for a bonus allocation factor if a bonus pool is earned in general.

As noted, MAP's core objective is goals-focused fairness, with the hope that the employee will be a hero. (Part of a leader's job is to create results-generating heroes that grow in the company.) A sense of fairness and accuracy are imperatives, as well as goals alignment. Challenges to scores should be afforded in a positive manner, and negotiated. Escalating an objection should be an option. Merit will prevail.

Allocating bonus or "gain sharing" results is important (Note: Profit sharing has some legal requirements). Once a bonus pool is established, the right allocation criteria are needed. Some might be:

- Must be employed for the full fiscal year of the bonus pool allocation
- 1/3 by relative pay percent
- 1/3 for absolute and relative MAP scores
- 1/3 for supervisor evaluation per established performance review criteria.

Challenges should be allowed, to foster trust.

Other performance review criteria should also be used, as set by HR.

End-in-Mind Project/Program Planning

These are usually a subset of operational plans for specific projects or programs. "Dynamic programming" is a spatial, end-in-mind tool for breaking a complex problem into its key parts and aligning strategies and tactics on the ends wanted (and the ends not wanted as well).

In this graphic, we start at the right side and list the goals we want, and what we do *not* want to happen as well. We then move *left* and name the up to six Key Success

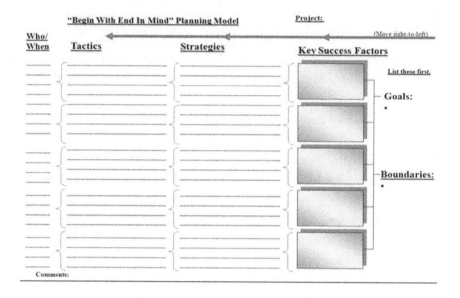

Factor (KSF) constructs that will be needed. We then move left again to the key strategies for realizing each KSF.

Tactics are then set for each strategy, including people and other resources needed, and deadlines. This Why, What (KSF), How, Who, and When flow is a powerful process. The How Much projections need to be provided also, for the business case.

This process is very good to help subordinates think through all kinds of issues: sales strategies; new programs or projects; proposals; exit planning, and more.

Dynamic programming can be used for all of strategic planning through to individual sales or partnering deals. The right-to-left flow is purposefully a "backward" flow to stimulate the mind to be spatial, like working the maze backward, per chapter 3.

Process Improvement (often called Continuous Process Improvement, or CPI)

Along with BPM (Business Process Management), these more tactical methodologies help with improving operations results, efficiency, and effectiveness.

Lean and Six Sigma are the popular, rigorous methodologies commonly accepted to do so. Design for Six Sigma (DFSS) and Eight Disciplines (8D) are alternatives.

A veritable language, including Business Process Model and Notation (BPMN) symbols, are commonly used by "Black Belts." Current state and Future state value steam maps are often constructs.

> "A useful way of improving processes successfully is to use a lean manufacturing technique called Value Stream Mapping (VSM). It originated at car manufacturer Toyota, where they called it 'material and information flow mapping.' VSM is now widely used in a variety of industries as a way of identifying improvement projects."
>
> —mindtools.com

Many Japanese words are used in Lean Six Sigma due to the fact that core improvement principles were most aggressively developed and applied in Japan in the 1950s, thanks to the influence of Dr. W. Edwards Deming, an American. The Japanese wanted to move out of their historical low price-low quality products paradigm to a quality paradigm. They sought help, and Dr. Deming responded. Dr. Deming once noted that if you cannot define your process you do not have a process. Thus, defining the process is critical. Mapping is its visual representation.

Actively Build and Use Business Cases

Just as a process does not exist if it is not defined, a business case is critical to prepare for business success. For a publicly traded company, preparing a business case is a fiduciary, legal responsibility. It should be standard practice in all businesses. It needs to be complex enough to capture all of the key Why vision and goals, What outside-in focuses, How plans, When timings, By Whom organization, and the How Much financial results (including the inputs-outputs, and capital and/or acquisition needs). Set a cash plan also.

Competitive positioning needs to be in the What section (for both absolute value for customers and for competitive differentiation). Risks need to be assessed and mitigated. Cascaded sub-plans may be needed. Good, Bad, and Most Likely plans are a good idea. Make sure key stakeholders have an input before being submitted. Tie the business case to the adopted corporate vision, mission statement, goals and adopted policies as applicable. Many business case examples and templates are online from which to choose.

Change Management

All changes, be they strategic, annual, operational, or process improving, involve changes to the organization. As will be shown in chapter 7, avoiding change resistance is critical, is difficult, must be done, and can be optimally achieved if correctly understood and approached.

> "The only human that likes change is a baby with a dirty diaper."
> —John Best, Master Black Belt (MBB)

When in doubt in regard to managing change, build this table and use it for your planning to best leverage the Primal Drives in each situation.

Program/Audience Focus:		
Date:	By:	
To Do's	Primal Drives To Leverage	Not To Do's
	Safety	
	Self-Interest	
	Hope and Transcendence	
	Honesty and Trust	
	Energy/Time Optimization	
	Sociability	

Learning

Every organization needs to be a continuous learning organization, starting from the top and on an ongoing basis due to constant change. This imperative is reflected by the famous quote by Robert Reich, former Labor Secretary in the Clinton administration: "The only unique asset that a business has for gaining a sustained competitive advantage over rivals is its workforce—the skills and dedication of its employees. There is no other sustainable competitive advantage in the modern, high-tech, global economy."

> "An organization's ability to learn, and translate that learning into action rapidly, is the ultimate competitive advantage."
> —Jack Welch

"A manager is responsible for the application and performance of <u>knowledge</u>."

—Peter Drucker

Adult education (andragogy) is critical, but significantly different from children's education (pedagogy). Redundancies, hands-on practice, time flexibility, accountability, engaging content and other variables must be addressed.

Summary

To achieve results, key business concepts and processes are needed in addition to the Why of the Primal Drives.

Getting financial liquidity results for shareholders is the major imperative for leaders of both public and private companies.

"Planning, planning, planning" is the needed framework. Multiple, cascaded levels of planning exist, with requirements for each. Getting employees' input regarding needs and plans has many benefits.

Project planning needs to use an "end-in-mind" approach, moving from right to left.

Aligning performance to organizational goals is an imperative, with monitoring and feedback. Bonus allocations need to be tied to performance, and fair.

Continuous Process Improvement is important, with several proven methodologies available.

Effectively managing change is an imperative.

Achieving a "learning organization" status has many valuable benefits. Training adults is a challenge.

Chapter Seven

Unleash The Results *Animal* in You...and in Others

PLANNING AND EFFECTIVE CHANGE MANAGEMENT

"It is not the strongest species that survive, nor the most intelligent, but the ones most responsive to change."

—Darwin

"You must be the change you wish to see in the world."

—Mahatma Gandhi

"To improve is to change; to be perfect is to change often."

—Winston Churchill

As we saw earlier, when there is no way out (to avoid the impacts of change) the answer is to "go further in" (leverage change). Thus the Judo Principle is a key success concept. Planning is the "further in" vehicle.

Planning and continual replanning are critical given the reality that not only is change an imperative, but it is even *existential*. Per this oft-repeated graphic, forces are constantly changing around us all the time—and changing the success rules constantly.

Nothing will stay the same for very long, and the change speed is accelerating. This change acceleration will . . . accelerate! Only planning will keep us ahead of this reality, and avoid us being caught short.

Darwinism, or the survival of the most adaptable, is real, and its power must be Judo-leveraged. The alternative to doing so is very bad, recognizing that change is constant and will define, and re-define destinies. All the success rules will change. Strengths will inevitably become weaknesses. We must "eat our young before others do." This can only be done via planning.

Look what happened to Research in Motion (the makers of the BlackBerry) when their planning missed the relatively rapid switch to sensory needs versus business needs by a major part of the mobile market, which even eventually impacted the business user market. Look at the US Republican Party when they missed the change from the past self-reliance value system to more of a government-dependent value system by many. Both dynamics could have been leveraged if better foreseen and strategized.

In the 1960s the Big Three auto companies' planning missed the quiet pivot toward higher quality and lower priced cars. They did not sufficiently understand the quiet power of Kotler's and DeBono's "Generic Benefits" (the core reasons we buy what we buy, which are also Primordially based), and how to continually reposition on them. Foreign producers' planning was much more robust, saw this benefits based shift and have taken advantage of it. The Big Three's marketshare is now a fraction of what it was. Many disruptions have occurred, including the need for massive government bailouts, at taxpayers' expense, to even survive for two of them.

As a planning zealot, Jack Welch's "Neutron Jack" label was due to his insistence that if a division could not plan and act to be number one or number two in its market it should be sold or terminated, even if profitable. He came to this view when he realized that 20 percent of his divisions were generating 80 percent of gains, and all of these were segment leaders with planning-based visions. He left buildings standing, but the people were gone, just like a neutron bomb causes. As a result, GE became the highest valued and most admired company in the world under Welch.

Plan, Plan, Plan

Good planning is the key to good change, and competitive advantage. Specific, quality strategic, annual, and operating plans are needed.

Strategic Planning

In *Future Shock*, Tofler noted that the generation at the time would see more innovation than all prior generations combined since any records were kept. Thus change is continual in humans (Transcendence), and is generally caused by four key forces:

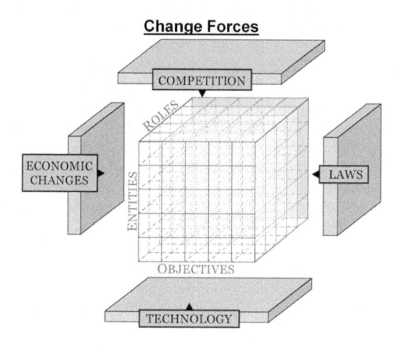

Change Forces

Technology. This is the fastest moving and most disruptive driver of change. It is also the best opportunity to change the fastest and best versus competitors. Tofler also noted that "experiation" would increasingly define technology products' success. Being able to <u>experience</u> a product doing something for us versus using the product would be a key differentiator. Moore's Law (named after the co-founder of Intel) correctly stated that computer hardware's capabilities would double every eighteen months "for at least ten years," and it has continued after that.

Most technology innovations or evolutions make today's capabilities easier, faster, safer, and more economical; all direct contributions to buyers' Primal Drives. The web, mobile technologies, social media, new devices, cloud computing, and other technology innovations continually change all the rules. More will constantly be coming. Some other innovations, especially in pharmaceuticals and medical research, are mostly innovative (as opposed to evolutionary).

Competition. Those pesky devils! They are always doing something to change the competitive rules. It's like Butch Cassidy said to the Sundance Kid when being pursued for weeks by a determined posse: "Don't they ever give up?" The answer is no, it will always be no, and their expected moves must be projected via planning—and leveraged. "Game Theory" and other methods are often used to do this. Whatever method is used, we must project what they will do to build on their strengths and shore up their weaknesses. They may try to create new spaces and find key differentiations. It is not *if* they will, but how and when.

I am not proposing industrial espionage, but many methods and feedbacks can be used to get a reading on what they are doing and why. These can be used to project the future moves. Trade articles, news releases, partner feedbacks, industry analysts, their customers, their prospects, and your salespeople can provide key feedbacks. Pieces of the puzzle can be connected to form a mosaic. Their patent submissions can be very revealing. Once directions are forcastable, then countering and leveraging plans can be set. Very important is to be zealously proactive and not just reactive in this planning process.

Laws. Laws and regulations constantly change, and enable or destroy businesses. This is especially true for Federal laws. Forecasting these is a major challenge. "What if" contingency planning can be used for quickly pivoting. For example, the Affordable Care Act will have profound changes on healthcare quality and costs, employment, taxes, and more.

|||||||||||||||||||||||||||||||||||||||||||||||||||||||||||||||||||||||||||||||||||||||||||||||||||||||||||||||||||||||||||||

PEOs Arose from New Tax Laws

These indirect employment firms, very popular and prevalent today, grew out of new laws in the early 1990s allowing PEO (Professional Employment Organization) companies to employ and lease back to the parent company their own employees, but at better cost. Payroll, benefits, training, and other services could be provided more cost effectively due to pooling and concentration.

If these laws ever change, PEOs will disappear.

|||||||||||||||||||||||||||||||||||||||||||||||||||||||||||||||||||||||||||||||||||||||||||||||||||||||||||||||||||||||||||||

Laws and regulations in regard to oil exploration on federal lands, and for coal-fired electricity plants have had major economic impacts. The Dodd-Frank financial industry law, and in-process regulations, will dramatically change banking. Recent

National Labor Relations Board rulings have been highly impactful to businesses. The new Boeing plant in Charleston, South Carolina is just one example. Many unplanned union demands were required, even though South Carolina is a right to work state.

Economic conditions. Booms and busts regularly occur. The "Kitchen" and other economic cycles are well known. Multiple forecasting services exist to help understand what is coming. While many economists were forecasting the 2007+ housing bubble burst, developers, banks, speculators, and the buying public took no heed, with disastrous results that will take many years from which to recover. The kinetic energy of Greed blocked the sober planning and envisioning that was needed.

The Federal Reserve's multiple "Quantitative Easing" monetary policy waves have had many impacts in the 2010–2013 era, and the implications will be felt for years in terms of interest rates, inflation rates, taxes, commodities (e.g., gold and silver), and more.

Globalization is a powerful economic change force also.

How the constant changes in these multiple forces affect us will vary by business type and market segment. Time-based "vectoring" ("where the puck will be") will be needed over time to align to leverage the changes. The introduction of products and services, which might take quarters or years to launch, needs to be vectored to the right timing relative to changes in demand and competitors' moves over time. If too early, unanticipated losses are going to be incurred due to costs existing but revenues not occurring as projected. If too late, a "first mover" might sew up the leadership position. Thus correct timing is critical to deduce. Forecast-based planning is needed.

For companies primarily offering products to a wide market, being the "first mover" can be critical. However, some feel that being second or third with a better solution is smart. The "bleeding edge" can be a difficult place to be, and requires waves of resources. Also, the first mover needs to proactively stay ahead.

But IBM Was Late...And Won!

After Digital Research's CP/M operating system and the Apple OS were out for several years in PCs, IBM belatedly introduced the MS-DOS OS (licensed from Bill Gates and Paul Allen). Via an "open" policy, more application software was made available, pricing was better, channels were secured, and other "open" competitive moves were made to eventually win with over 80 percent market share for MS-DOS, and then Windows (eight versions thus far, and counting). Their differentiated value-adds carried the day.

Trout and Reis, in their book *Positioning*, provide many value positioning constructs and examples. A key revelation is that we should position as better relative to something *already known and believed* versus trying to (expensively) establish a new mental state. This would support being a better follower. For example, Netscape's first web browser was eclipsed by Microsoft, Mozilla, Google, Apple, and others, who often positioned *relative to* Netscape, and to Internet Explorer later. Netscape did not stay ahead enough.

Employees Know!

When taking over a new company or strategically consulting, structurally soliciting ideas, optionally anonymously for candor regarding the culture and climate, it always becomes clear that employees have it figured out as to what is needed, internally and externally.

Solicit their inputs. It might be limited to hundreds, but thousands of feedbacks can be sorted through with modern online tools.

Rewards are good to consider, especially recognition (Herzberg). Use the ideas.

Besides the input value, their Primal Drives are addressed, similar to the Hawthorne Study (see chapter 1).

Make sure they know that the ideas were truly valued and considered, and were used. If not used, explain why.

Regardless of the right timing, correctly knowing what changes are coming, and the threats and opportunities to be prepared for to Judo-leverage, is critical. How do we do that?

First, recognize that just using internal views is silently self-limiting. The hidden, inherent "as is" (change resistant) bias versus the "could be" or "should be" (change causing) is a critical challenge to be overcome from the beginning. Many methods to do so exist, including using facilitators and outside experts. Since they have no "as is" vested interests and can leave, are experienced and skilled at managing the games that will occur, and use proven processes, several types of value are provided. Relative to managing change itself, see below.

‖‖‖

Watch Out for Research!

Both the Ford Edsel and New Coke (replacing old Coke) were products of exhaustive market research before being launched. Both failed, and quickly. Flawed research inputs to planning can be dangerous.

‖‖‖

Per *Outside In* (by Harley Manning, Kerry Boudine and Josh Bernoff), an "outside-in" learning process needs to be used. Per the Golden Rule ("they have the gold so they rule"), they, out there, have the money we want, so beauty is first in the eye of the beholder. Therefore, we need to set up effective processes for:

- Customer inputs*
  - Including their forecasts and plans*
- Prospect inputs*
  - Including their forecasts and plans*
- Partner inputs*
  - Including their forecasts and plans*
- External media articles, etc. summaries
- Sales force inputs
- Service personnel inputs
- Operating personnel inputs[4]
- Think-tank/analysts' or consultants' inputs (often acquired)
- Other relevant inputs.

---

4   Which may include paid, lawful snoopers on competitors.

*Under a protective confidentiality agreement, so they will be more open and complete.

||||||||||||||||||||||||||||||||||||||||||||||||||||||||||||||||||||||||||||||||||||||||||||||||||||||||||||||||||||||||||||||||||||||||||||||||||

Don't Just Ask!

Henry Ford once noted that if he just asked what prospects for his new-fangled car wanted, they would say "faster horses."

When innovations are planned, and prospects don't know what they don't yet know, benefits-based "could be" education will be needed to improve planning an subsequent demand. Prototypes often help.

Position against what they already know for the best grasp and results.

In chapter 2 we saw that "new and improved" tweaks the Transcendence Primal Drive and also positions against the old, which is known. Different and better are powerful value-add messages.

||||||||||||||||||||||||||||||||||||||||||||||||||||||||||||||||||||||||||||||||||||||||||||||||||||||||||||||||||||||||||||||||||||||||||||||||||

In-crowdsourcing

Whether the chosen timeline is three or five years, structured feedback processes are needed for each information source. Per chapter 5's discussion of "in-crowdsourcing," employees' inputs are important to gain, organize, consider, and use as possible. Incentives may be needed to get the quality of responses that will be needed for an optimal plan. Some in-crowdsourcing questions might include:

- What will be the major technology changes in the next n years that can affect us?
- How will those affect business actions?
- What will be the major competitive changes in the next n years?
- How will those affect business actions?
- What will be the major legal requirements changes in the next n years?
- How will those affect business actions?
- What will be the major economic conditions changes in the next n years?
- What "megatrends" are coming that will affect us?
- How will those affect business actions?
- Who are the three major competitors?

- How, in some detail, is the company strong or weak relative to them?
- Per the positioning graphic's principles, what new solutions will be needed (for different target markets)?
- What will become obsolete?
- What are the company's internal strengths?
- Weaknesses?
- What recommendations do you have?
- What are your go-to-market ideas and plans?
- What internal culture improvements are needed?
- What are your organization ideas?
- Who should lead them?
- What resources are required?
- What should be the priorities?
- Any other questions, general and/or specific, that should be asked.

The feedback will be eye opening (and perhaps embarrassing, but embrace it). Importantly, when changes are later made, this participative process will have many change acceptance benefits. It is easier for employees to change to *their* ideas versus others'. Also, by this process they start to understand the external pressures and the validity of having to change relative to the pressures. They more easily grasp that the alternative to change can be worse.

"Fit" Must Be Considered

Most customers want evolutionary versus revolutionary change. The Microsoft Windows 8 operating system was initially highly criticized. PC sales dramatically slumped (the Associated Press just reported a 14 percent drop in PC sales in 1Q13). In the strategic, revolutionary jump to be cross-platform (PC, tablet, smartphone), perhaps trying to get close to Apple's interface style, Microsoft's new look and much different functionality were significantly different than Windows 7, Vista and XP. Having a touchscreen unit helped, especially for a PC. But most did not have touch screens. The learning curve was high, the usability howls were loud, PC vendors complained, and Microsoft is reported to be issuing v.8.1 to have a

better "fit" option to Windows 7 functionality. "Fit" should have had
a larger role in planning.

||||||||||||||||||||||||||||||||||||||||||||||||||||||||||||||||||||||||||||||||||||||||||||||||||||||||||||||||||||||||||||||||||||||||||||||||||||||||||||

As noted, once this information is gathered and organized for consumption,
and before proceeding, it is important to understand "as is" sales volume levels,
gross margin levels, operating margins, etc. Product line profitability, business
unit profitability, and other key performance metrics are important to define and
publish. What is strong and weak in the existing business are important baselines.
What expertise exists? What assets, present or coming, are to be monetized? What
limitations should be removed?

Example Desired Vision Positioning*

*From the Chief Strategy Officer Summit, May, 2013

What objectives over the next n years will be set, using SMART (Specific,
Measurable, Action-focused, Resourced, and Time-based) goals?

With these outside and inside inputs plus objectives, established brainstorming
on SWOT (Strengths, Weaknesses, Opportunities, Threats) analyses can now be
conducted; with a facilitator looking out for and guarding against turf protection
and paradigm rigidity. Both will exist—which is certain since the participants are
breathing. It is in our DNA's Primal Drives to be biased, as explained, for Safety, Self-
Interest, Hope, and Ease, and to keep Social circles intact. If this external objectivity
process does not occur, Pogo's observation will prevail: *we* become the enemy. How

sophisticated and rigorous these SWOT analyses are will be determined by the size and complexity of the company.

"What is our driving force?" is a key question to ask and address also, very early. It reflects our core culture and biases. Between eight and fifteen have been identified as possible:

1. **Products offered**: produces specific products (things) for its markets.
   Examples: General Motors, Coca-Cola.
2. **Services offered**: delivers specific services (human efforts) for its market.
   Examples: Wells Fargo, Charles Schwab.
3. **Market needs**: focuses on meeting the needs of specific markets.
   Examples: Fisher-Price, Seattle University.
4. **Customer needs**: focuses on meeting the needs of a specific set of customers.
   Examples: YMCA, Mayo Clinic.
5. **Return/profit**: focuses on the achievement of predetermined returns or profits.
   Examples: United Way, Goldman Sachs.
6. **Size/growth**: focuses on the achievement of a specific size or growth rate.
   Examples: Network Associates, University of Phoenix.
7. **Technology**: applies its technological capabilities to innovative products or services.
   Examples: Intel, Microsoft, 3M.
8. **Human resources**: leverages its employees' specific qualities, skills, or training.
   Examples: Kelly Services.
9. **Service capability**: leverages the depth or uniqueness of its employees.
   Examples: Value Line Publishing.
10. **Production capacity**: leverages its investment in a physical plant.
    Examples: Boeing, International Paper.
11. **Sale/distribution method**: has a unique or distinctive way of marketing.
    Examples: Dell Computer, amazon.com.
12. **Natural resources**: owns or controls significant natural resources and has the capability to process these into usable forms.
    Examples: DeBeers, Exxon.

13. **Land**: owns or controls land and the uses to which it can be put by itself or others.

    Examples: King Ranch, Arctic Slope Regional Corporation.

14. **Assets**: owns or controls assets whose preservation is paramount.

    Examples: Noble Drilling.

15. **Image**: seeks to maintain a specific organizational image within its markets and the products or services it produces. Examples: Cartier, Gucci.

Source: Dr. Terry van der Werff, *Global Future*

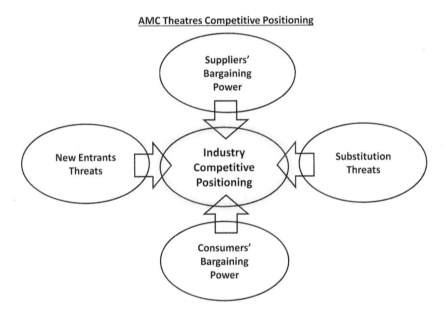

AMC Theatres Competitive Positioning

A specific agreement on the driving force (or multiple driving forces, if the company has multiple divisions) is needed as a key planning framework. Be prepared that this discussion will be very animated, usually.

Another element of the strategic planning process is target market segmentation and selection. Some key considerations are:

- Referenceable customers exist or can be acquired.
- Word-of-mouth processes exist to be leveraged.[5]

---

5   In *Crossing The Chasm* Geoffrey Moore noted that a market is people who talk to each other (and have somewhat homogeneous needs).

- Differentiated solutions exist, or can exist, or can be acquired.
- Domain expertises exist or can be acquired.
- The market is large and rich enough to sustain good growth.
- The market is not "owned" by a major competitor, and no major entry barriers exist.
- An effective sales program can be established.
- Partners exist or can be acquired.
- The market can be addressed via Marketing Communication.
- No legal or other limitations exist.
- Entry barriers can be introduced.
- Other success criteria may exist in certain industries.

(Note how these segmentation criteria match the VC investment criteria provided earlier.)

Also important is the consideration of risk in possible strategic actions, be they internal (organic), by acquisition, or a hybrid. This graphic is a simplified look at four quadrants, each with different degrees and types of risks. Specific risk assessments are thus needed.

Solutions/Markets Planning

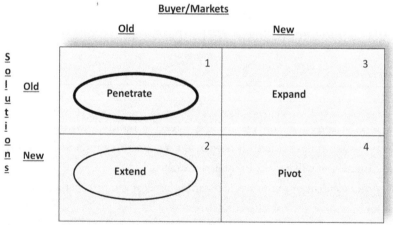

1=lowest risk and entry cost; 4=highest

The corporate vision, purpose and board policies need to be defined, as a framework.

Out of this participative, research based process, often using "forced choice" synthesizing (e.g., if twenty ideas exist, each person rates the top five in order, and these scores are aggregated), a draft strategic plan can be produced, including:

1. Vision (and higher "meaning")
2. Objectives
3. Key success factors
4. Strategies (including target markets and value positioning differentiations)
5. Tactics (including organization, resourcing, etc.)
6. Financial forecasts
7. Policies and procedures

Via the forced choice method, all have their inputs, and the aggregate highest score often is the best plan (per "the jury of executive opinion" method--Rand Corporation). Also, key people more readily rally to the final direction even if it was not their top direction due to the participative process used. They got their say, but they perceive that perhaps "We is indeed better than me." If any do not then acquiesce, Plan B may be needed for them. All energies need to be focused on the derived plan, so none "leak" to the side and waste precious Energy, Time and resources.

Then the plan needs to be "socialized" with the board and perhaps key stakeholders under an NDA to assess "fit" and other factors that may determine success.

This strategic process should be repeated at least each year, inclusive of an early assessment of how well the last planning results were in terms of accuracy. Also, the results versus the past annual plan can be reviewed. A new three year plan is then developed by the same process.

The plan is a means and not an end. If during the year strategic changes in assumptions occur, then the strategic plan can be revisited.

New annual plans can then be developed within the strategic plan roadmap.

Annual Plans

As noted, annual plans exist within the context of the strategic plan. The annual plan should first restate the key elements of the strategic plan to link to the framework. After that, the nature of the annual plan will vary greatly according to the entity doing the

planning. A corporate annual plan subsequently needs to include divisions' or departments'
incorporated operating plans.

This is an iterative process of working through:

- The strategic plan's framework and its implications
- Initial goals
- Strategies and tactics
- Competitive positioning[6]
- Target markets
- Organization plans
- Products/services plans
- Operational plans
- R&D plans
- Pricing and related policies
- Marketing and marketing communications plans
- Personnel plans are needed as well, as a critical resource
- Compensation and benefits plans
- Capital plans
- Budgets projection (P&L, balance sheet, and cash) (base, good, bad)
- Program plans (which will vary sharply by company type and unit).

These iterations culminate in the initial annual plan for the entity(s). Leaders' rewards are often tied to reasonably exceeding the base plan/budget.

When submitted in draft to senior management and/or the board they will aggregate the plans, suggest revisions, adjust goals, ensure inter-group coordination, and initially allocate resources. They will want to see a balance of potential and capabilities. Relative IRR (internal rate of return) calculations will often be used for resource allocation, as well as core values and implementation weightings to align with corporate strategy. Investment risk, investment size, timing, and return likelihood will be used as well.

The final annual and operating plan(s) are then re-planned and re-submitted. One more round of revisions are then likely, and then all will be finalized, published, and communicated.

---

6   Per Kenachi Ohmae (McKenzie) in *Mind of the Strategist*, all strategy is competitive positioning oriented. Also, protect what you have before launching into new areas.

Operational Plans

Operational/departmental plans can thereby be set and actioned as a sub-set of the Annual Plan. These can be by business unit, division, department, or all of the above as applicable.

Goals and policies are "cascaded" down from the Annual Plan, as a framework. Generally, the same planning components as the Annual Plan will be used.

Other components can be added as needed. The Operational Plans will be very detailed, and specific. At this level is "where the rubber meets the road."

Strategic Versus Organic Growth

If acquiring versus growing internally, the same planning principles generally apply to choosing what and generally who to acquire. The subsequent deal process has its own dynamics.

Protecting the acquired value, usually at great cost to shareholders, including if earnouts are used, is key.

Integrating the acquisition is where the challenge is. As Muhammad Ali, an HP's strategy officer noted recently, "77 percent of acquisitions fail." He explained that the integration quality is often the failure point. HP's approach is to begin the integration planning early in the discussions, per this graphic:

HP's Acquisition Integration Process

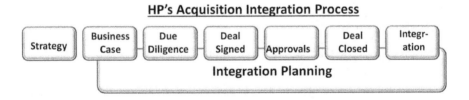

I have been part of seven mergers, on both sides. Most were successful. I quickly learned that the smaller company was always concerned about their Primal Drives, especially Safety, even before the deal closed. Key people either had their resumes ready, or they were already in recruiters' hands. Of the three key intangible assets (customers, partners, and employees), the key one to protect is employees (unless purposeful "mashing" is planned, of course, which I have done). This is consistent with the Whole Foods CEOs observation that employees take care of customers, who take care of shareholders.

When key employees "bail," the institutional knowledge goes. Customer contacts go. Competitors are often strengthened, or born anew. The value that was purchased is consequently lost. Shareholders are damaged.

‖‖

Protect Your Acquired Employees

The acquired CEO, if still in place, needs to be willing to proactively buffer employees from any insensitivities by the acquirer. Keep the "bleep" from flowing downhill, even if it is job threatening. You owe your people that. If you cannot and then leave, they will follow you to a new company that can then kick the acquirer's ___. Make sure you let the acquiring management know the costs of any stupid actions by them as early and candidly as possible. You owe that to them.

I had to do this twice; once effectively, but not the second time. The acquirer's errors were a tsunami that never ended due to internal power plays by the acquirer's team. I left after a few quarters.

‖‖‖

Thus the key is to proactively put a high floor under the acquiree's feelings of Safety, Self-interest, Hope, etc. Some ideas are:

- The acquiring CEO actively talks about this concern, and counter plans; as always, "an issue identified is half solved."
- Let employees of both entities know how they will benefit, and to not fear n concerns.
- Help all to understand the Newco vision and purpose, how it will create 1+1=4 value externally *and* internally (external value creation is the key; it will mask over many internal sins if successful in the marketplace).
- Put their COO or CEO into a top spot in Newco. The symbology is much more than would be expected. Safety, Hope, the potential for Selfish rewards, etc., are signaled.
- Make him truly powerful and not a figurehead.
- Place other key acquiree's employees in prominent places in Newco.

- Set incentives based on Newco results (approximately 66–75 percent) and acquiree results. This fosters both execution and synergistic cooperation.
- Incentivize leaders to have near-zero loss of acquired personnel, customers, and partners—especially employees.
- The acquiring CEO needs to spend much personal time with the acquiree's people, to reflect importance, Safety, etc. (Here is a very good place to use Tom Peters' "Management By Walking Around."). Have the board participate also.
- Use frequent recognition.
- Use teams as appropriate.
- Create joint team-building programs.
- Let customers and partners know how they will benefit, and to not fear n concerns.
- Regularly report results, pro and con. As possible, confidentially share plans.

||||||||||||||||||||||||||||||||||||||||||||||||||||||||||||||||||||||||||||||||||||||||||||||||||||||||||||||||||||||||||||||||||||||||

Jump In to Help

In one public company that acquired mine, Europe operations (seven countries) were merged for efficiency (versus effectiveness), over my constructive but firm objections. It quickly failed. I was then asked to get things back on track. Effectiveness moves were enacted, and it worked. Even if I had not been the second largest shareholder in the public company I would have helped.

||||||||||||||||||||||||||||||||||||||||||||||||||||||||||||||||||||||||||||||||||||||||||||||||||||||||||||||||||||||||||||||||||||||||

A common problem is integrating marketing and integrating sales groups with counterparts. Often times efficiency thinking will override effectiveness. They key is to focus on what is best for customers. Always. per Drucker, "Be effective first, then be efficient."

The same is true for R&D and for Operations. Admin is often the easiest to integrate.

"Gainsharing" vehicles can be set up to foster the sharing of ideas, technology, materials, processes, etc. The receiving group gets new, different value, and a portion is credited back to the providing group. Fair "transfer pricing" is another option. The key is to reward transferred value.

Change Management Is Too Late, and Too Reactive

The only human who likes change is "a baby with a dirty diaper." Thus, resistance is a pervasive threat to the needed change and must be avoided (if possible), overcome if it exists, and turned into a change seeking dynamic optimally.

In 2009, the iSixSigma organization's large survey of business and government process improvement leaders found that overcoming internal change resistance was the number-one process improvement (change) challenge. This was closely followed by the challenge of winning executives' support for process improvement efforts (another face of change resistance, perhaps—"let's not rock the boat," or "if it ain't broke, don't fix it," or "I might lose out in the change, so slyly resist it"). This factually documents the critical importance of either avoiding (best option) or overcoming change resistance.

Some ideas about how to avoid resistance or to overcome it, and to even have change to be *sought*, are the subject of this section.

Sources of Change

Change can come with many faces. Just a few are:

- Lean programs
- Six Sigma programs
- Mergers
- Acquisitions
- Divestitures
- Joint ventures
- New business lines
- Eliminated business lines (e.g., Saturn being liquidated by GM)
- Reorganizations
- Globalization
- Right/downsizing
- Outsourcing
- Technology retooling (e.g., robots vs. people)
- A combination of the above.

Each of these disrupts the status quo.

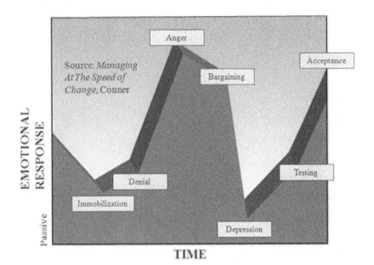

Understanding Change Resistance

The change resistance cycles in this graphic must be avoided if possible, or sharply shortened in time. Not doing so will be costly in many ways, both tangible and intangible.

> "…I have determined that the single most important factor to managing change successfully is the degree to which people demonstrate _resilience_; the capacity to absorb high levels of change while displaying minimal dysfunctional _behavior_."
>
> —**Daryl Conner**, _Managing at the Speed of Change_

Resisting Change Is Based in the Primal Drives

The brain processes information in several different ways. In neuroscience tests, areas light up in response to changes, pro and con (usually the latter). (In Google Images, search on "neuroscience" for some examples.) What is important is that the information is always processed through the Primal Drives. If not handled properly, and proactively, change can threaten _all_ of the Primal Drives of employees. Depression (the powerful amygdala being energized) needs to be avoided.

Some examples of negative Primal Drives reactions to change are:

Safety
- Job safety?
- Role safety?
- Lifestyle safety?
- Local tasks control?
- Company safety?
- Destiny control?

Self-Interest/Greed
- Present pay?
- Potential pay?
- Promotion?
- Bonus?
- Career?

Hope and Transcendence
- Company stability?
- Company growth?
- Promotion?
- Easier tasks?
- Retirement?

Energy and Time Optimization
- Work harder?
- Work longer?
- Learn new tasks?
- Find new job?
- New training?

Trust and Honesty
- Are they lying to me?
- How long have they known?
- What are they not telling me?
- When will the other shoe drop?
- Who can I trust?

Sociability
- Will I lose my friends?

- Will I have to make new friends?
- Will they accept me?
- Family's reaction?
- Friends' reaction?

Obviously change can engender many Primordial concerns; that must be pre-considered. (Applying the Judo Principle for having these change issues work *for you* is explained later, below.)

Of special interest is research by Larkin and Larkin in *Communicating Change*, where first-level employees want the information to come from direct supervisors (90%-92% in the U.S., UK and Canada), followed by middle management. It seems as though through more frequent interactions they have calibrated Supervisors more, so they have more trust as to reading them. C-level leaders can follow up, but the first contact should be with first-line supervisors. It seems C-leaders carry some credibility problems, deserved or not.

Of course, this means supervisors and management must be pre-empowered with the Why, What and How of the change, and the worse impacts of not changing. They must believe in it also, so time spent answering questions is time well spent. If unionized, arming them and HR to overcome possible union resistance is often a key need as well. They will have ideas of how to do so, thus careful listening and reaction are needed.

In union shops, the union leaders need to be pre-briefed as well out of respect. But this must be *just before* the supervisors tell the employees, to control information quality and completeness. Other possible agendas cannot get in the way. Also, never forget that oftentimes the union leaders' focus is not exactly the same as the members. I have observed that members often can grasp the change's overarching truth and wisdom, but labor leaders can often see any change as something to be resisted— perhaps for its own role sake to further bolster the union's power. (The workers' lower value of union-provided information, reported by Larkin and Larkin, probably reflects workers' understanding of the union leaderships' varying objectives, which can cloud the truth. So, *enable your supervisors!*)

Before you make any change, understand the work rules and other rules in the labor agreement, and be ready to defend why and how the changes are not a violation that might result in a wildcat strike. If some labor agreement conflicts do exist, then upfront negotiation will be needed. Be prepared with "giveaways" (politically powerful but not economically costly ones are best) that are valued by them but can be sacrificed for the greater gains to be made. Never show your final ideas early. There will always be an iterative negotiation process. To get to an agreement, several "walkaways" by each side might need to occur. "Lesser of the evils" positioning is also a factor (more on this below).

Also, make sure you check Federal and local regulations about force reductions, and EEOC and ERISA rules. I have had 100 percent EEOC success when thus challenged because I had pre-planned actions to avoid conflicts that could not be won.

Contracts with customers, distributors, suppliers, etc., should also be pre-evaluated before a change.

The "Muddy" or "Frozen" Middle (Managers) Must Be Managed Also

These people are already caught in the unenviable "shock absorber" position between:

1. Management's incessant pressures, changes, restrictions and more;
2. Floor or desk level pushbacks by the people that have to execute the change.

Also, they fully realize that the position numbers on the promotion pyramid get smaller and smaller with each upward rung. Thus jockeying relative to competing peers is a key success factor. Probably the major elements of that process are:

1. Do no wrong (make no mistakes);
2. Avoid losing power (turf, budget, people, control, etc.) in a shuffle.

Thus they generally go through the same Primal Drives concerns as above. How much top management allows mistakes to be made culturally will directly control how change risk taking they are. See chapters 4 and 5.

Also, performance reviews can incorporate change orientation, change support, and change success ratings. Some question "360 reviews" generally, but this might be one exception to consider for evaluating change leadership. Change is critical, and this area lends itself to less risk of personal vendettas being played out compared to other possible evaluation efforts.

*Ways to Foster Change Acceptance
and to Overcome Change Resistance*

"Discretionary performance is that extra level of performance we exert when we <u>want</u> to do something, as opposed to when we <u>have</u> to do something (compliance)."
—**L.W. Braksick**, *Unleash Behavior, Unleash Profits*

John Kotter is a recognized change expert, with eighteen leadership and change books. His famous book *Leading Change* laid out an eight-step process for successful change leadership:

1. Establishing a sense of urgency
2. Creating a guiding coalition
3. Developing a vision and strategy
4. Communicating the changed vision
5. Empowering broad-base action
6. Generating short-term wins
7. Consolidating gains and producing more change
8. Anchoring new approaches in culture.

However, I believe numbers 3 and 4 must come first: developing and communicating a vision and strategy. Without these, steps 1 and 2 are harder. Steps 5 through 8 can then follow.

Foster Change as a Competitive Weapon

One Fortune 50 company has put over 70,000 line supervisor and managers through Lean Six Sigma and change management training, to foster continual improvement. They see having the best change culture as the number-one competitive weapon in a very fast-changing market.

This gets us back to chapter 3, the power of spatial-based envisioning as a first order of leadership. Without a good change vision and strategy from the outset, confusion will reign, politics may run amok, energy will be lost, and suboptimal (or perhaps even negative) results will be experienced. (chapter 5 provides guidance for defining the optimal vision to focus on, and to communicate.)

For people's Primal Drives, one can Judo-leverage each of the above fears, and should. Putting the fears out front for all to see is one option. It is like in the Army when running they sing about "Jody's got your girl and (is) gone" (copyrighted by a different Duckworth, who was an Army drill instructor). Also, they sing about going to war. These songs are to get the lingering fears on the table and confronted so they are socialized, rationalized, accepted, and then go away. Thus, openly raising the concerns early shows that you are empathetic with them, and care. Also, they can then better internalize and accept them. Additionally, it gives you the chance to address each one and turn as many as possible into positives. In summary, these actions are needed:

Primordial Drive	Summary Action Plan
Safety	Position the change as increasing Safety (and its corollary of control) for key people, and vs. not changing
Self-Interest	Show a path to better potentials
Hope and Transcendence	Enable more Hope and show how to Transcend
Energy and Time Conservation	Show how ease and speed will be enhanced
Honesty and Trust	Make sure they trust the Why, What, and How of the change. Explain each.
Sociability	Spend personal time. For reorgs, arrange for mentors, personal gatherings, and other ways to bond and establish new Sociability. Keep relationships intact as possible and smart. (Sometimes the opposite is best overall, even if more disruptive initially.)

Lesser of the Evils Positioning

Most people will put up with a change if they understand that the alternative is worse, relative to impact on the Primal Drives. However, this is not always true.

||||||||||||||||||||||||||||||||||||||||||||||||||||||||||||||||||||||||||||||||||||||||||||||||||||||||||||||||||||||

Lesser of Evils Positioning Does Not Always Work

In late 2012, Hostess Brands declared Chapter 7 bankruptcy liquidation and closed its doors. Eighteen thousand were permanently laid off. Five thousand bakers would not take wage and other cuts even though they knew from management that all would lose their jobs if they didn't (other unions had settled). *All* 18,000 lost their jobs! It is expected that buyers of the brands' assets will acquire the brand names and formulas, distributor and customer contracts and contacts, and some equipment, but will not use the same facilities or employees. Pensions have been lost as well.

||||||||||||||||||||||||||||||||||||||||||||||||||||||||||||||||||||||||||||||||||||||||||||||||||||||||||||||||||||||

Building a Change-Resilient Culture

"Effective leaders are capable of reframing the thinking of those whom they guide, enabling them to see that significant (continual) changes are not only the imperative, but achievable."

—Conner, *Managing at the Speed of Change*

Gaining change acceptance can have stages. These few steps, regularly and consistently practiced, will insulate people from the change impacts and will help align Primal Drives to change:

- "Knowledge is power!" Relative to change's imperative, educate, educate, educate—on the Why, What, and How levels.
- Openly and often educate about our natural, Primordial, *emotional* resistance to change.
- Regularly communicate, top-to-bottom, that change is the *number-one competitive critical success factor*. Who manages it best wins, and vice versa.
- Constantly communicate the changes going on around the company, and the impacts.
- Note that competitors' employees are the same, so this is a change competition between us and them to best self-manage. "Let's beat those guys!"
- Educate about the *worse-evil* costs of *not* changing.

- Get ideas to adapt to the changes. Reward them, especially wins. Get buy-in.
- Solicit ideas to become the future innovator, driving changes. Reward them.
- Set up "Change Agent of the Quarter"–type reward and recognition programs, at multiple levels. Make them real, visible programs. Celebrate successes.
- Do not permit change resisters, openly or quietly, to prevail. Listen to objections, looking for merit in the views. If is just for backside protection, shut it down. Sanction if necessary.

Initially Small May Be Smart

If evolving to become a change company, find a highly likely, controllable change project that can be "horsed" to success. Size may be key. Provide the needed support, including executives' support. Then sequentially expand the size and complexity of projects. Ballyhoo successes.

Project leader quality will be important. Choose carefully. Set up metrics-based results incentives. Provide political support as requested. If the KRD's (Key Results Descriptions) of players includes change management support (like in chapter 6), then helping with change (versus resisting) will be more natural in the organization because Primal Drives are engaged.

Change Views Will Vary by Generation, Individuals, and Culture

As possible, these differences in expectations need to be taken into account:

- **Matures (1909–1945):** Driven by ideals of duty and sacrifice, value quality over speed and efficiency.
- **Baby Boomers (1946–1964):**"Me" generation, focus on prosperity, being in charge, committed to the "team."
- **Generation X (1965–1979):** Question authority and institutions, dislike hierarchy, embrace technology. Very mobile.
- **Millennials (1980–2000):** Protected, used to security, extremely tech-savvy, want to be recognized individuals. Very mobile.

When one-on-one, key personality factors will be involved. Pre-assess the environment and set plans accordingly.. A few key constructs are:

- Givers vs. takers
- Confident vs. not
- Secure vs. not
- Positive vs. contrarian
- Ambitious vs. not

And finally, how change will be managed in the US vs. Europe, vs. Asia, vs. South America, vs. Africa, etc., must be carefully considered. Individual Why, What, and How approaches will be needed due to material culture differences, and different Primal Drives views.

Summary

It is a law of nature that who best plans and changes wins. Darwinism, or the survival of the most adaptable, is real, and its power must be Judo-leveraged. The alternative to doing so is bad, recognizing that change is constant and will define destinies. All the success rules will change. Strengths will become weaknesses. Rigorous, effective planning is the key antidote. It will allow changes to be leveraged versus the company being ravaged; as so many have.

Strategic, Annual and Operating plans are needed. Each has its key elements. All should "cascade" from the Strategic Plan. Especially important is deciding what is the core "Driving Force" of the company. Then, planning can be conducted within that framework.

Well-thought-out change is important to purposely pursue, regardless of the resistance. Avoiding that resistance is usually the best path: "an ounce of prevention is worth a pound of cure."

However, change is a threat for many Primal Drives if not properly and proactively handled. Not doing so is a major inhibitor of progress and may even become debilitating. Special legal factors must also be considered. Often positioning a needed change as the lesser of the evils can work.

Proactive methods exist to hopefully preclude change resistance from arising, or to quell change resistance as much as possible. Proactive leaders position the company to see change seeking (which is even stronger than change resilience) as its key competitive advantage.

Chapter Eight

Unleash The Results *Animal* in You...and in Others

SOME SPECIAL LEADERSHIP SCENARIOS

Your Best Friend Will Tell You Something You Need to Hear Even if You Do Not Want to Hear It

That helpful spirit is the thrust of this chapter, for the following special situations:

- Government sector leadership
- Non-Profit leadership
- Engineer-type leaders
- Women leaders
- Older leaders
- Turnaround leaders
- Military leaders.

"Effective leadership is not about making speeches or being liked; leadership is defined by *results* not attributes."

—Peter Drucker

Each of these above situations has special aspects that justify special summary coverage in terms of experience-based observations and helpful leadership thoughts. These insights are not meant to be judgmental per se, but to highlight special challenges, opportunities, and leadership needs, in the spirit of "an issue identified is half solved." The intent is to help achieve results, and the resulting personal rewards and success. As Yogi said, "You can't hit 'em if you can't see 'em."

Leading Government Entities

When you meet effective government leaders, congratulate them. They have a much tougher job than most realize. Without the natural rationalization of a profit motive like in a commercial business, many end goals factors, some conflicting, can exist. Except for outsourced or "privatized" public services (like I did for several years), the common end focus of profit is rare in the government sector, and is a major leadership challenge. Several other factors are also a leadership challenge. All this opens the door to the additional challenge that "friends come and go, and enemies accumulate." Thus good government leaders are good jugglers and adroit in persuasion, prioritization and politicking.

||||||||||||||||||||||||||||||||||||||||||||||||||||||||||||||||||||||||||||||||||||||||||||||||||||||||||||||||||

Example of Conflicting Public Transit Service Standards

- On-time performance
- Route directness
- Route coverage levels
- Travel time vs. auto
- Passengers per mile operated
- Pay hours to platform hours
- Mean time between breakdowns
- Revenue/cost ratio.

Several of these conflict with multiple others. Improving one impacts others, so prioritization is needed. Policy makers need to approve the criteria and priorities.

||||||||||||||||||||||||||||||||||||||||||||||||||||||||||||||||||||||||||||||||||||||||||||||||||||||||||||||||||

This section is written for the professional leader in a government entity that is not satisfied with just having a comfortable, safe, 9–5 job, but truly wants to continuously improve service quality as a personal, citizen mission. If mere existence is the core drive, then these points will not be helpful, because nothing will be. (If turf building for Safety in size exist, as sometimes occurs, these views will be challenging.)

||||||||||||||||||||||||||||||||||||||||||||||||||||||||||||||||||||||||||||||||||||||||||||||||||||||||||||||||||||

Government Employment Levels and Pay
Are Hard to Control Without the Profit-Focused Brake

"Public employment grew by nearly 2 percent over the past three years, while private employment has dropped by 7 percent.

"Private-sector workers have also seen their wages decline, while those working for the various levels of government have held their own. Federal workers now enjoy an average salary roughly 10 percent as high as their private sector counterparts, while their health, pension, and other benefits are as much as four times as high."

—*Forbes on MSNBC*, April 2010

||||||||||||||||||||||||||||||||||||||||||||||||||||||||||||||||||||||||||||||||||||||||||||||||||||||||||||||||||||

While not politically correct, these below general realities, to which there are some exceptions, make goals-focused and excellence-focused leadership more of a challenge than in the private sector. While not all of the below special challenges always exist, many do.

Political leaders can change the goals and standards at will, and do. Such changing "end-in-mind" targets are difficult for leaders to respond to. The changes might be sudden, such as when an adopted policy is suddenly criticized by vocal voters and quickly changed politically.

Without goals rationalization, performance reviews are much less relatively clear cut, more often leading to acquiescence by leaders, versus knowing that a complaint or fight is likely.

The lack of clear-end criteria also leads to promotions that more often validate the "Peter Principle" (i.e., a person is promoted to a position where he is incompetent). Pay inflation can also result.

Adding a job position in private industry usually has an ROI analysis behind it and multiple approval levels. This is often less so in government entities. New politically based programs are, by nature, relatively more often for politics and not economics. Larger "turfs" are seen to be more Safe so as to enjoy Selfish rewards with more Hope, so "body creep" is relatively more prevalent. End of year spending sprees of un-used funds to protect next year's budget size are frequent.

Winning a Union Grievance Is an Interesting Process

Rather than an individual in a non-union private company having the responsibility of taking an action when disciplined, virtually always a public union will file and pursue a grievance for a disciplined member employee. Or a civil service protest will be introduced.

In one case an employee claimed workers comp for a shoulder injury. Being self-insured and skeptical, I had the employee "tailed" by a licensed PI. Photos showed the employee carrying roof tiles on his shoulder up a ladder, lifting weights, and more. When terminated for fraud, the union acted as though the Pope had been shot and filed a grievance.

Since I had negotiated a grievance "loser pays the arbitrator and other party's costs" clause in the last contract, they dropped the grievance just before arbitration costs were to be incurred. I had privately briefed my union interface friend on the coming facts. They then knew they would lose based on the photos and PI testimony, and a mediator's view of fraud. I was able to use the cost avoidance issue to override members' zeal to not let management win. He stayed fired. Subsequent workers comp incidents went down too.

Unionization of government operations is substantially higher than in the private sector, almost four times as high. AFSCME (American Federation of State, County, and Municipal Employees), SEIU (Service Employees International Union), ATU (Amalgamated Transit Union), teachers unions, etc. are good examples. They do contribute to the size of the middle class.

I was a member of four unions while in college, my father was a United Mine Workers steward, and the need for unions historically was reviewed in the chapter 1 History. I have also directly or indirectly led companies with over twenty unions. Thus I can attest that unions pose a material leadership challenge in numerous ways versus the larger number of non-union shops. The two most challenging areas are *not* negotiated pay and benefits; they are work-rules limitations and grievances management.

Most work rules have the purpose of job security behind them. Mostly, they want to limit productivity gains so that employment levels and pay (supply-demand) will stay high, often to limit the impacts of automation, improved productivity, or jobs outsourcing. While this might be sustainable in the short run in private companies, over time competitors or other external forces will change the competitive rules and render damage to the slower-changing unionized company, perhaps lethally. The US auto industry is the poster child for these types of problems. Interestingly, employment is only about 20 percent of its highest level.

However, such competition or external challenge forces do not similarly exist in the government sector, so fewer pressures exist to limit a union's power over time. Only a diligent "watchdog" process and strong, merit-based political leaders can help control this.

In addition, in the private sector the "open shop"/"right-to-work" states, mostly in the South, have attracted thousands of companies and related jobs to the South, to escape the North's "closed shop" requirement that all belong to a union and pay dues. However, it seems that in most states and the federal government an assumption exists that "closed shop" type rules will exist for government unions. Even in a Southern state, a new government employee often becomes part of the union automatically. This is true in most federal programs as well.

Therefore, for government sector entities, putting the brakes on employment and benefits costs, and changing work rules for increased productivity, are materially more difficult than in the private sector. Strike rights are not the core issue, since many cannot strike by law. A major factor is that the unions are often the top contributor to elected officials and expect protection by them. Pay, benefits, rules, etc., are materially determined at the political level, not the managerial level. Also, the ROI linkage between costs and non-numerical benefits is harder to establish and defend.

These were the bases of the major battle in 2012 in Wisconsin, where the legislature and governor passed laws to trim campaign financing by unions, upheld by courts and a recall referendum. The state was then able to turn large, growing (statutorily illegal) deficits into surpluses, and lower taxes. The state's economy has improved also, and jobs have been added. Local governments were given more power.

||||||||||||||||||||||||||||||||||||||||||||||||||||||||||||||||||||||||||||||||||||||||||||||||||||||||||||||||||||||||||||||||||||||||

Minority Employment Is Relatively High In Governments. Good.

An April 2013 *Atlanta Journal Constitution (AJC)* article reported that while minorities made up 45 percent of Fulton County residents, 89 percent of County employees were minorities.

Good. These people work hard, provide for their families, pay taxes, buy goods and services from others (for a multiplier effect), show the value of work to children, and more. They are contributors.

||||||||||||||||||||||||||||||||||||||||||||||||||||||||||||||||||||||||||||||||||||||||||||||||||||||||||||||||||||||||||||||||||||||||

Discipline in government is also much harder because of the civil service, EEOC, and unionization challenges. Protecting government workers from political whim is important. The degree of application is debatable. Fair and accurate "due process" is always important to have, but often is not enough even when used. This tendency results in leaders often being more flexible and accommodating of performance variances than in private industry. They have to more carefully pick their battles, which is unfortunate for taxpayers. (I have been 100 percent victorious in such challenges, none of which should have been brought. Most of those were when I was running a government entity, even though it was only about 15 percent of my professional time as a leader.)

In private industry, substantial margin exists for sanctioning those who do not produce. This accountability element, whether for the Safety, Hope, or Self-Interest drives, energizes and rationalizes results focuses, and is a source of individual drive and effort. Also, it is generally accepted that merit-based sanctions can and will be applied. This merit-based control environment is less prevalent in government operations.

In government entities, powerful, special civil service protections exist, where the reviewing commissioners or arbiters are often politically sensitive and are by role less interested than the leader in assuring excellence. While civil service protections should bar politically based decisions, which was the original purpose of the laws, my experience is that this has morphed into a type of extra protection for poor performing employees compared to the non-union private sector. It is often somewhat like having a pro-union mediator protecting them, sometimes openly, where appointed or elected arbitrators may have constituencies as the focus versus performance merit; they may want to be chosen again, versus being "stricken". They often start out as viewing the burden to be on the employer to meet a higher standard versus a neutral, "What are the facts?" stance. All have read the stories of the punishments of egregious acts being reversed or reduced for reasons that remain a mystery. Employees fired for seemingly correct reasons are often brought back, usually with back pay. This is certainly a leadership challenge.

||||||||||||||||||||||||||||||||||||||||||||||||||||||||||||||||||||||||||||||||||||||||||||||||||||||||||||||||||||||||||||||||||||||||||||||||||||||||||||||||||||||||||||||

Civil Service Protections Do Have Value

Employees need reasonable protection from politicians who may be trying to use political patronage over merit.

However, merit based leadership actions need to be protected.

In private industry, if a senior leader would invoke the Fifth Amendment to not testify, like has happened at the IRS recently, it is likely that the "moral turpitude" clause or general "at will" rights of the employer would be invoked to fire the person, or put them on unpaid leave. In the government they are often just placed on paid administrative leave. This is a challenge for government leaders.

||||||||||||||||||||||||||||||||||||||||||||||||||||||||||||||||||||||||||||||||||||||||||||||||||||||||||||||||||||||||||||||||||||||||||||||||||||||||||||||||||||||||||||||

It is also my observation that EEOC protection standards are higher in the government sector. This is possibly due to the relatively high percentage of minorities who work in the public versus private sector. (One DOL report stated that 65 percent of working blacks work in the public sector, for example. This is good for overcoming past discrimination's many impacts, but it is a leadership challenge also related to EEOC issues' strength.)

The purpose of the EEOC standards are important to having a free society where all have equal opportunity to "pursue happiness" as protected in the Constitution without discrimination based on non-merit factors. However, becoming a shield for suboptimal performance, where it occurs, is bad for all elements of society.

While not politically correct, the above general realities, to which there are some exceptions, make goals-focused and excellence-focused leadership much more of a challenge than in the private sector.

Needed Actions by Government Entity Leaders

Covey had it right to start with the end in mind as a first act. This means that service standards, metrics policies, and procedures have to be set by political and operational processes, deep into the organization. Have them be officially and visibly adopted by politicians, and then by personnel (even signed for). They then need to be widely communicated and consistently applied, with visibility and due process.

These objectives and policies need to be core to the entity's mission, measurable, and driven deep into the organization via departmental goals. At all levels SMART goals are needed (Specific, Measurable, Actionable, Resourced and Time based). Use Key Results Descriptions (KRDs) at all levels, as presented in the prior chapters. They then need to be used to drive operating programs, performance reviews, compensation, promotions, sanctions, etc. The Milestones Achievement Progress (MAP)-type performance reviews, documented, are vital.

Very well constructed, mission-supporting Standard Operating Procedures (SOPs) are also needed. These spell out policies, programs, rules, and variance sanctions. These often become an Employee Handbook that all receive (and sign for them after thirty days, including a statement that they have or will read it and are bound by all elements as continuing employment criteria).

In order to harness Safety, Self-Interest, and perhaps Hope and Energy/Time Optimization deep into the organization, all pay, bonus, and promotion levels need to be directly tied to these SMART goals and SOP elements. They need to be tracked quarterly via the Milestone Achievement Progress (MAP)-type program defined in chapter 6. Politically adopted compensation and reward policies need to exist and be used.

Semi-annual (twice per year) performance evaluations need to be tied to the goals results and SOP compliance. Customer and taxpayer surveys can provide good performance metrics. Rewards and sanctions need to be applied as applicable. If not, employees will see the goals and SOPs as lip service only and will pay them no mind. Anarchy is then a possibility. This process will help with EEOC, civil service, and union grievance "due process" defenses as well. Merit can then better prevail for all.

The second need is in the hiring area. Pick a good assessment tool, like the Hartman Values Profile, or better. Set the desired profiles by testing the (documented) best people in each group, and then use the profiles as one tool of several in helping hire or promote A-players. Background checks, references, education verifications and sometimes lie detectors can be used. Like on any team, if you get the right athletes aboard, the go-to players, then results take care of themselves.

Avoid seniority based promotions alone if possible. Set merit based standards for promotions by using per-goal results, SOP performance, supervisor evaluations, validated testing versus criteria, and education. Be careful of EEOC guidelines and civil service and union rules, if any, to promote the best leaders. Seniority can be included (and may have to be by contract or law), but should be one of five or more criteria.

By these acts "meritocracy" will become the defacto culture vs. mediocrity. Just like a culture takes its lead from the CEO, when the government leader sets and implements a meritocracy, people's self-interests will align to it. The upward spiral begins and is self-fueling. Pride and personal commitment can flourish. The public directly benefits.

Next, give high visibility to the results, positive and negative, versus the goals. Provide visible rewards (but sanction privately). This will reinforce the goals-based meritocracy culture. It will also help provide political value that is protective based on merit. A politician is much less likely to change a successful program for political expediency for several reasons. Be prepared to defend the rewards program when legal challenges are raised, as they likely will be.

Additionally, be a good steward of taxpayers' funds when negotiating labor contracts. Once, when with a management services company for public works and public transit management, we treated all such negotiations as though it was my company's own money. Get the politicians behind you in this. The unions hated it. So, be proactive in establishing, and protecting, fair and mission-focused work rules.

Selling Management Outsourcing Contracts Was a Consultative Selling Art!

Our benefits were many. However, our experts' costs were about five times local people costs, the politically contributing unions did not like our negotiating and merit-based management skills, and all had to be done in front of TV cameras covering public meetings by Authorities, Councils, and Commissions.

Finding a truly community-good dedicated, powerful politician champion was the key to success. They would lead the selection and contracting process through the political "thicket" of getting enough political votes to win. After finding that A-personality political champion our job was to arm him or her (it was often a her, due to high community good commitment) with benefits "ammo," and with documentation that we would do a better job for the community in myriad ways. It was pure consultative selling, and fun.

For the future, use the planning methods in chapter 7 to forecast the future, and what changes will be needed by your organization to be well positioned to support the projected needs in coming years. To do so, some changes may be needed now given implementation lead times. Submitted plans and budgets need to have a Why, What, How, When, Who, How Much flow. The mission statement might have to be tweaked. Enabling statutes might need to be updated or changed. Roles might even be dropped or moved to other entities.

Then work with political leaders to explain why the future suggestions are good for their constituencies. Once approved, proactively communicate the plans and underlying reasons, and the benefits to the public being served. Then execute. Keep the media informed.

Make sure you have the political backing needed to be a highly effective leader. In a minority of situations, employment is a political patronage payoff. In some situations that is the true "end," versus public service quality that needs good leadership. If while interviewing you perceive this, withdraw (unless you want to be part of that process, but then, by my standards, that is not what a true leader does). Relatedly, make sure you understand how strongly excellence is politically supported. Take a read as to whether the political "stomach" is there to truly support goals-focused leadership. Why and how the last leader left can be an insight.

Leading Non-Profits (Especially Charities)

Thank goodness for these unsung leaders who do us a great service. This is especially true for charities.

Having been on the board of several non-profits, I know that this leadership role has many challenges versus running a private business. So, we should all admire the leaders of non-profit groups, especially charities. They are special people and represent the best in us. Capitalism is the best economic system there is compared to alternatives, but it is imperfect. Such non-profits fill key roles for society.

The most important challenge is that the organization is often too dependent on the Sociability Primal Drive and its sub-element, altruism. As noted in chapter 2, this is the weakest of the Primal Drives to depend on and has many limits that must be outmaneuvered. Altruism embodies relatively less native energy and causes extra efforts to be needed to succeed. Variance risk is higher.

The lack of a commonly rationalizing profit drive is a challenge in this sector also; although sufficient cash flow may come close to a functional profit drive. Perhaps to a lesser degree, the same goal setting, SOPs, reviews, hiring, and promoting needs exist as above for government entities to assure "the racer's edge."

The key leadership need is to find a way to harness the higher Primal Drives-based must-do energies of individuals and organizations that can be leveraged by the non-profit. Local and national governments, non-government organizations, corporations, churches, and foundations have mission-related needs that might be leveragable via contracts, agreements, relationships, etc. With these stronger Primal Drives as energy more results can be achieved. Better personnel can be attracted and retained. Aligning with businesses that either truly want to help and/or can directly and materially benefit from the effort for their own Primal Drives is good for Judo-leveraging potential.

Thus the core issue is to get closer to the stronger Primal Drives than Altruism without losing the essence of the core altruistic mission, and not having too many unacceptable "strings" attached. This is mostly a marketing strategy problem for the leader to address. Normal leadership actions per chapters 4 (not to do) and 5 (to do) then apply. Chapters 6 and 7's methods and tools can also be used.

Engineers, Mathematicians, and Accountants as Leaders

Not to be obtuse, but they can be the best and not-so-best leaders. Bill Gates, Steve Jobs, Jack Welch, and many others are or were unequaled. These and many other engineer or technically trained leaders have excellent leadership track records. They have the well-deserved respect of many.

Are they the exceptions that prove the rule that engineers, etc. sometimes have special challenges as leaders? Here are my observations about this question after twenty-plus years of working with engineers and in one management services company being the go-to executive for relating to customer contacts that were city or county engineers.

First, engineering, mathematics, and accounting schools are extremely rigorous and all but the very smart students tend to wash out and change to other fields. So, graduates need to be deeply respected for their native intelligence. They have big brains and are great problem solvers.

It has been my observation that engineers, mathematicians, accountants, etc., generally pursue those vocations because they have an emotional need or value system to put definable, certain structure on things; in order to be comfortable with understanding and dealing with the surrounding world.

Thank goodness they do. Planes fly. Bridges handle traffic. Spacecraft make the exacting mathematical journey to Mars. Software works. New electronic products regularly are released. Business financial books balance.

The challenge for some is the native "grayness" of leadership, including constant change over time. Very few issues are "in the box." Most events are, or soon will be, outside the box, are not structured, and are always changing. The term "simultaneous tight and loose properties" reflects that leaders need to be naturally (emotionally) comfortable with both realities.

At the worst, engineers, etc., who are emotionally challenged by grayness and rapid change can become some combination of introverted, uncertain, too slow to act, over-controlling, stubborn, and possibly negative to be around. Any and all of these acts, if they occur, are limiting to the Primal Drives of others being achieved and are therefore suboptimal for the organization, and for personal goals. Great visions can sometimes overpower the limitations for awhile, as has been discussed.

"Founderitis" Can Be a Key Challenge in Technical Companies

Very smart software or other types of engineers often start a company in regard to a new technology idea. While many can take it all the way to an IPO and beyond, many cannot. They have to be replaced, often by investors. In many cases they become the CTO. This can work well if the founder is a giver and emotionally understands the wisdom of this move for all, including him and his family. If not, the founder can be on the sidelines with his stock under someone else's control. Strengths can become weaknesses (which is true in *all* of us).

As in all things, defining the issue is half the battle. For these individuals self-awareness, perhaps via testing, is the key remedial need, including how the ramifications can be self-damaging in terms of personal goals and Primal Drives being realized. Perpetual personal growth is needed also. Learning to be able to better control the outcome by emotionally giving up over-control of the process is a very personal, emotional challenge. It is vital, however. For some, doing so is like Cortez burning the boats. The engineer, mathematician, and accountant who can combine brainiac powers with grayness comfort when needed have a special, valuable talent. Hire and promote them.

Engineer leaders need to seek objective inputs and feedback from others, including anonymously. Act on what is heard.

Remember that spatial thinking/envisioning governs the pecking order. If you have the grayness handling problem, make sure your vision is compelling. Or hire someone with vision and support them—or at least put up with them when they scare you to death.

"Dancers" Scare the Thinkers!

In one leadership seminar for my people the lady trainer was reviewing the four key personality types. She started to go on and then observed that the "Thinkers" (engineers, etc.) were secretly, deeply scared of the Marketing people's ("Dancers") thinking processes.

Women as Leaders

Many would say this is a no-person's land and only fools knowingly enter. Perhaps so, but the purpose is pure, which is the only important test. My purpose is *for* women who want to be leaders, and effectively break through the very real "glass ceiling" that exists in certain situations As a matter of fact, I believe that when a society can evolve to a matriarchal status then we have reached the pinnacle of safety, security, opportunity, and hope.

"Matriarchy"

"Three types of matriarchy exist, according to the Encyclopedia of Psychology and Religion: gynecocracy refers to a mother leading a group, whether a family or nation; matrilineality is a social system that passes inheritances down through the female lineage; and matrifocality refers to the centrality of women in society, especially mothers."

—eHow.com

Women and men are both similar and different. Scientific studies have shown this: "The scans also showed that men's and women's amygdalas are polar opposites in terms of connections with other parts of the brain. In men, the right amygdala is more active and shows more connections with other brain regions. In women, the same is true of the left amygdala. Scientists still have to find out if one's sex also affects the wiring of other regions of the brain. It could be that while men and women have basically the same hardware, it's the software instructions and how they are put to use that makes the sexes seem different." (Source: *livescience.com*, April 2006.)

Another study cited by *livescience*.com, January 2005, reported that: "Men and women *do* think differently, at least where the anatomy of the brain is concerned, according to a new study.

"The brain is made primarily of two different types of tissue, called gray matter and white matter. This new research reveals that men think more with their gray matter, and women think more with white. Researchers stressed that just because the two sexes think differently, this does not affect intellectual performance.

"'Their findings show that in general, men have nearly 6.5 times the amount of gray matter related to general intelligence compared with women, whereas women have nearly 10 times the amount of white matter related to intelligence compared to men. 'These findings suggest that human evolution has created two different types of brains designed for equally intelligent behavior,' said Haier...Scientists find it very interesting that while men and women use two very different activity centers and neurological pathways, men and women perform equally well on broad measures of cognitive ability, such as intelligence tests.

"These findings suggest that human evolution has created two different types of brains designed for equally intelligent behavior..."

A February 2005 report in *livescience.com* found that: "Popular culture tells us that women and men's brains are just different. It is true that male and female hormones affect brain development differently, and imaging studies have found brain differences in the ways women and men feel pain, make social decisions, and cope with stress. The extent to which these differences are genetic versus shaped by experience—the old nature-versus-nurture debate—is unknown.

"But for the most part, male and female brains (and brainpower) are similar. A 2005 *American Psychologist* analysis of research on gender differences found that in 78 percent of gender differences reported in other studies, the effect of gender on the behavior was in the small or close-to-zero range. And recent studies have debunked myths about the genders' divergent abilities. A study published in the January 2010

Psychological Bulletin looked at almost half a million boys and girls from 69 countries and found no overall gap in math ability. Focusing on our differences may make for catchy book titles, but in neuroscience, nothing is ever that simple."

According to Amber Hensley in *mastersofhealthcare.com* (June 2009): "Women tend to communicate more effectively than men, focusing on how to create a solution that works for the group, talking through issues, and utilizes non-verbal cues such as tone, emotion, and empathy, whereas men tend to be more task-oriented, less talkative, and more isolated. Men have a more difficult time understanding emotions that are not explicitly verbalized, while women tend to intuit emotions and emotional cues... women typically solve problems more creatively and are more aware of feelings while communicating... Psychologist Shelley E. Taylor coined the phrase 'tend and befriend' after recognizing that during times of stress women take care of themselves and their children (tending) and form strong group bonds (befriending)... Women typically have a larger deep limbic system than men, which allows them to be more in touch with their feelings and better able to express them, which promotes bonding with others... Men typically have stronger spatial abilities, or being able to mentally represent a shape and its dynamics..."

These differences and similarities can be material success or failure factors in differing leadership situations. (As we will see, events and "nurture" can open new vistas for female leaders today.)

From many observations I believe the "software" differences emanated from the human species' primordial genes survival-based *roles*, that played out in distant prehistoric times. The genes perpetuation roles were different for men and women but complementary, and are *still deeply programmed (nature) into us* at the Primal Drives level today, to support genes perpetuation; possibly going as far back as Homo erectus ("upright man"), more than two million years ago). These include genes perpetuation roles based differing situational views and applications of the Primal Drives "software" for species Safety, Self-interest, Hope and Transcendence, Honesty and Trust, Energy and Time Saving, Sociability, and more.

To generalize (and there are a few exceptions), these differences evolved because in ancient times there were two different, interdependent environments to be navigated for human species to have the best chance of survival and genes perpetuation, with neither being better or worse, or more important, than the other, just different—and complementary:

1. The non-village external, "out there" world: This is where the larger, physically stronger male hunter or warrior had to go (Ayla, in Jean Auel's entertaining *Clan of* *the Cave Bear* fiction series, would have been the exception), that was dangerous, physically challenging, constantly changing, and had major negative repercussions if hunting (or fighting) failure occurred. If so, people starved, or were decimated by enemies. Failure, like a missed spear throw, had to be quickly shaken off, even if one had to lie to himself about prowess, or blame another. There was no time or room for extensive self-recrimination or self-doubt that could negatively affect the next effort. The idea of self-doubt had to be expunged as dangerous. Personal survival was often at risk as well, requiring strength, guile, spatial awareness, instincts, and purposeful risk taking. Safety was very low, so courage had to be innate. Knowing when to be on the offense or on defense had to be quickly decided.

Also, hunters had to keep moving to find moving pockets of game. They literally had to "think on their feet" while moving so as to find the quarry, and how to position to kill it for the community's need for food. For battle, finding the preferential terrain was key. The testosterone (an energizing steroid) levels would very high in anticipation of the challenge, to be successful.

||||||||||||||||||||||||||||||||||||||||||||||||||||||||||||||||||||||||||||||||||||||||||||||||||||||||||||||||||||||||

Pacing While Thinking

Men do this more than women it seems, probably harking back to ancient hunting styles. The deepest thought was about how to find and kill game for the village while moving and searching through the woods or across savannas. Or, how to position forces for battle advantage. Thinking on your feet was literally needed. Today's pacing is likely a hunting movement surrogate that intrinsically supports deep thought. The author is guilty, as my wife sometimes observes. "Please stop pacing!"

||||||||||||||||||||||||||||||||||||||||||||||||||||||||||||||||||||||||||||||||||||||||||||||||||||||||||||||||||||||||

Self-belief, and even egotistical hubris, was important when trying to succeed against physical and other challenges. Individual skill was a key to success. Also, team hunting was often needed for success, so merit-based teamwork was needed at times. Rivalries could not interfere with results. Personal prowess was important to the pecking order that always formed; especially the best vision of where to go and how to execute for success.

A clear leader may or might not emerge, but all supported the envisioning process because of the greater good. An injured teammate meant lower potentials, so help would exist if needed to be ready for the next hunt or battle. The feelings of others were not important unless they interfered with the hunt's success; and feelings were often a sign of personal weakness that could be exploited by others. A personal feud had to be put aside for the greater good of the hunt, at least until the hunt was over.

Thus, each man had to be both an individual hunter-warrior and often be part of a functioning killing team. In both cases end success goals were always top of mind, and the process to be used variable to the situation and goals. It was an outside-in/top-down thinking process, and time-in-motion thinking. The ends and situation determined the means. Spatial thinking was significantly needed because tactical warfare and hunting are time and motion processes.

How can we gain the high ground versus the enemy? Would the prey be at the valley waterhole over the next ridge, or grazing in upper meadows? When the herd would be stampeded, where would it run so that an ambush point could be preset? Who would play what roles based on expertise (stampeders vs. the best weapons experts)? If the group was to split, where and when would they meet, and what were the best paths to get there, long before maps existed? Who would guard in the rear to warn of pending attacks by other tribes or four-legged predators (e.g., saber tooth tigers were probably masters of the food chain)?

Every minute would bring new relationships between the challenges and opportunities. These intangibles had to be quickly spatially sensed and juxtaposed at all times, including changes in the cause-effect relationships, what new goals had to quickly arise, and what should not be done now. Timing sense, spatial envisioning, logical thinking, experience, common sense, and cool-headed ("icewater in veins") judgment "under duress" were critical to hunting success, and perhaps even to battle survival. There would often be little time for debate, and communications were often terse and solely goals-focused. Seriousness of purpose was the commanding emotion. Each man knew his job and each expected the others to do theirs. Forgiveness of serious, harmful errors was in short supply.

Tidiness's costs versus gains were often in conflict with constantly moving to new hunting potentials, including that the past location's tidiness added little to a new location and effort. Using Energy and Time were net negatives.

Interpersonal communications were somewhat sparse, often with grunts or gestures being sufficient. There was a native sense about what to do, and the roles of each in the hunt or battle.

Weapons quality was important and a continual focus. Quality and sufficiency of the "tools" were important to success for the village's needs being met. In battle, this was even more important.

Weapons proficiency was also important. A missed spear throw or arrow was a costly, perhaps dangerous, waste.

If a battle was in process, bravery, skill, offensive attitude, and teamwork were important. There was an orientation to move towards the challenge; to be on offense. Except possibly for gathering slaves, a "no prisoners" hardness existed. Sensitivity to the plight of the vanquished was very low. The captured might even be disdained for not dying in battle (this was a key element of the Japanese Bushito code right up until WWII was over, and later on some islands). Leaders in subsistence times like Tamerlane were known to kill almost all in a village who opposed him, as a message to others to acquiesce. Those purposely released bore the surrender message to others to surrender without fighting, who often did (many villages that did not resist were spared).

Strictly personal feelings were held tightly. Any feelings of inadequacy had to be expunged. What the hunting or fighting team needed was controlling. Any merriment would be saved for when back at the cave or village, if they made it.

||||||||||||||||||||||||||||||||||||||||||||||||||||||||||||||||||||||||||||||||||||||||||||||||||||||||||||||||||||||||||||||||

"Anything But No!"

In the Army, HUA! (Heard, Understood, Acknowledged) actually means "anything but no" (aka, "will do," even at great personal peril). "Hoorah" is the same in the Marines.

||||||||||||||||||||||||||||||||||||||||||||||||||||||||||||||||||||||||||||||||||||||||||||||||||||||||||||||||||||||||||||||||

Sexual mores varied by culture, with monogamy often required, and sometimes not. (According to author Stephen Ambrose, Lewis and Clark learned that different Native American tribes had differing mores in this regard.)

Back in the cave or village, relative laziness was often a norm. The work could be left to others, and Energy saved for the next hunt.

As a result of the above, primordially men had to be:

- Spatially intelligent, for envisioning what to do next for success, and where danger may be lurking

- Committed to their family's and village's welfare
- Hunt or battle goal oriented and committed
- Constantly striving
- Individually skilled
- Team player when needed
- Able to push past fears
- Rationalize away failures
- Only communicative as needed
- Able fend off rivals or attackers when needed
- Confident and self-motivating
- Constantly seeking new advantages in weapons, methods, and insights
- Good providers for their community
- Good partners with their spouses back home, who had important roles also.

2. The internal cave or village world: Also for genes perpetuation purposes, keeping a functional, harmonious, stable, peaceful, clean, safe social community (cave or village) and rearing healthy young was, of course, a prime role for those who remained in the village, primarily the women. These factors were critical to perpetuation of the genes, no matter how well the hunters or warriors did. Relatively more physical safety existed here versus "out there."

They endeavored to keep the provider partner strong, happy, and successful. They raised the children. The interpersonal burdens and expectations were heavy. This started with childbirth, child rearing, nurturing and doctoring.

Myriad details, tangible and intangible, had to be known and applied in the complex interpersonal culture of the cave or village. Continually gaining information was vital.

The quality of collective life was a key success factor. Many challenges regularly existed. Discord, disease, and injury were to be avoided at all possible costs because:

1. The "entropy" dangers of negative discourse could mean collective weakness in the face of ever-possible external challenges, with women being the prime peacemakers.
2. The remedies for disease were so weak or nonexistent that avoiding such problems was important. Cleanliness/tidiness was an accepted imperative, as well as providing nourishing food. Women would often be the healers,

and would experiment with cures using what nature provided. They would also make the clothing needed to keep warm, and for mates to hunt or fight successfully. Details and quality were critical.

The "strength (Safety) in numbers" Social harmony imperative meant a socially stable cave or village, where the quality of interpersonal relations and positive cooperation were key to the group's aggregate strength and survival potential. Intuitiveness and sensitivity to the feelings and emotions of others was vital to both personal relationships and to cultural harmony and smooth functioning. Being able to read people intuitively was a mandatory skill, including body language, personalities, values, motivations, and more. They needed to have a deep sense of interpersonal relationships quality.

Common sense was also highly important.

Creativity was vital.

Sensitivity and care giving to others in need was vital to the community's well-being.

A keen eye for detail would be a vital skill for the gatherer.

Power in the personal pecking order was important to harmonious life enjoyment in the Social community, and to being in personal control. This status was often a combination of the mate's perceived prowess and stature, family wealth, personal attributes to offer, and sensitivity to others' interests (resulting in helping others' Primal Drives be realized, with return benefits). Being concerned about and protective of one's own social status in the pecking order was important to safety, power, and political success. Slights could become ostracisms or even attacks if not perceived and controlled.

Slights had to be quickly perceived and dealt with, as they might affect the women's stature in the community's politics. Safety, Self-Interest, Hope, etc. could be affected. Relatedly, often there was a level of competition, often unspoken, with other women for power and influence, and for material rewards This often went beyond competitively attracting a strong mate for gene pool quality. Errors were to be assiduously avoided owing to these key success factors, especially stature. How others felt about them was critically important.

Constant information gathering was very important, because, then as now, information is power. Thus the information grapevine was continually vibrating and had to be participated in and be influenced. Being the most knowledgeable was a power source.

||||||||||||||||||||||||||||||||||||||||||||||||||||||||||||||||||||||||||||||||||||||||||||||||||||||||||||||||||||||||||||||||||||||||||||||||||||||||||||||||||||||||||

Killing the Shirt and Leaving

In the very funny *Defending the Caveman* play, the author states that women are information seekers and shopping is a native information gathering event with many details being important to gather, no matter the time or patience needed. They thus do it well.

Men, on the other hand, go into a store, kill a shirt, and leave.

||||||||||||||||||||||||||||||||||||||||||||||||||||||||||||||||||||||||||||||||||||||||||||||||||||||||||||||||||||||||||||||||||||||||||||||||||||||||||||||||||||||||||

Joining a small like-minded group for joint success and Safety was often smart to do, often forming into what we call cliques today: a strength in numbers survival and prosperity action. Access to it would be very guarded. The sharing of feelings and emotions in the group was considered to be important. Honesty and openness were cardinal rules. Loyalty was important. Giving to the group's greater good was important. Anyone seen to be disloyal was sanctioned, early and often. Any rivalries were kept inwardly.

Thus women developed very strong intuitions, sensitivities, knowledge, and insights in regard to relationships and group harmony. In many such societies, matriarchal wisdom was the highest wisdom. The councils would weight those inputs very heavily, and they were controlling in many.

Thus women's abilities were not different, but the Primordial Drive roles were different, requiring different "software" in the form of Primal Drives application.

Women Will Rule!

Today, these ancient female primal roles are still important, *and* are evolving as we enter times of more plenty and surrounding Safety, to evolve to new roles. The surrounding, expanding ecosystem surplus allows growing Safety variances, opening new opportunities. Women are shaking off the "tyranny of the either-or"(Collins) and breaking past Primordial boundaries in many areas, and will continue to do so in the future. They are often more educated and more sports-minded and competitive today. Risk taking is up. They see males as less and less protecting false "glass ceiling" limitations (more work is needed). More have entered leadership ranks, have validated potentials, and have mentored others. Confidence is up. They see more avenues for personal contribution and success. They want to share in the merit-based rewards, and achieve rapidly evolving self-realization goals.

In the US, with over 50 percent of adult women working, they want to contribute outside the home and be recognized for those contributions. Many women are getting married much later in life and want to be financially successful. Many working women want to be able to focus on the job's responsibilities, and find ways for traditional home caregiver activities to be simultaneously realized with quality. More and more women are entering the very competitive political world and are making major contributions. Coming combat roles for women will have many ramifications for the future. Thus, I believe women are evolving better than men!

||||||||||||||||||||||||||||||||||||||||||||||||||||||||||||||||||||||||||||||||||||||||||||||||||||||||||||||||||||||||||||||||||||||||||||

Nurture Can Change Nature!

At a recent Sunday School class, the teacher put tape around the six-year-old children's hands, sticky side out, to get them to "stick together." Invariably the boys immediately started pushing each other like Sumo Wrestlers. No exceptions. The girls would hold hands and dance around each other in cooperation and warmness, laughing together. No exceptions.

When going to lunch after church, while raining, my six-year-old granddaughter held her mother's hand and skipped around and over the puddles. My four-year-old grandson, in his Batman outfit and cape, walked alone and made sure he *stomped through every puddle in the lot*.

Some "Nature" differences can exist.

However, when coaching my middle school daughter's soccer team, we won the city championship. One of the reasons was "Blood Drills," to get them comfortable and even enjoying legally aggressive physical play. In practice the player that legally touched the loose ball the fifth time won an M&M (symbol). The loser had to do a push-up (different symbol). We literally ran every other team, even older ones, off the field physically, with no Yellow or Red cards. I am convinced that if we played with boys of the same physical size, the girls would have smoked them.

Nurture *can* change the Nature programming! Men must help!

||||||||||||||||||||||||||||||||||||||||||||||||||||||||||||||||||||||||||||||||||||||||||||||||||||||||||||||||||||||||||||||||||||||||||||

Leadership Advice for Women

In July 2005, *livescience.com* reported that: "We have found that women will focus on the emotional response to stress. In contrast, men typically think only of the (stress) sensation itself, which may explain their higher thresholds and tolerances."

||||||||||||||||||||||||||||||||||||||||||||||||||||||||||||||||||||||||||||||||||||||||||||||||||||||||||||||||||||||||||||||||||||

Avoid Dwelling on Variances or Risks

On a flight talking to a female diversity consultant to large corporations, one of the insights about how to help female managers was her observation that a major challenge versus men is that females tend to over-dwell on actual or potential negatives or errors, then try to avoid them too much, and let them affect them too long.

Remember: Bleep happens. Be confident. Learn and move on.

||||||||||||||||||||||||||||||||||||||||||||||||||||||||||||||||||||||||||||||||||||||||||||||||||||||||||||||||||||||||||||||||||||

So, what advice should be given? It all depends on the selected playing field.

Where interpersonal skills and delivering on promises are the key, no one is better than a female. Service companies (based on delivering on promises) stand out as significantly requiring these skills, and healthcare, as well as government entities, especially local and state governments. No better skill set exists. Politics also.

If, however, one wants to go into the "jungle" as a figurative big game hunter, mostly dominated by high testosterone men today, where new challenges (stress), opportunities, and rewards exist, but where the "glass ceiling" is strongest, then some advice can be helpful. Owing to the higher risk and greater difficulty, the rewards are higher, both financially and emotionally, than less stressful and risky environments. The requirements are higher also.

Margie Warrell's tips in *Stop Being Safe*, cited in chapter 5, definitely apply.

Larger, often global, fast-growing product and service companies are more complex, fast moving, assailed by powerful competitors, have demanding shareholders and boards (with legal fiduciary requirements), and are more risky than service companies. The bets can be big, including fearlessly betting the company at times (for example the new Ford CEO Alan Mulally fearlessly borrowed $24.7 Billion, leveraging virtually every asset at high debt service costs, and it paid off). Future spatial envisioning and planning are keys. While intellectual carefulness is important, emotional fear has no place.

Most of these product companies are still led by males, especially outside the U.S. "Hunter" *attributes* are required to be competitively successful relative to other companies usually run by hunter males, who are not prisoner oriented.

Metaphorically, it is like playing NFL football, with the opponents being male, big, tough, spatial, goals-driven, and highly competitive. They seldom let failures or setbacks bother them. They are both individualistically ambitious and team players, as needed. They set high standards and forcefully enforce them. Self-doubts are expunged. They suffer no fools. Nurture is a means, not an end. The three imperatives are Goals, Goals, Goals. A friendly style is a means, not an end.

Thus, an effective opponent needs to match or outdo these *attributes*. When the ball is hiked, the one who pushes the other team back is attitudes and attributes based. As one coach once noted, "Desire is not enough. You must also have the skills, attitudes, and performance."

The "glass ceiling" is thicker in this realm because the attributes have been practiced more by males for the millennia as Nature based, paradigms exist, with spatial envisioning the major force, and the attributes will always exist to be leveraged and not resisted. Males are larger in numbers in this realm, understand what the success rules are, are natively skilled at them in general, know that competitors are hunters also, will be attributes-judgmental, and will not materially lower their standards and paradigms for several reasons, including the fact that many do not know how to lower them and feel comfortable. They feel that their attributes are applicable, since most competitors will have them.

So, as imperfect as it is, the "glass ceiling" is more attributes based than anything else. In this regard, I have twelve key points of advice for women breaking through the glass ceiling in these types of companies:

1. Remember that spatial thinking/envisioning is key to the pecking order. Envisioning is a spatial process that needs to be strong. Being able to spatially see the affective power forces in the future and around you, and how to best spatially position for goals as a result is a critical big-game hunter skill, both offensively and defensively. Be spatial, or have someone you listen to on your team that is spatial (people will see what is happening but go along if it is working, and will admire you for being open to good advice. Even the historically great white hunters in Africa had skilled trackers who were spatial, but the hunters got the trophy credit.) (E.g., Meg Whitman just hired a new, male Chief Strategy Officer to help.)

If this spatial thinking is not a natural attribute, practice it by studying maps and relating to how places fit together. Find other spatial development resources. Practice with a compass and your spatial mind will strengthen. When driving spatially, envision the street patterns and the locations in general. Practice spatial drills; many association drills are on the Internet to be practiced. With these spatial practices you are building new mental synapses, just like you would if learning an instrument or language. Use the outside-in, tomorrow-to-today planning tools in chapters 6 and 7 to help.

2. Relatedly, begin with the end in mind in all things. What do we want to achieve before we start, and what do we want to avoid happening? Then set Key Success Factors (KSFs), strategies, tactics, assignments, and financial plans, in that order. (A format for doing this is in chapter 6.) Start meetings by setting results goals, work the related agenda, and end by determining if those goals were met. All plans should have a Why, What, How, Who, When, and How Much flow. Top-down is an unnatural act for some, but vital.

3. Practice the Judo Principle to leverage the Primal Drives in chapter 2 and Appendix A, for both self-management and for getting the most out of others. Practice the leadership principles in chapter 5, and avoid those in chapter 4.

4. Use the other leadership tools and methods in chapter 6. This includes using the planning processes in chapter 7. Study the four key power forces of changes in technology, laws, economics, and the competition (direct and indirect, reflecting that McDonald's considers Kroger a key competitor also, for the "food wallet"), and the impacts they have had and will have (have formal processes to forecast these changes, as they will define the challenges and opportunities in the future—see the Gretsky "where the puck will be" quote in chapter 6).

5. Find and use mentors. Actively seek self-improvement inputs. "I'm good, so how do I get even better?" (And, if doing well, mentor others, male and female. You will learn by teaching and giving.)

6. In larger organizations, know that your biggest competition for success is *inside* **the company.** Make sure you have a spatial, time and motion understanding of this dynamic as well; watch your flanks, but do not let undue caution limit results-focused leadership actions. Do not dwell on how others think. Just deliver results ahead of plan.

7. Leverage your exceptional interpersonal skills and sensitivities, but as means and not ends. Ethical results relative to goals are the only end. Period. As Drucker said, achieving results is the test of the effective executive. But it takes people to achieve results, so harnessing their Primal Drives via sensitivity to them is generally good, and women excel at this sensitivity. However, since this is an imperfect world, too much nurturing can be bad (as McGregor found at Antioch). Be willing to "shoot" when needed, with emotional inner comfort. Like with our kids, all people we rub elbows with in business, internally and externally, will try to find the "edges" for their own benefit. It is not a question of if, but how often and how strongly? As a result they will go over the line and hope to skate past. If the leader allows the skating, the line will move out further the next time because they might be able to get away with that new action also. So saying no and possibly even sanctioning is equally as valid as being sensitive when done at the right time for the right issue. The word will quickly get around that merit-related performance is the rule of the day and the extreme variances will subside. Testing the edges will especially occur initially, perhaps from males mostly but not solely. Act!

8. Be willful and determined, but *attitudinally* and *not emotionally*. Emotions are housed in the frontal lobes of the brain, and determination elsewhere (to me it is at the bottom of the brain, the cerebellum, where the spinal cord starts). Quiet determination and inner toughness will be non-consciously "read" and respected, and reacted to. Emotionality will be negatively reacted to and perhaps even resisted because it is a threat to others' Primal Drives. Make sure your willfulness is a "means," however, and not an "end." Know and practice the difference.

9. Never take counsel of your fears (as FDR advised during the Great Depression), and persevere when "bleep" inevitably happens. Shake them off as self-limiting. Be part of the solution and not part of the problem. It is not if bleep happens, but how often and how badly; Murphy is ever present and has uncanny timing. Perseverance with calmness under stress requires some "icewater in the veins," or coolness under fire, so that better logical versus emotional thinking will prevail. This self-control will also help with the correct "know when to hold them and know when to fold them" or "what not to do" decisions that may come.

Being able to emotionally accept defeat and still feel good about yourself is also important. "Who gets mad (or blinks) last wins." If your arrow misses, shake it off, retrieve it, find new game, be confident, shoot again, and bring home the results to feed others. It is on you to persevere "no matter how hopeless, no matter how far." Again, be part of the solution and not part of the problem. All leaders have failed tactically, and some strategically, several times. Like the male hunter, find a way to rationalize away a failed result and press on afresh. No prisoners.

‖‖‖

All Leaders Have Detractors

Even George Washington faced the very serious "Conway Cabal" in the fledgling government back in Philadelphia to oust him as general while Washington was at Valley Forge (before the successful Trenton raid across the Delaware at Christmas). The cabal was led by a general who was envious. When the twenty-one-year-old Major General Marquis de Lafayette, from France, would not go along because of his respect for Washington's leadership, it dissolved.

Lincoln's detractors were legion.

When Ulysses S. Grant was to be the new Union Army commander, Lincoln's cabinet openly fretted about his drinking. The savvy Lincoln noted that "That man wins battles. Find out what he drinks and send a barrel to all my generals!"

The more effective you are the more envy will exist by some, and the more cabals perhaps. Enjoy them. Stay ahead via results.

‖‖‖

10. Relatedly, do not overreact to slights, disses, envy, and worry. I am convinced that a person cannot be successful if they are over-fearful of criticism. Intellectual carefulness is good, but emotional fear is bad. Absorb the pain and concern without emotion, learn and move on—as a better, wiser person. Shake it off. Let their pettiness be their problem and not yours. The only thing that counts becomes future results. The needed "food for the village" has now moved over the next hill, so we need to press on and go get it. Now.

11. When you sense that hiring, promotion, or termination criteria are unfairly stacked against you:

- Make sure you stack up well regarding the present and future attributes *that they need for business success.*
- Check the selection criteria for true job performance applicability.
- Seek independent, objective inputs in this regard. Listen and learn.
- Objectively determine if you are part of the issue relative to the winner being stronger.
- If you feel not, maturely meet with the decider(s), state your case, and get their feedback. Learn from it no matter what is said. Their weightings of certain attributes might have been the tie-breaker, and they have such rights

related to job performance, and choosing the best accordingly. You would also. So number-one above is key.

- If you feel non-job performance prejudice is involved, calculate the gain vs. the pain of possible actions. Small gains vs. political costs may cause disappointment to be accepted as the lesser of the evils. Level-headed judgment is needed. Life can be unfair at times.

- If material net gain potential exists and internal efforts fail, then seek possible remedies. Use the chain of command first. Be respectful, objective, and non-threatening. Appeal to ethics and the value of the company using the right criteria, and fostering meritocracy. Listen to what they say, and learn.

- If still convinced that bias exists that cannot withstand independent scrutiny, meet with HR and make your case. Listen to what they say, and learn.

- If still convinced of bias and the stakes are large you have external remedies. The EEOC is a free source. Attorneys are an option, with employment specialist lawyers being needed. You must carefully decide between retainer, fee share, or a combination.

- If mediation or arbitration occurs, have your facts ready, be confident, and state your case. Per Sun Tzu's "attack the strategy" and the Judo Principle, use the company's points against them. Be prepared for a range of possible offers, from no, to yes, to something in between.

- If you win, overcome the company's hurt feelings by exceeding expectations. Win-win always works best. Give them room to have been imperfect. Help them grow. Based on the merit of results the tide will turn, as a natural act, because their Primal Drives are being met.

- Keep your head high at all times; learn and grow.

- Mentor others, male and female.

- Always seek mentors. Listen and learn.

12. Take personal responsibility for your success…or failure. Have others help you. They will, if you help yourself first. Regardless, it is on you unless being patently discriminated against. Also, help others, female and male.

The very good news is that as growing economic plenty allows more Safety perceptions and comfort in general, more attitudinal room will exist for males to vary the long-held leadership attributes they have for leadership success, especially where those attributes are less of an imperative. Women are becoming more prevalent and proven as leaders, such as Meg Whitman and others. You are probably more competitive than your female ancestors. Once in the door, set new success standards based on results. This will help upcoming female leaders have more room for success. Results success is the best favor you can do for them. It sets the stage for Hope, Safety, and Self-Interest needs to be met by coming female leaders.

But remember that desire is necessary but not sufficient. Per the football metaphor, bring the needed skills and attitudes under that helmet and behind that chinstrap. Hit somebody (in football, you do not tackle their front, you tackle through the backbone-and hear them grunt). Like the soccer girls, bring your game! Be on the balls of your feet, and put competitors, inside and out, literally on their heels. High-five yourself internally (internal conceit), but keep it to yourself. Build others. Give-to-give. The "get" will be automatic.

Older Leaders

Thankfully I am now one of those (I made it!), and I have studied myself and other leaders.

While there is a long history of septuagenarians and older leaders just reaching their prime, in general many older leaders are considered by many to be past their prime as a general paradigm. Perhaps some seniors themselves fall into this self-image trap. Perhaps it is only perception based on surface observations that can be reversed with focus and effort.

"The apocryphal tale that you can't grow new brain cells just isn't true. Neurons continue to grow and change beyond the first years of development and well into adulthood, according to a new study. The finding challenges the traditional belief that adult brain cells, or neurons, are largely static and unable to change their structures in response to new experiences."—*livescience.com*, February 2005

"Scientists know that our brains shrink with aging, but does less gray matter really matter? Apparently not, according to a new study of 446 people in Australia. 'We found that, on average, men aged 64 years have smaller brains than men aged 60,' said Helen Christensen of the Australian National University. 'However, despite this shrinkage, cognitive functions—like memory, attention, and speed of processing—are unaffected.'"—*livescience. com*, June 2005

"Scientific wisdom once held that once you hit adulthood, your brain lost all ability to form new neural connections. This ability, called plasticity, was thought to be confined to infancy and childhood...Later studies found more evidence of human neurons making new connections into adulthood; meanwhile, research on meditation showed that <u>intense mental training can change both the structure and function of the brain.</u>"

—*livescience.com,* June 2005

First, the author feels certain that the faculties of a senior leader are not diminished by age alone, absent disease. Also, no one has more experience, knowledge, and memories to draw on, including what not to do. That is very valuable in a leader.

"The modern brain is an energy hog. The organ accounts for about 2 percent of body weight, but it uses about 20 percent of the oxygen in our blood and 25 percent of the glucose (sugars) circulating in our bloodstream, according to the American College of Neuropsychopharmacology."

—*livescience.com,* June 2005

||||||||||||||||||||||||||||||||||||||||||||||||||||||||||||||||||||||||||||||||||||||||||||||||||||||||||||||||||||||

Use It or Lose It

"Your brain is a thinking organ that learns and grows by interacting with the world through perception and action. Mental stimulation improves brain function and actually protects against cognitive decline, as does physical exercise.

"The human brain is able to continually adapt and rewire itself. Even in old age, it can grow new neurons. Severe mental decline is usually caused by disease, whereas most age-related losses in memory or motor skills simply result from inactivity and a lack of mental exercise and stimulation. In other words, use it or lose it."

—*The Franklin Institute*

||||||||||||||||||||||||||||||||||||||||||||||||||||||||||||||||||||||||||||||||||||||||||||||||||||||||||||||||||||||

When young we had children depending on us and much time to get a Selfish payback on efforts (Energy use), with Safety. It is the author's observation that in the Primal Drives there is a false "marbling" calculation with later age, that with less time left to enjoy the extrapolated Selfish fruits of hard work and Energy use, and with no imperative need to support children (Safety) who are now gone and on their own (unlike when we were leading young families). This allows the Energy Savings Primal

Drive to attain more control to save Energy calories. The gain potential is not worth the high energy costs. The shorter time might not Safely provide enough returns. A new Primal Drive calculation occurs.

This parallels investment strategy changes in later life. With less error/loss make-up time available, older persons get more conservative in investment strategies. When young, time existed to make up losses, so more risk could be tolerated.

When this deep Energy use vs. Selfish payback calculation occurs, we just innately, non-consciously dial back somewhat in intensity of thinking and action, and mental and physical calories use; and are not even aware of it, even though all the abilities are still there if called on. Less proactivity-causing hormones are autonomically released, for Energy conservation. The shorter term gains versus cost ratio does not call for the Energy calories to be expended as when young.

Use it or lose it is a very controllable internal calculation that can be reversed by conscious attitudes and actions. Thus, have confidence now that you understand the undiminished capabilities, facts, and underlying Primal Drives causes. Some purposeful actions could include:

- Accepting the use it or lose it bromide, and re-energize.
- Place a vast majority of your assets in irrevocable trusts for others' benefit so that you must get back to that "no prisoners," must-do leader you were for your own needs, reflecting the value of being lean and mean. Become primordial and "eat what you kill." You *will* kill to survive!
- Set a stretch goal of $n you will leave in your will, whether it will be to family members or charities or others, and challenge yourself not to fall short as a self-worth standard. Internalize it.
- Get yourself overstretched with giving programs in addition to your work. The stress of it will cause the brain to go back to that hyperactivity you always had, which is still there if brought out. Many will benefit in the process also.
- Adopt or become a legal guardian of one or more children, which will scare the _____ out of you and fire up the needed Primal Drives.
- Or, as Stanley Bing says in *What Would Machiavelli Do?*, "just lie to yourself" if you cannot find such a path to reenergizing the brain's powers. Perception becomes reality.

All of these will reset the Self-Interest and Hope Primal Drives to overpower the Energy Saving Primordial Drive and get you back onto that proactive leadership thinking and striving path that is still there. With this energy, and with the unequaled life experiences, a juggernaut results. Pity the poor competitor… internally and externally.

It is easy to imagine that the legal guardian idea especially sent an electric charge through you; hopefully not a shudder, but an electric charge. The author hopes you understand that if it would come true, you would immediately become just as smart and driven a leader as at 35, without any conscious thought, and much more experienced and skilled. This would harness Safety and Self-Interest Primal Drives as motivators: the two most powerful of all.

Thus your native leadership abilities are still there if energized. Whatever energizing path is best for you, overcome the Energy Saving Primal Drive that is holding back the Self-Interest-supporting hormones needed to have the brain as proactive as it was, and can be again. It is as simple as that. As we have all heard, "If not you, then who? If not now, then when?" The ball is in your court, and all will see and appreciate the result. It is fun, also, to be the sharpest in a room of young "whippersnappers," especially when none expect it. With a smile, put them on their heels intellectually. Then help them. Mentor them. Be a giver. Those youngsters need all the help we can give them.

Also, take Jimmy Buffett's advice, to die while you are living, and not just be living while you are dead. There is no need for the latter in reality, only in attitude.

Like with females, the very good news is that as growing economic plenty and its impacts on the young's motivations, more attitudinal room will exist to vary the attributes for leadership success. Additionally the growing view that "70 is the new 40" provides opportunity. Once in the door, set new success standards. The Boomer's higher work standards help also.

Older workers are not to be discriminated against by law. If such bias is suspected, generally follow the above steps for females.

Remember that spatial thinking/envisioning is key to the pecking order. Now, mount up! Move out! Lead the cavalry to save the day. Lead those kids!

Leading Turnarounds

These are often very difficult leadership situations owing to the additional challenge that the internal culture often becomes negative and resistant to success requirements. Extra conviction is needed by the leader, including accepting that a component of the enemy is possibly within.

By definition, a turnaround has not had success and is going the wrong direction; the longer the worse. Several ramifications of this slope can be:

- Results per plan are not realized; or worse, results are diminishing.
- Value positioning may be wrong in several ways.
- Execution programs are likely weak.
- There is weak or no alignment of rewards relative to results.
- Good people leave.
- Too many people may not be A-players.
- People look to avoid responsibility and to be blameless as the downward slope continues, for job security.
- Such people may often resent A-players' efforts to right the ship because they know their inadequacies will eventually be surfaced in a successful company, and their Safety Primal Drive will be triggered.
- They may exhibit many negative styles such as undercutting, deception, political posturing, blaming others, avoiding responsibility and accountability, and more.

Thus, only being externally focused is not enough in turnarounds. Two endeavor fronts exist, as a special challenge for leaders, with internal issues possibly the most challenging.

|||||||||||||||||||||||||||||||||||||||||||||||||||||||||||||||||||||||||||||||||||||||||||||||||||||||||||||||||||||||||||||||||||||||||||||||||||||||||||
Resentment

One study found that people resented a new, effective person because it disrupted their Safety and comfort.
|||||||||||||||||||||||||||||||||||||||||||||||||||||||||||||||||||||||||||||||||||||||||||||||||||||||||||||||||||||||||||||||||||||||||||||||||||||||||||

Previous chapters were mostly externally oriented. For the internal battlefront, here are some ideas:

- Begin your efforts on a "glass is half full" basis, but be vigilant. Let them determine their own fate. Tell them that. They begin with a "1000 batting average," and where they go from there is up to them. You are there to help and to hold all accountable for results for pay.

- Openly and actively surface this internal challenge possibility or general reality, in the spirit that "an issue identified is immediately half solved;" in light of what you expect to happen and not to happen, and the rewards and the sanctions that will apply. Document it for possible "due process" EEOC defenses ahead if needed.
- Find those who want to contribute, and figure out who the detractors are. Get private feedbacks. Document all. Take needed actions.
- Openly reward the A-players, to set an example and culture.
- Where a detractor exists, counsel him, specifically (with metrics) set what you want to improve and the time frame(s), define the results if not improved, including specific consequences if results are not improved in a specific period and per specific goals, and document all (a memo to the employee with his acknowledgment is a good idea, and all sent to HR).
- Where there is no or inadequate response, strongly sanction (privately), with indirect visibility to all. Do not personally criticize the individuals to others, but take very discernible actions. These could include demotions, pay cuts, non-promotions, horizontal moves, time off, or even termination. Everyone will get the word and will then take actions to avoid the same fate for their own Safety, Self-Interest, and Hope. Some will do better than others with this. Where major problems exist at the start, some very visible, justifiable, defendable terminations can be a great tonic. Reorganizations for "business requirements" can be used.
- Be prepared for EEOC or employment litigation actions with proper criteria and due process for terminations, demotions, and non-hires. Of course, never discriminate on any criteria other than "business requirements" merit.
- Show conviction to lead, and walk your talk. Do as you say. Lead from the front.
- Get your exterior value positioning right, both absolutely and relative to competitors.
- Execute a highly effective go-to-market program.
- Operate excellently internally. The MAP method (chapter 5) can be very helpful.

Leading in the Military, by Col. (Ret.) Roger L. Duckworth

At the request of the author, my brother, I am adding a few thoughts on leadership in the military from an Army perspective, based on experience at West Point, my

Masters in Public Administration, commanding a Field Artillery Battery, two Blackhawk Helicopter Companies, an Air Assault Battalion, and a Joint Unmanned Aerial Vehicle (UAV) Program.

Why is the military unique to lead? There are a number of reasons but these are a few:

- The military is a unique environment in that it assaults the primary Primal Drive, Safety.
- Likewise, Self-Interest is not a factor due to the pay.
- That Hope may not be realized is not a deterrent. As matter of fact several Hopes exist; Hope to do well in the career or time; Hope to come home safely and in one piece; Hope the family will be safer; and Hope for the country's safety.
- An employee that violates his company's regulations may get fired. A soldier who violates military regulations can be fined, or even imprisoned.
- Employees work their shift and go home. A soldier goes home when the job is done. "Stop loss" orders can keep him in the field perpetually.
- There is no Easy for combat soldiers, and time marches on—hopefully.
- Honesty, Trust, and Social contributions form the bedrock of soldiers' drives. They will literally die for each other. Many Medals of Honor are posthumous and related to helping others.
- A military unit's missions are usually very well defined. Their execution may have to vary due to "fog of war" conditions.
- Warfighters have no union representation to negotiate their pay, allowances, or benefits.
- Personnel turnover of from 33 percent to 50 percent per year are expected.
- Military jobs are generally very technical and require intense training to master. Much of that training occurs on the job.

This is a short list but sets up the primary question. How does a leader train and motivate soldiers to willingly go in to battle where there is great and real risk to their lives? Where the core Primal Drives are assaulted? One can imagine the guts it must take to kick down the door and be the first in to "clear the room." Or fly directly into ground-to-air missiles. Or sail through mines. Or to launch a rescue boat into 20-foot seas. These actions are counter-Primordial, and to be honored by all. This will be further exemplified by the women that volunteer to become combat soldiers, sailors, and airmen.

I feel that the primary leadership requirements are:

- Unquestioned honesty
- Trust in the unit
- A commitment to achieve the mission, regardless
- Total self-confidence
- The soldier having inordinate confidence, in himself, in his unit, in his leader, and in his country
- The Sociability drive to do for others, including his country, which is commanding of all Primal Drives
- The commitment to his unit and job, which is 100-percent character and giving based. The cost may be his life, but the giving benefits make the risks worthwhile.

How a leader creates each of these is below.

Soldiers trust that their mission is valuable to the country and to those who are oppressed. Soldiers always want and need to know "Why." A good leader insures that they understand "Why." Soldiers must have confidence in their chain of command. This confidence is gained through observing that their leaders are technically competent, tactically competent, honest, and fair. The military is physical. Warfighters expect their leaders to be in great physical condition. They disdain those who are not. A leader must look and act like a leader. Merit-based style is important.

Leaders must be fair. Every soldier has to know that they will be treated fairly whether the reward is positive or negative. The leader must follow the West Point guideline, "An officer on duty knows no one." You have no favorites, no losers, no special classes.

As Sun Tzu noted, leaders must love their soldiers. You might call this empathy or something else but if one of your soldiers has a problem, it is your problem. It is not only your problem because his performance affects your mission, but because he or she is one of "yours." My "Golden Rule" is "Do the right things for the right reasons and I will stand by you, no matter the consequences."

||||||||||||||||||||||||||||||||||||||||||||||||||||||||||||||||||||||||||||||||||||||||||||||||||||||||||||||||||||||||||||||||||||||||

Some Fighting Overlooked

A soldier was called in for punishment for fighting. His commander asked him why he was fighting. He said, "No one calls my CO (Commanding Officer) an SOB!" Do you think he was punished?

||||||||||||||||||||||||||||||||||||||||||||||||||||||||||||||||||||||||||||||||||||||||||||||||||||||||||||||||||||||||||||||||||||||||

The leader must be decisive. My philosophy is, "Always make a decision when you have to, but never make a decision before you have to." If a decision has to be made, make it on the best information and advice that you have. When the chain of command leader makes a decision, that is it! Assuming it is lawful, all must execute the order, regardless.

The leader must know what is going on. Get out of your office and walk around and talk to your leaders and soldiers. Do your paperwork after everyone else has left for the day. Tom Peters calls this "Management by Walking Around." It not only works, it is the only way to lead.

And finally, the leader must trust his leaders and followers. You do your job and you let (and insist) that they do theirs. They will be proud that they are trusted. But, always, when giving a soldier a job, insure that they have the training, help, tools and equipment to get it done.

So the soldier, seaman, or airman trusts his mission, his leaders, and himself. He is ready for anything. I do not think there are any secrets to achieving this, just the unique desire for excellence, and for giving. How do they get confidence in themselves? First, they have been through at least six months of rigorous training to learn their skill. Second, they are further trained and mentored on their particular skill by their leaders. Third, they participate in endless (to them) repetition so that they can perform their skill perfectly in rain, snow, darkness, under duress, etc. This is important. They must know internally that they can do their job, no matter how much they dislike the repetition. Fourth, the unit must train as a whole all of the time, often in warlike conditions. You cannot get a unit ready for combat in garrison.

Let's pray for them!

||||||||||||||||||||||||||||||||||||||||||||||||||||||||||||||||||||||||||||||||||||||||||||||||||||||||||||||||||||||||||||||||||||||||

Clap For Them. Shake Their Hand. Buy Them Lunch.

In the Atlanta airport, the busiest in the world, traveling military personnel are everywhere. It is the norm for people to come up and shake their hands and thank them. Lunches and dinners are bought. When a group moves through spontaneous clapping breaks out. They deserve all of it! They are always very appreciative. Do the same, everywhere.

|||||||||||||||||||||||||||||||||||||||||||||||||||||||||||||||||||||||||||||||||||||||||||||||||||||||||||||||||||||||||||||||||||||||||||||||||||||||||||||||||||||||||

Summary

The Primordial Leadership principles in this book are for general application to better achieve results as leaders. Special situations exist that require special insights and actions. These are:

Leading government entities: The lack of a profit motive rationalizer, changing political winds, civil service restrictions, and higher unionization all need to be understood and navigated. (As a citizen, the author thanks strong government leaders.)

Non-Profits: These important entities, especially charities, also lack the profit motive rationalizer. Thus, the leadership efficacy methods in chapters 5, 6 and 7 are especially important to use. Finding success energies beyond Sociability-based altruism is important.

Engineer, accountant, and mathematician leaders: While many are able to deal well with the grayness of leadership vs. black and white, these very smart people need to be "open systems" in regards to proactively harnessing the Primal Drives in themselves and others, and external change dynamics, to keep the organization achieving results over time.

Female leaders: The future is bright; the skills are the best in many business areas. Where a "glass ceiling" exists, consider the views and action ideas presented relative to the needed attributes being applied, and why those attributes exist. A process for doing so is provided as well.

Older leaders: The very strong abilities and experiences still exist and need to be valued and put into action. Ideas for doing so have been presented.

Turnarounds: These intense situations may require relatively more actions to achieve the needed redirection. The problems often evolve to include internal problems, which are the most difficult in some ways; but the most immediate to address if they exist. Ideas are presented.

Military leaders: These are special people to lead, and important requirements exist to do so. Trust is the top one.

CONCLUSION

To repeat the opening: thank goodness for leaders! They create jobs for families, enable spending in the economy and its multiplying effect, pay taxes to support governments, contribute people and monies to charities, are the backbone of our economic wealth, and supply the resources for defense from foes. They are sometimes maligned by the envious, but they are essential to all of us.

Your family, present or coming, especially depends on you to enhance their quality of life. That is your job; it is on you. If not you, then who? If not now, then when?

Being different and better than other leaders is key. Continually improving leadership skills is a hallmark of A-player leaders. They are constructively dissatisfied at all times, including about their own capabilities and contributions. These Primordial Leadership insights, plus to how-to ideas, will help the A-players to do more, do it better, sustain improved results, and be even better, and differentiated, providers and citizens as a result. Coming leaders can learn from these insights.

We are…animals. Per the many findings from neuroscience and other fields, our deepest, DNA-level drive is to perpetuate our species' genes. This drive is enabled by the key Primal Drives in all of us, that can be consistently applied in all situations for improved results. But it is up to you to do that now that these insights, ideas and experiences are provided.

Recognize that your people are your key asset, and *their* Primal Drives are the "fuel" for your organization's success, now and over time. Beyond not being in the way, bring out the best in them. *UNLEASH THE BEAST(S)!*

Study and practice the Primal Drives in ways that are creative and additive. Teach others. Use the insights, methods and tools that have been provided. Study the Appendices to further learn much more about our brain structure, especially envisioning, values, and the Primal Drives, and Values.

Per the Judo Principle, proactively practice envisioning and related planning. Apply good values. This framework is essential to good results being achieved, and the above many benefits.

Proactively get your organization to welcome change as a competitive weapon.

Now, go lead. *Cause* your and others' future to be rich, and contributing to society—and to families. Go out and achieve more. Lead!

Be Purposely Kind

(Excerpts from a 2013 University of Syracuse Commencement Speech by Author and Professor George Saunders; from an August 2, 2013 report by Liz Klimas)

"Although achieving a goal of being kinder can be helped by education, meditation and spiritual tradition, Saunders said, some of it comes with age.

"'We get our butts kicked by real life, and people come to our defense, and help us, and we learn that we're not separate, and don't want to be,' Saunders explained. 'We see people near and dear to us dropping away, and are gradually convinced that maybe we too will drop away (someday, a long time from now). Most people, as they age, become less selfish and more loving.'

"The 'cure' to the 'sickness' in us, which Saunders cites is selfishness, is to 'seek out the most efficacious anti-selfishness medicines, energetically, for the rest of your life.'

"'Do all the other things, the ambitious things – travel, get rich, get famous, innovate, lead, fall in love, make and lose fortunes, swim naked in wild jungle rivers (after first having it tested for monkey poop) – but as you do, to the extent that you can, err in the direction of kindness,' he said. 'Do those things that incline you toward the big questions, and avoid the things that would reduce you and make you trivial. That luminous part of you that exists beyond personality – your soul, if you will – is as bright and shining as any that has ever been.'"

Coming in the future will be *Primordial Marketing and Sales.* This book will show how to apply the Primordial Drive and enabling Primal Drives to persuade others to "facilitate exchanges of value in the marketplace," per Dr. Philip Kotler's definition of marketing in his famous textbooks (from which I once studied in my MBA program, and later taught marketing).

Many of the book's tables, tools and examples can be found, for free, at www.primordialleader.com. Also, I can be contacted at lduckworth@primordialleader.com.

Appendix A

THE UNDERLYING PRIMAL DRIVES

"Because the light is better here."

This section will shine a beacon light on the key Whys for leadership success, referencing recent neuroscientific findings.

As noted in the *ezines.com* article, "The Power of the Mind: Unlocking the Secrets," "What if someone told you that the only thing stopping from achieving your dreams was you?" The incredible mind power that each has inside of us is literally unstoppable if harnessed correctly and in the right way. In reality, the power the mind exerts over us influences our daily life, career, families, relationships, and every aspect that we may never have even thought about. How do we harness this mind power?

> "The number one thing that we have to do in order to increase our mind power and become aware of our true potential is to realize that we are capable of being number one!"
>
> —Stephen Hughes

This Appendix uses a direct-use observational flashlight to *find where the keys really are* vs. past traditional, less powerful leadership methods and views that looked in more convenient but insufficient places. The light is moved to shine on the Primal

Drives that most strongly assure the most-basic Primordial Drive. This section contains the "reessstt of the story": six (of eight) key "Primal Drives" that serve and directly enable and protect our most basic, Primordial, DNA-level "engine." The Primal Drives can be then be powerfully, consistently and purposely harnessed by applying the Judo Principle.

Metaphorically, just as anthropologists could just guess at hieroglyphics, when they unearthed the Rosetta Stone, it unlocked ancient Egypt's hieroglyphics secrets. Here we unlock the Primal Drives (hoping to inspire more research also).

The thing this book *cannot* do is assure you actively use these insights and thinking and action construct to better perform as a leader. *That is up to you, once armed.*

The Primal Drives Are Always There...
To Be Better Exploited Than in the Past

infosource.org explains the genes perpetuation drive as follows: "*Genetic imperative* refers to the instinct of an organism to pass on its genes or reproduce. The phrase can be used to describe the behavior of specific organisms or a species as a whole."

In 2008 *Neuromarketing* observed that "...neuroscience is creeping into many areas of business endeavor. In a few years, a manager discussing Neuromarketing may find that she shares a common vocabulary with other managers attempting to adapt traditional management methods to the findings of brain science."

Earlier quotes observed that Sociobiologists are focused on the genes perpetuation imperative that drives us as well.

As noted, as a result of the unique tools, methods, and insights, we will see that *nothing* done at the conscious level is accidental or ad hoc. Actions, views, feelings, priorities, emotions, values, etc. are secretly determined at deep, hidden, "software" levels in us, and all are controlled by the Primal Drives to protect and enable the core Primordial Drive of genes perpetuation. Being better than others by leveraging them to be different and better is the key focus.

Dr. C. George Boeree of Shippensburg University stated that "There are certain *patterns of behavior* found in most, if not all, animals, involving the promotion of oneself, the search for status or raw power..."

Understanding the scientific truths/contexts *behind* these powerful Primal Drives is important. We did not try to learn algebra, geometry, calculus, and higher math on our own, but instead used the published experiments (in textbooks) and findings of others (Copernicus, Pascal, Pythagoras, etc.) developed over the 4,000+ years of math research. Similarly, we can also benefit from the studies and opinions of smart Neuroscientists and other scientists. These are presented (and repeated) via a few representative excerpted quotes that best explain the nature of the Neuroscience and sociobiology findings and views, for use later in this leadership book to differentiate from others, and be much better than them.

Learning from the Scientists

First, Aristotle's famous fourth century BC "hylomorphism" talks about our "matter" (*hyle*) or the "substance" being of what we are intangibly made, and our form ("morphism") as our matter/substance in physical actuality. This construct is a vessel for how to think about who we are below the surface (substance) and how it forms into a physical leader being (form). The important need is to better understand the underlying, controlling intangible (*hyle*) substance elements of who we are, from scientists.

According to Dr. Gazzaniga of UC Santa Barbara, "The human brain is a bizarre device, set in place through natural selection for one purpose –to make decisions that enhance reproductive success."

A Harvard publication noted that "The central theoretical question of sociobiology is explaining how cooperative behavior may have evolved between unrelated individuals."

According to *plato.stanford.edu,* sociobiology is "the application of evolutionary theory to social behavior. Sociobiologists claim that many social behaviors have been shaped by natural selection for reproductive success, and they attempt to reconstruct the evolutionary histories of particular behaviors or behavioral strategies... Sociobiologists are engaged in the construction and evaluation of theoretical models of evolutionary change and in the empirical testing of aspects of those models for particular cases. The result is an expansion of standard Darwinian evolutionary theory (which traditionally explains morphological adaptation) to a new domain: namely, animal sociality."

evolution.berkeley.edu describes natural selection as follows: "Fitness is a handy concept because it lumps everything that matters to natural selection (survival, mate-finding, reproduction) into one idea. The fittest individual is not necessarily the strongest, fastest, or biggest. A genotype's fitness includes its ability to survive, find a mate, produce offspring — and ultimately leave its genes in the next generation."

According to *public.wsu.edu*, "...an animal doesn't necessarily have to survive on its own. Another aspect of personal survival is the forming of social groups within a species. When staying alive is not just the responsibility of the individual, but other members of the species help the individual to survive, and vice versa, all members' chances are enhanced... The purpose of a social group and the level it takes is often dictated by how well it serves to promote the survival of the members."

Thus the Primordial imperative is to survive the very competitive, unsympathetic "natural selection" process that is required *for survival and to perpetuate the genes of the species;* which is the most basic, "primordial," "DNA-level drive of all.

The field of sociobiology represents strong, leveragable scientific thinking about the hidden, low-level, enabling Primal Drives that support and enable our many actions and attitudes for ensuring genes perpetuation over time. Thus, we need to proactively understand, appreciate, and leverage that core drive and its enabling Primal Drives in all human interaction ways—as an imperative.

The Six Key Primal Drives Contexts for Differentiated Leadership

Advantageous social behavior to get the most results via people is the strength-in-numbers vehicle! Per the Preface, in a hypercompetitive, people-to-people social world like ours, we must find ways to stand out as better, different leaders from those around us and competing with us; in order to get them to respond in a desired way. We need a *differentiated advantage!*

Unsettling as it is, we are just like all animals in terms of basic drives. As business people we are after results and are on a constant quest to better achieve results by having an unfair advantage, a "racer's edge."

Even though the six Primal Drives interplay with each other in different situations, and are somewhat affected by personality factors, values and emotions in specific situations, no better, more consistent construct than the Primal Drives exists to harness and Judo-leverage to gain unfair "advantageous social behavior."

Many additional Primal Drives quotes could be provided, but the above from very smart people help us to realize *several very important, useful, Judo-leveragable things*:

- There is indeed a deep, primordial "factory" or "engine" that drives our genes survival probability.
- Along with strong, spatial cognitive envisioning skills, and Values, leveraging the Primal Drives provide strong, *differentiated* capabilities relative to those

still looking for the keys under the easier streetlight. This allows us to stand out as different and more valuable.

- While we may know the term "Primal Drive," until now we have not deeply understood and applied on a purposeful basis the powers of the Primal Drives for better and different business results.

- While not consciously aware to us, *the Primal Drives are even more pervasive and powerful to utilize than leadership training and management books to date have identified!* New insights allow new skills and actions.

- In our professional race for success *versus competitors, obstacles and for potentials,* who best learns the underlying, genes perpetuation enabling Primal Drives (called the "proximate mechanism(s)" structure by the Sociobiologists), and harnesses them proactively (Judo), have better, stronger leadership action levers to push and pull *than others.*

- Some individual variances are caused by socially learned ("nurture") personality factors that must also be understood and harnessed in specific situations; but *the controlling, over-arching, driving Primal Drives are shared by all in ways that can be consistently and purposely applied. The "marbling" combinations are the "art."*

- Cognitive skills ("gray matter") are important, especially spatial thinking skills, including being able to envision "ends" beforehand. More insights into this key envisioning skill, that brings out the Primal Drives in others, are presented in chapter 3.

- Using the six Primal Drives may seem harder at first versus seat-of-the-pants thinking, but as always, "The hard way is the easy way, and the easy way is the hard way." Using them becomes quickly natural, and powerful.

Think of the Primal Drives as being the quiet but all-powerful "operating system software" that manages everything we do, but well below the conscious/awareness level. While this is disconcerting in regard to being controlled in reality, it *can* be harnessed with awareness and purposeful actions. The payoffs are many.

Through my direct observations and experience, I have identified eight Primal Drives, but two are not readily leveragable for leadership (but do drive much of our autonomic systems):

- The reproductive drive
- The will to live

The six key, leveragable Primal Drives, to be further explained below, in approximate power order, are:

1. Safety
2. Self-Interest (including greed)
3. Hope and Transcendence
4. Honesty and Trust
5. Energy and Time Optimization
6. Sociability (including altruism).

My observation is that the first three, in order, are the most powerful and prevalent, and the second three slightly secondary in power. "Marbling" (interacting) combinations in certain situations will be important to understand for situation correctness. The "art" of leadership is in the correct marbling for results.

Each Primal Drive will be reviewed below, including many sub-Drives and examples for each. These are generally ordered in importance. In given situations several will be involved, in a "marbled" sense. Their mixture and weightings will vary according to the situation and will be determined by what best assures the perpetuation of the genes. *Learning to assess each situation's Primal Drives hierarchy and marbled combinations is a skill that needs to be mastered, and the results applied.* Specific tables can be used in all human interaction areas to assess how to leverage the Primal Drives in each situation. Examples are in chapter 5.

1. Safety

This from *LiveSciences* shows just how strong the Safety Primal Drive is: "The brain's 'fear center' doesn't need to be working for an animal to learn to be afraid… If the region is damaged, another area can take the reins and allow the brain to continue to form fear-driven, emotional memories."

In a November 2008 *LiveSciences* article, "Brain Encodes, Controls Responses to Fear: Study," author Wynne Parry noted "As a basic survival mechanism, fear helps to keep us safe from danger. We react with a 'fight or flight' response — tensing our muscles, freezing in place or taking off. Our heart rate and breathing quicken.

"The walnut-sized amygdala is the region of the brain responsible for recognizing and responding to fear in these ways. New research zeroes in on the part of the amygdala that controls the messages our brains send out: the central amygdala. In fact, two studies have shown how the central amygdala encodes memories of fear and controls learned responses to fear."

Thus, as noted in the below excerpts from the journal *Nature*, risk/danger avoidance is unconquerable. "Flight or fight" is always the *first read, even if we are not consciously aware of it.*

"Fear is a universal emotion. New research...has begun to explain how this part of our brain works...two studies have shown how the central amygdala encodes memories of fear and controls learned responses to fear."

—*LiveSciences*, **November 2010**

"Freezing in the face of danger is an old, emotional response which probably was evolutionarily adaptive in our ancestral past."

—*LiveSciences*, **December 2005**

Safety is the most controlling and pervasive Primal Drive we have and it needs to be proactively harnessed *at all times;* yet its power and pervasiveness are usually not sufficiently understood, or not used strongly and purposefully enough. It is the elephant in the room, and we must harness it to avoid getting trampled.

When change or a new opportunity or a challenge comes up we will, far below the conscious level, instantly first determine if the contemplated action or situation is Safe or not; or if not acting is perhaps even more unsafe. The scope and importance of the issue will determine the degree this factor plays. A low-impact, tactical action will naturally be less unsafe due to scope. However, a major action will have more Safety concerns due to scope and potential impact. If Safety risks are not major, Self-Interest, Hope, Energy and Time Optimization, Sociability, etc., may override Safety concerns in a give situation.

"Change management" is such a challenge mainly but not solely because of the Safety issue. There are ways to make that Drive work to support change, but it is almost never used. chapter 7 will show you how.

In the Safety area resides the core source of political turfs in companies (along with Self-Interest and Energy Optimization, but mostly Safety). They protect what they have, even if it is now obsolete. This Safety-based protection force is why eventually strengths become weaknesses as things continually change around the company, but the company is locked in place by the Safety ("don't rock the boat") drive. "Change management" exists as a purposeful management challenge because it is hard to change people and programs where the changes are deemed to be unsafe, not in their best interests, or harder to do. (We will review handling change management in chapter 6.)

Safety is the unspoken, key reason bureaucracies incessantly grow in size, purporting to add new value to justify survival and growth.

Unions form for workers' collective power. Unions often have a short term Safety (and Self-Interest) drive that often endangers longer term Safety (and Self-Interest) rewards, and Transcendence. Works rules may improve Energy Optimization and job Safety. Elected union reps know their members are mostly today-oriented, even if harmful over time, so their leadership Safety is in maximizing short-term success. That the plant may be closed later is often not strongly on their Safety radar, even if they know the consequences. The 2012 Hostess Twinkies shutdown is just one example.

This short-term versus long-term Safety is always a construct to be considered in general, in all situations.

Safety is also a key driver of Sociability, the sixth Primal Drive.

Some aspects of how Safety deeply and quietly, but controllingly, works in specific situations include:

Job Commitment Safety

Do I work for a giver that will be fair and positive, or a taker that I cannot trust? Does management find the right first? Does management take credit and pass blame, or the reverse? Will merit prevail, or brownnosing? Is inward political jockeying and undercutting the operating rule and an open opportunity for selfish opportunists? Will we be allowed to learn from mistakes, or get our head handed to us in a basket, possibly accompanied with a pink slip? Is management visionary enough to protect us from the future? Does management respect and protect the Safety power of quality? Is management fast to act or bound to hide? Do they listen and heed advice from those on the front line? Is decision making decentralized to give us some control, reflective that top management is trusting? Does honesty prevail at all levels? Does management truly appreciate new ideas and challenges, or not? Can I bring bad information to management and survive?

Can I meet my autonomy needs as long as I produce well? Can I self-determine a future if I perform? Should I make an emotional commitment to the company versus just showing up and holding a spot?

Buyer's Personal Resources or Career Safety

When selling a product or a service solution to a buyer's decision team, the seller probably will not get a bonus for a good decision, but can get career-sanctioned, and even fired, for a bad decision. There is not much room for Safety error in marketing and selling. In all such purchases the career Safety factor needs to be carefully identified and thought through beforehand, and harnessed via the Judo Principle. When the prices and/or features are about the same, Safety will be the determinative elephant in the room, and often hidden. Be aware that doing nothing is often Safest for them versus taking an action. Or, an internal solution might be safest, even if suboptimal. "Not Invented Here (NIH)" is Safety based.

Thus, Safety differentiation needs to be proactively elevated as a *positive* differentiation factor (Judo). Payback period and ROI/IRR are not only Self-Interest drives but also Safety factors. Winning the Safety battle is crucial to winning the sales war. Being on the wrong side of perceived Safety is bad positioning. Reputational Safety can be important ("the defacto leader"—nobody gets fired for buying from IBM), as well as return policies. Overcoming a Safety barrier by "buying the business" can be an option.

Product or Service Use Safety

For consumer and business purchasers of products and services, solutions Safety is always a key, even if an unspoken concern. Car warrantees (now up to 100,000 miles from some), home warrantees, electronics warrantees, products money-back guarantees, conditional service payments, "claw-back" contract provisions, product return policies, convenience cancellation contracts, drawdown returns if you lose your job, performance insurance, software escrow accounts, etc., are all reflective of the strength of this Safety issue in business. So is the need for customers or prospects to check with Dun and Bradstreet in regard to the company's solvency and credit worthiness, for buying or selling.

Perceived Safety is a major customer need force to be *embraced and leveraged* (Judo) as a differentiator versus being criticized as a negative thing to be avoided. Lead with Safety. The retailers Orvis (I'm a fly fisher), Nordstrom, Sears, Lands End, LL

Bean, and many others figured it out long ago and often get the differentiation nod as a result of Safety.

Investors' Safety

For potential investors, will the Safety concerns offset the greed drive when considering an investment? Will the cash be enough to get to net cash critical mass, even if a downturn occurs? Will "liquidation preferences" for investors exist? For public companies, these types of considerations are really what is going on related to the P/E multiple, often unspokenly. The major types of risks investors look at are:

- Market/growth risk: Is there a large enough market that wants this type of solution in large enough quantity and at value pricing?
- Competitive risk: Do dangerous competitors exist or does the company have compelling differentiations that can be extended over time, and can even raise entry barriers? Is the market "owned" by anyone?
- Financial risk: Will the plan, even if underperformed, allow the company to survive with minimum added investments, and have an exit or value improvement potential? For public companies, what are the earnings risks, and the risks of the sector's P/E multiple being lowered due to uncontrollable events (like a competitor having bad quarterly results)?
- Management risk: Does the company have the skilled, experienced team it will need to grow the company and take it through an exit of continually higher share value? For a board, will the Safety of keeping a management team in place outweigh the Safety and/or greed of making changes? The net answer will be situational.
- Valuation risk: Is the initial valuation too high to get a strong return?
- Syndication risk: Can we get others to invest, to spread the risk? For public companies, is the stock "float" sufficient for liquidity Safety?
- Legal risk: Are there any existing or pending legal risks? This could include others having patents, limiting regulations, pending or active litigation, and many more possible variables? Are dangerous new laws or regulations expected?

These risks are very real in investors' minds, so leverage this! (Specific criteria used by potential private equity investors are provided in chapter 5.)

Other Safety Arenas

Is the bank's debt loan going to be safe in the bank's eyes (are the key financial ratios solid, and is the "Times Interest Earned" net income factor large enough for Safety)? Are the covenants sufficient? Does solid collateral exist that can be monetized? If personally guaranteed, what assets exist, what is the credit score, etc.? Does my credit committee reference group endorse the direction? Can the loan be syndicated? Will the company be around to repay principle? Are my peers doing this, and how do the balance sheet debt-to-equity ratios compare? Will we be consistent with the law, present and coming (especially Sarbanes-Oxley, Dodd-Frank, and the Affordable Care Act now)? Will this investment be state-of-the-art and competitive for a reasonable period? Do suppliers perceive Safety? Will trade credit be paid, to avoid senior debtor liens being applied?

These and many other such Safety "reads" are taken many times per day by each employee, by prospects, by partners, by investors, and by others at the Primal Drives level. How should we harness the near-manic need for Safety? If we do not, resistance will arise, often unspoken, but will be determining in many situations.

Communicate Safety!

Leaders need to be conscious of Safety perceptions 24/7/365. Many methods exist, to be applied situationally. For change management, see chapter 7.

Humor is a very strong tool to use. It communicates Safety in multiple ways. Touching is good (appropriate touching). Smiling is Safety bearing. Be upfront about the fears, and they may well go away. The real key is inward confidence and courage, to feel Safe yourself. See chapter 5. Being a giver is important inner Safety, because your purpose is good.

2. Self-Interest, including Greed, Selfishness, Self-Realization, and Some Narcissism

Even though second in power of the Primal Drives to Safety, Self-Interest is the most controversial Primal Drive, especially if no Sociability is involved (what is also good for others) as a brake. Self-Interest and greed are a derided Primal Drive, but are a key to business, democracy and capitalistic prosperity. It is key to wealth being generated for others, versus all being at subsistence levels (again). The envious and their protectors deride it. If marbled with other Primal Drives such as Sociability, then perceived reasonableness can occur.

Adam Smith spoke of the Self-Interest drive in his 1776 *Wealth of Nations*, noting "the invisible hand of self-interest" as being pervasive and vital to success. He was correct. However, since money begets money, beyond individual work rewards, unbridled Self-Interest results in a growing wealth gap that will eventually erupt—as it has many times in the past, like in 1917 Russia, Venezuela today, and Cuba in the late 1950's. A balancing is needed to keep such disruptions from becoming too excessive. Such a balance must:

1. Not hinder endeavor energy (aka minimize defeating handouts) to those who can work
2. From the wealth surplus that is generated, provide "safety net" benefits to those who cannot work.

Without Self-Interest and Hope overriding Safety, no investment would happen, and the result would be stagnation. Instead of the "pie" growing larger for wealth sharing, destructive arguments over the sharing of a fixed, or even shrinking, pie would ensue. Not pretty, or productive. Why would a person get up and go to work, which takes Energy? Or endeavor for a promotion via extra Energy efforts? Or attempt to exceed budget plans and goals? Or leave a company for a better, more rewarding one, with all of the uncertainty of doing so, including Sociability losses (loss of work friends)? Answer: the Self-Interest Primal Drive (mostly). While some will put themselves in unsafe situations for greed, this is not the norm—except for risk-taking entrepreneurs or intrapreneurs.

Personal drive seems to be centered here. See chapter 4 for more insights.

Self-Interest is vital and well practiced by all in varying degrees, with some being less constrained than others by Sociability and values. Therein lives destructive greed. Narcissism also resides there. Larceny and deception also, combined with weak Honesty and Sociability drives. Jealousy and envy are rooted here. If we did not have the Self-Interest drive, there would be no basis for these emotions to start with. A balanced combination of the Self-Interest, Honesty, and Sociability drives are needed.

However, we *must* take care of ourselves first as a survival Primal Drive. Hard work, smart work, greed, larceny, lying, deception, political jockeying, pay insistence, unionization of blue collar or government jobs, protecting against unfairness and many other sub-Drives are involved in different situations to support Self-Interest.

W all want something for nothing if we can get it. Why The Self-Interest Primal Drive secretly compels us. For example, smart TV commercials offer the Shamwow absorbent towel for $19.95; then at the end they offer you two for the price of one. They could just price one at $9.95 but want to proactively harness Self-Interest, for more gain than originally offered…FREE (not)! The buyer feels he or she got something for nothing (the second unit), driven by the compulsive need to do so, to gain a Selfish advantage (something for nothing).

Most retail pricing is a Self-Interest starting point for final pricing. Smart leaders know that end buyers, and especially those with professional purchasing departments (e.g., GE, Walmart, Selectron, Sears, etc.), will *always* negotiate on price to get the most selfish possible advantage. The term "bloodsport" often applies to purchasers in retail companies, with the view that "we make our money on the buy." They are driven to do so for their own Primal Drive reasons, and political expectations to support the company's primal Self-Interest needs. Otherwise, why would so much energy and cost be expended on the purchasing function? Purchasing departments, buyer legal departments, etc., who need to justify their resourcing, will *always* want to extract selfish advantage to justify their net value versus costs, and related Safety (and personal rewards Self-Interest) reasons. These truths must be Judo-leveraged at all times by sellers. Never start with your final terms.

Today's "reverse auctions" are growingly popular. Done by Purchasing, the best three prices are given to the economic buyer/decider. Thus, winning there is the key.

In international markets, negotiation is *expected*. For example, closing a deal in Tokyo is pure art. Ditto in China. Other types of art are needed in the Middle East.

As they say about Self-Interest, "It's human nature." Unfortunately in business negotiation most of these acts are short-term oriented and can hurt all parties long term. (On the other hand, as the famous British economist Lord John Maynard Keynes noted, "In the long run we are all dead.")

The "political class'" Self-Interest (to be re-elected to posh, powerful positions) drives them to avoid negative decisions and often to bribe constituents via more benefits or earmarks. They know that in politics "friends come and go, and enemies accumulate."

Taking is in all of us to some degree, to get something for as little as possible, perhaps, in some, even if moral dishonesty is involved (determined by how strong the Social and Honesty Primal Drives are—or are not). However, taking does not wear well long term, so never give in to it becoming ingrained. Per Covey, balance courage and consideration.

Narcissism is an aspect of Self-Interest, defined by Twenge and Campbell in *The Narcissist Epidemic* (following *Generation Me*) as "having an inflated or grandiose sense of self. A narcissist thinks she is special, unique, and entitled to better treatment than others. Narcissists aren't particularly interested in warmth and caring in their relationships. They might enjoy being around people — and certainly can be charming, flattering, exciting, and likable — but they are in relationships for their own narcissistic needs. Narcissists also spend a good deal of their time and energy doing things to make themselves look and feel good and pumping up their egos. A narcissist might brag, turn all conversations back to himself, try to associate only with important people, want to have the best and newest of everything, or steal credit from others. When things don't go his way, the narcissist might get angry or even violent. Narcissists can be fun to be around in the short term, but awful to work for or be in a close relationship with in the long term."

They also note that the narcissism trend is worsening: "We know that narcissism has increased over time among individuals based on several datasets. College students now endorse more narcissistic traits than college students did in the 1980s and 1990s; in one large sample the change seemed to be accelerating after 2002. An Internet sample of the general population also showed higher narcissism scores among younger people than older people. Perhaps most disturbing, a 2005 study using a large, randomly selected sample of Americans found that nearly 1 out of 10 people in their twenties had experienced NPD (narcissistic personality disorder) — the more severe, clinical-level form of the trait. Only 1 out of 30 people over 64 had experienced NPD in their lifetime — even though they had lived 40 more years than the people in their twenties and thus had that much more time to experience the disorder. This suggests a large increase in NPD over time."

"*Ego*" in our personality mainly rests on Self-Interest. An egotist is self-absorbed to the detriment of sensitivity to others. They don't need others for "we" Sociability-based Safety, but will manipulate them for "me" Self-Interest. It's Primordial, and they were never given the "veneer" of Sociability-based otherness in their upbringing.

Hedonism is an aspect of Self-Interest, where wanton self-indulgence without any regard for the needs or perception of others, or common sense, prevails. Buying or acquiring what we "want" versus what we "need" introduces much waste, but has fueled many economies, and many bankruptcies and divorces.

Autonomy is an aspect of Self-Interest (and Safety also), to not have to deal with others' pressures. If we are unconstrained we can have a better chance of meeting personal needs. Being out of control due to others is also a Safety issue to the individual.

Envy of others is centered in the Self-Interest drive and is never productive. Envy is one of the worst aspects of human behavior, and is Self-interest based. It often leads to blame versus self-responsibility to close the gap by constructive self-improvement. It never works long term because Mother Nature does not reward win-lose over time, only win-win. Envy often causes win-lose, zero-sum thinking.

Growing religious secularism (in times of plenty where the Safety of Sociability is not as needed) versus the personal actions constraints of Socially oriented religion (e.g., the Ten Commandments, the Golden Rule, the Koran) is Self-Interest based. Increased surrounding Safety (economically and otherwise) leaves margin for room to recover and survive, where in subsistence situations there is no such margin, where conforming to the self-limiting strength-in-numbers requirements of others is important. This is not true in times of plenty. The secularism, hedonism, and narcissism increase as surrounding Safety increases, where strength-in-numbers-based but self-constraining Social rules are less needed for general Safety. The obverse is that "there are no atheists in foxholes," where Safety is very low and the need for others, including deity support for Safety comfort, is very high.

The differing values of different generations with varying Safety contexts and resulting varying Self-Interest and Sociability drives is a parallel example of the above, where increasing macro or aggregate Safety allows individual Self-Interest-based narcissism, etc., to emerge, to overcome Safety enhancing Sociability restrictions. While not meant to be pejorative, the Millennials and "Gen Y" generations are great examples, and to lesser degrees the Gen X and Boomers groups. Each had more contextual Safety than their parents before them due to continually improving surrounding economic circumstances and world events. Sociability pressures for inconvenient conformance could be downplayed. Religious pressures could be downplayed. For example, Boomers' parents had values based in Great Depression and World War II Safety threats (fear) and less economic-plenty-based Safety; it took pervasive Social cooperation rules and suppressing Self-Interest to collectively survive. They then further shielded their children from those Safety concerns and helped them have "a better life." This was aided by an improving Safety ecosystem.

Thus, Boomers had more economic Safety margin and only had the abstract Cold War nuclear threat. Narcissism began to increase due to more Safety and less need for Social "Safety in numbers" self-constraints, to the point that some Boomers became the "flower children" and the "me generation" (versus previous "we" views). More began to turn to government to be the answer versus individual endeavor like their parents. Subordinating Self-Interest for strength-in-numbers Social good limits was less vital.

Then Boomers raised Gen Xers with even more Safety, so narcissistic Self-Interest could ascend even more. Xers were followed by the Gen Yers, and then the Millennials. With the progressively increasing physical and economic Safety, strength-in-numbers and resulting Sociability-based self-control was less important, and increasingly inconvenient. Each generation could then focus more on "me" and increasingly forsake "we" limitations due to less and less Safety concerns and the sensitivity to Social constraints that stress the "we." Not only were "me" physical needs (hedonism) stronger, but emotional "self-realization" (Maslow) needs grew stronger also. Religious mores, in place for societal quality and stability, were constraints on hedonism and narcissism that were no longer needed for Safety in Sociability numbers.

In the 1950's Isaac Asimov in his famous *Foundation* series coined the term "psychohistory" to reflect this dynamic in humans. In summary, in difficult times good decisions were made, and in times of plenty less good decisions were made. Many feel this dynamic is the underlying reason that past great democracies died—from within as narcissism, hedonism, secularism, and so on allowed the fabric of a Social, values-based society to atrophy to the point of collapse. Threats could no longer be defeated due to internal weakness.

With increased Safety also comes more Transcendence potential, which helps explain, in addition to more Safety due to more prosperity and opportunities, the younger generations' openness (and some would say drive) to change jobs versus their elders' higher level of Safety-based loyalty.

As shown, Self-Interest is a Primordial need in all of us. Leadership challenges have continued to evolve as a result of the generational changes due to increased Safety and the ascendance of Self-Interest and Transcendence needs. The great thing is that these Self-Interest Drives are very easy to leverage. Proactively Judo-leveraging Self-Interest is a great opportunity in virtually all situations. Selfish persons are easy to leverage. Using "avoid" positionings are often needed, to get them to do the right things as "the lesser of the evils."

Employees need many things to meet their Self-Interest needs, and leaders need to understand and leverage that truth. Compensation, recognition, autonomy, "avoids," and many other needs exist to be leveraged. Herzberg's findings (chapter 1) highlighted this. chapters 4 and 5 review what not to do and what to do in this regard.

Always figure out how to get Self-Interest working for you, and not against you. Judo-leverage it!

3. Hope and Transcendence

I consider these linked drives to be a forward-looking Primal Drive that leads to Safety and Self-Interest *in the future*, recognizing that change is inevitable over time. It is like the brain intrinsically knows that "the only constant is change" and wants to judo-harness it for Safety and Self-Interest later. It is impressive how strong it is in our "primordial soup" ("Hope springs eternal"). I have seen it trump seemingly impossible Safety dangers. Short-term Self-Interest can be put aside due to future Hope. Energy calories are purposely expended now on the Hope of a better result later. When consulting I have seen employees stick with a seemingly failing company because they sensed that there was Hope (often versus change Safety risks). Employees will stay with a destructive leader due to near-term success Hope (but only for a short period usually).

Leadership that evokes a vision, hopefully correctly, automatically communicates Hope. The loss of Hope is when most relationships finally end, including at work—and home as well.

Transcendence is a Primal Drive for constant change and improvement over time, again to help assure improved Safety and Self-Interest in the future so that change will be protected against. Abraham Maslow picked up on the impacts of this in his "Hierarchy of Needs", but did not explain the underlying Why of the Primal Drives.

Among labor negotiators it is well understood that no matter how lenient and benevolent management has been in the past, a "what will you do for me now?" commanding Hope force will exist, to support Self-Interest and job Safety. The rank and file want to consistently Transcend from where they are for Self-Interest, etc., even if it is currently better than the average. Of course, this has Self-Interest and Safety elements mixed in—and perhaps Energy savings as well if they want easier work rules such as seven hours of work for eight hours of pay (such as one situation I was in when working as a union employee at a manufacturing plant). Transcendence and Self-Interest Primal Drives have been seen to overpower Safety, resulting in major job losses over time, such as at GM, Ford, NCR, Hostess, etc.

The Transcendence Primal Drive provides a change openness mentality if properly positioned and explained. A key is to credibly paint a vision of what the planned actions will *avoid* in the future, or even now.

I believe that *curiosity* is a derived sub-force to help with Transcendence to situations that are more Safe, have more Self-Interest potential, and benefit other Primal Drives. Why else would it exist since it takes Energy, and the change may incur Safety concerns? Seeking new information and knowledge is a path to possible Transcendence—and Hope.

Ambition is sourced in Hope and Transcendence, plus Self-interest.

Likewise, *boredom* seems to be centered here. We need to continually transcend. "Wanderlust" is probably located here also.

Power seeking is Transcendence based, to position for more Safety and Self-interest gains.

Always figure out how to get Hope and Transcendence working for you, and not against you. Judo-leverage it!

4. Honesty and Trust

I believe these drive elements are protectors of Safety, Self-Interest, Transcendence, and Sociability, today and tomorrow, and are kind of a "third dimension" protective Primal Drive for managing results via people relationships over time. These are powerful drives and important to Judo-leverage, but truth must be pervasive to be successful. The Honesty and Trust drive results in all of us having a good barometer of the character and thus dependability (Safety) of other parties in a relationship relative to our own self-interests. Others' self-interest (Safety, Self-Interest, etc.) will unconsciously calibrate our own trustworthiness, and they will react accordingly. A relationship without Honesty and Trust will be a weak one over time and not fulfill its promise for any of the parties. Thus, being dishonest and untrustworthy hurts the untrustworthy person also, and most.

Stephen M. R. Covey's *Speed of Trust* (as summarized by Gather.com) states that: "After summarizing why trust is so important, Covey explains the 4 Cores of Trust: integrity, intent, capabilities, and results, and how these 4 Cores of Trust will impact the way people view you and trust you. The 4 Cores of Trust are part of the First Wave in the 5 Waves of Trust Model. The first wave is Self-Trust. In the 5 Waves of Trust, Covey explains each wave in detail and what makes up each one using examples and even in some cases giving charts for readers to fill out. The other 4 Waves of Trust are: Relationship Trust, Organizational Trust, Market Trust, and Societal Trust. In the second wave, Covey explains the 13 behaviors that make up a trustworthy person, varying from talking straight to creating transparency, to showing loyalty and to simply clarifying your expectation of someone, among others that are just as important."

That "the truth hurts" reflects that some believe that being evasive or dishonest is the easier path. However, other people have very rich "antennae" and will subconsciously pick up honesty and trustworthiness concerns (women are especially good in assessing this; a result of their role in genes perpetuation safety, as explained in chapter 7). The Primal Drives of a person, through the unconscious mind, will "read" the non-conscious mind and Primal Drives of another person and assign a trust rating. Goleman et al called it "latching." How we "walk our talk" over time will constantly be calibrated by others in terms of trustworthiness, or not. A negative rating will cause caution and possibly even rejection. Potential impacts will be diminished. Those that unconsciously reflect "do as I say and not as I do" will be quickly found out and diminished. That "95 percent of communication is nonverbal" will reveal the truth rather quickly.

The imperative for ethics, and unconditional ethics, is centered in the Honesty and Trust drive, marbled with the Sociability and Safety drives for strength in numbers. It always has to be Judo-leveraged for us—and for others as well. Always.

Per an article I once read in the *Duluth Herald Tribune*, "See the Child in Him," and observations, I believe that we all come into this world wanting to be honest and loving for survival reasons, and to be dealt with lovingly and honestly. (Think about the pure honesty of children, and how they are hurt by dishonesty.) That we or someone else turns out differently than being honest and trustworthy is mostly due to personality factors that emanate from a difficult adolescent environment ("nurture") where deception and perhaps aggression became survival factors emotionally, and perhaps even physically.

We "learn" to be dishonest and/or aggressive as a desperate survival tool in such dangerous situations, and often become "takers" in general for Safety and Self-Interest. Untrustworthiness results, with many negative consequences in personal life and in business. Thus, if one has that problem it does not have to be the real you, so see someone for help (and I also refer you to *Unlock the Secrets of Childhood Memories* by O'Connor). The problem source will be found and then a happier path to honesty and trustworthiness, and life in general, can be taken. Others will benefit also.

It should be noted that if a non-trust situation is seen to be short term and will end, the other person's Self-Interest and other Primal Drives may override this concern. This will not endure, however.

For self-management, leadership of others, marketing, sales and other relationships, Honesty and Trustworthiness are critical to sustained personal success (Safety, Self-Interest, Hope, etc.) on a consistent basis. In reality, "the truth will set you free!" As a small example, if you make a mistake, as we all do, be the first to openly raise it. That act takes energy out of the problem, reflects character, and will automatically increase your Trustworthiness quotient. The obverse is true also if you try to protect what everyone knows was a mistake. The emperor will then have no clothes, and might even be dethroned as a consequence. "White lies" may seem innocent, but do start to raise Trustworthiness and Safety flags that are not helpful. Just always tell the truth—as tactfully as possible.

Honesty and Trustworthiness are powerful Primal Drives to be Judo-leveraged, for you and not against you. Such drives must come from the core of individuals to be received as real and not just "put on."

Always figure out how to get Honesty and Trustworthiness factors working for you, and not against you. Judo-leverage it!

5. Energy and Time Optimization

The Energy and Time savings Primal Drive is responsible for very innate, DNA-level, important sub-drives such as laziness, procrastination, continually seeking easiness and convenience, having the dropsies (holding an object too loosely and it drops), taking shortcuts, and saving time. There is a drive in us that says to save Energy calories for emergency use when needed, and to do so purposely. Thus, laziness and procrastination are no accident; they have a core, DNA, genes-protection purpose.

When the Energy cost is worse than the gain we do not act, which may seem lazy or procrastinating, but it is deeply calculated. A good analogy is a trout's habits. It hides behind the rock where the current is slow and fewer calories are needed to hold the position. When an insect, minnow, or crayfish comes by it auto-calculates the calories to be gained versus those to be expended and decides whether to bite or not. Zero conscious thought is engaged; it is even below the instinct level. It is primordial.

We are primordial also. Below our awareness level we auto-calculate a do, don't-do, or do-later decision in each specific situation, far below the conscious level.

We constantly strive to get more results from our Time use. We see Time as a priceless resource and try to optimize its use for gain. We understand the truism of "tempus fugit." The truism that "time is money" is also reflective. We constantly look for more results in a time period. We also understand that "timing is everything." It is an underlying Primal Drive.

What are some everyday examples of business or personal actions to support the critical, underlying Energy and Time saving Primal Drive (think about the Why behind each of these)?

- Easy-open packages
- Fast food drive thrus
- Mouse and icons vs. a keyboard (Windows vs. DOS; Mac vs. PC)
- Speech-to-text software versus keying
- Express lanes in the store
- Shortcuts through lawns or bushes vs. using the sidewalk
- Self-checkout lanes
- Pre-packaged foods
- Meals Ready To Eat (MREs)
- Microwaves, and microwave products
- Jets vs. prop planes
- Bullet trains
- Express buses
- HOV lanes
- Quick Install instructions vs. the full manual
- FedEx or UPS vs. USPS
- Fax, e-mail, and now IM, texting, Twitter, Facebook, etc.
- Elevators and escalators vs. stairs
- Cruise control
- Bookmarks vs. typing URLs
- Delegation to subordinates
- Preset travel packages
- Welfare vs. work for some (even if self-liberties are surrendered)
- The "nanny state" where everything is done for us, until George Orwell's *1984* "Big Brother" world exists
- Many more examples could be listed for Ease, Speed and Time savings actions.

All of these and hundreds more save us Time and mental or physical Energy. IT IS IMPORTANT TO NOTE THAT THESE ABOVE EXAMPLES DID NOT JUST HAPPEN. THEY WERE CAUSED TO HAPPEN BY THE LOW-LEVEL ENERGY SURPLUS /TIME SAVING PRIMAL DRIVE. WITHOUT THAT PRIMAL DRIVE'S CAUSATION NO SUCH RESULTS WOULD HAVE OCCURRED. THIS FURTHER REFLECTS THE POWER OF THE PRIMAL DRIVES FAR BELOW THE CONSCIOUS MIND!

Habits are a result of this Energy Optimization Primal Drive. Habits allow proven, automatic actions with no mental calories needed to act. Pavlov showed that dogs do what they learn is in their best interest. Net "input-output" gains result. Pavlov's dog quickly learned correct reactions and had to use no mental calories when the stimulus was introduced.

Also, they (and we) form habits, as a kind of Energy-saving shortcut to ensure Safety (not get shocked) and to conserve mental Energy calories use in getting rewarded. We do the same, and the truisms can be fully leveraged.

Comfort zones also form due to ease and Energy savings control—and Safety probably, since the present outcome is pre-known versus variable. These comfort zones become the enemy over time due to changes constantly occurring. We get comfortable with the status quo (where perceived Safety, Self-Interest, and Energy saving also reside), and do not want to expend the energy to change or accept the risks. The lack of a cognitive vision of how to successfully change is often at work also. As a result, change is often even resisted (chapter 6 addresses change management).

Related *Complacency* is partly lodged in the Energy and Time Optimization Primal Drive. We get lazy to save Energy. The problem is that when an emergency arises due to complacency, as it always will, the problem is far advanced and much more expensive to resolve—and it may not be resolvable. When Rome was sacked by the Goths, this was due to pervasive complacency. When the German army launched the Battle of the Bulge attack, the allied forces' initial losses were due to complacency. In business, sitting on a lead is bad business.

Paradigms are derived from the Greek *paradiegma* (pattern) and defined in *Dictionary.com* as "… (a) set of forms all of which contain a particular element…a display in fixed arrangement of such a set…an example serving as a model; pattern…"

Paradigms are centered in Energy saving also, with some Safety (proven) and Self-Interest marbling also. Paradigms are pattern-based filters that allow situational views and judgments to be made with no mental (Energy) effort. Coveys' *Seven Habits of Highly Effective People* warns us that paradigms can become our single biggest impediment to correctness in a situation. Things constantly change, and often past paradigms provide an incorrect filter for later situational thinking. Constantly check and validate your paradigms. For example, the military has to purposely not try to fight a new war like it did the old one.

I believe that the "*memes*" concept is based in Energy saving. These ideas that become viral are an energy-saving way to organize the mind with certain beliefs in a low-energy use way, as reflected in this quote from *The Brainsqueezer Newsletter:*

"The Gender Idea Virus (aka Meme)

There is the male, and the female, idea virus. Associated with the male idea virus are stereotypical thoughts such as men are stronger, prefer the color blue, are more aggressive and ambitious and all the rest. We know them well. On the other hand, the female idea virus is that women are more submissive, like pink and pretty things, are gentler, more emotional and more family orientated. In modern times, many people have cured themselves of these 'traditional' idea viruses, and they've busted free of the narrow precepts of those particular memes. The remnants of those meme idea viruses live on in people unwilling to explore beyond them. And the gender idea virus itself seems to be fighting for its survival in pockets of resistance around the world. It is also perpetuated by marketers who know that there is money to be made from pitching to the infected."

Memes, be they right or wrong, somewhat like paradigms, let us instantly structure issues so that we can perceive them with no cognitive calories needed, and with some certainty. Memes change over time, just as our much less-confining memes about female leaders today. However, they always remain an Energy- and Time-saving, paradigm-like structure.

Acronyms are a purposeful Energy-saving element. Ask the military (e.g., DoD, DLA, JSOC, TRADOC, SOCOM, NATO, SEAL, AFCENT, and thousands more). In business, terms like "SOX (Sarbanes-Oxley)," IRR, NPV, ROI, SBA, SEC, IRS, DAGMAR (Define Advertising Goals, Measure Advertising Results), VC, CEO, COO, CFO, VP, EVP, SFA (sales force automation), ERP, HRIS, and thousands of others exist to get a point across with near-zero mental calories used. As can be seen, these are symptoms of a lower level drive to save Energy (and Time).

Shortcuts and summaries save Energy. Cliff Notes, executive summaries, briefs, PowerPoint slides versus full documents, etc., are used to convey core information with optimal Energy and Time saving value.

As noted, in *Blink*, Malcolm Gladwell referred to the Primordial nature of the unconscious mind for making correct assessments very quickly, in a blink, and drawing on (lower-level) non-conscious sources to do so. But we go to an even more basic, more powerful level. This "blink" is an instantaneous, low-Energy-use "read" by the Primal Drives construct in a given, marbled situation.

Kinetic energy in people ("a body in motion tends to stay in the same motion; a body at rest tends to stay at rest," per Isaac Newton) is a result of the Energy saving protection drive. A pattern or process tends to move forward as it has in the past.

Changing a direction is very hard to do, but often vital. If nothing is being done, getting it started is hard and requires a "compelling" reason to expend Energy and Time resources (that may become "the lesser of the evils").

As seen, the Energy and Time Optimization Primal Drive is pervasive and affects all that we do, far below the conscious level.

Always figure out how to get Energy and Time Optimization working for you, and not against you. Judo-leverage them!

6. Sociability (Constraints on Self-Interest, to Enhance General Safety)

Sociability has a genes perpetuation purpose far beyond just being nice. Per Dr. Gazzaniga of the UC Santa Barbara Center for the Study of the Mind, "...Social relationships are merely byproducts of behavior originally selected to avoid our being eaten by predators" (or today, being beaten by competitors, technological change, the economy, or legal changes-author's add).

The below excerpt reviews findings about that part of the brain that controls Sociability. But what drives it to do so? Answer: the Sociability Primal Drive.

NEW YORK—Do you spend time with a lot of friends? That might mean a particular part of your brain is larger than usual.

It's the amygdala, which lies deep inside. Brain scans of 58 volunteers in a preliminary study indicated that the bigger the amygdala, the more friends and family the volunteers reported seeing regularly.

"That makes sense because the amygdala is at the center of a brain network that's important for socializing," says Lisa Feldman Barrett, an author of the work published online Sunday by the journal Nature Neuroscience.

For example, the network helps us recognize whether somebody is a stranger or an acquaintance, and a friend or a foe, said Barrett, of Northeastern University in Boston.

But does having a bigger amygdala lead to more friends, or does socializing with a lot of friends create a bigger amygdala? The study can't sort that out. But Barrett said it might be a bit of both.

She said her study now must be replicated by further research.

The work, supported by the federal government, was aimed at uncovering basic knowledge rather than producing any immediate practical payoff, she said.

But it might someday lead to ways to help people maintain active social lives, she said.

People have one amygdala in the left half of the brain and another in the right half. The findings of the new study held true for each one.

Arthur Toga, a brain-mapping expert at the University of California, Los Angeles, who didn't participate in the study, called the work well done and the statistical results strong. The idea of linking a brain structure to human behavior is "interesting and important," he said.

—*excerpt from* Associated Press, *December 2010*

Sociability is not a whim or accidental. It is a key survival drive, varying in intensity across individuals, is most strong in trying situations, but is the weakest Primal Drive generally. The power of "strength in numbers" causes us to protect Social circles and ties that can contribute to our Safety, Self-Interest, Energy saving, and Hope/Transcendence. This drive requires us to obey mores, customers, ethics, etc., such as the Ten Commandments, the Golden Rule, and the Pillars of Islam. Elaborate rituals and practices exist to keep the Social fabric strong. It provides some control over our Self-Interest excesses.

(As noted earlier, owing to improving surrounding ecosystem Safety, Sociability constraints are less accepted today. Let's hope that continues, because the obverse would be worse overall. We would be hypocritical to complain about needing to motivate younger employees while not recognizing that the many surrounding positives that enable their narcissisms have broad, powerful benefits.)

Owing to nurture variances some are obviously better than others at Sociability, and some need it less than others due to the confidence and comfort of operating alone, or having insecurity about being around others. Some even have an anti-Social personality, perhaps because they were "potty-trained at gunpoint" when growing up in a negative environment where they had to emotionally pull within themselves to psychologically survive. (This is an example of "acquired" (learned, nurture-based) personality traits occasionally affecting an individual's Primal Drives.) Some have depression, resulting flawed genes causing glands to not naturally produce the needed chemicals and hormones for the brain.

Cultural Sociability norms (and values) vary by region of the world and even in regions of the U.S. For example, "Southern hospitality" is a truism. Evolving from a history of agrarian-based poverty in the South versus the more industrial, richer North, Social inter-dependence need was higher in the South so the Sociability norm was higher. "Southern hospitality" is the result, and it is real even today. (However, in the South less direct talk exists than in the northern industrial, richer areas. Social gentility means one has to carefully read between the lines to accurately understand what is truly being said, and not being said. Also, one has to be more circumspect in inter-personal style due to Social style expectations.)

That there is Sociology, the study of groups, attests to the existence of the Social Primal Drive. Social drives will exist inside a company (a key for "organizational development, or OD"). When the informal organization is actually in control, Social factors are very strongly at work in a company, for good or bad (for good if top leadership is flawed, and bad if leadership is correctly focused but burdened by a bad culture it has inherited—where some purposeful, selected firings or demotions will invoke Safety and Self-Interest drives in the remaining group and start a cooperative spiral). The existence and strength of a "grapevine" reflects Social Drives at work. Political cliques are the Social Drive in action, and strength in numbers for Safety and Self-Interest.

"Service society" norms vary by country and even within countries. I have observed that in crowded environments people tend to draw inward somewhat into their own space, and are less other-directed service oriented.

Driven by Safety, Self-Interest, Hope, etc., "pecking orders" form in all animal species' Social orders, reflecting how the Primal Drives interact. Pecking orders are true in households, communities, businesses, governments, and among nations. In formal or informal organizations different sub-drives determine the power pecking order for each. A striation of power and influence will form and generally be accepted by most (for their net Safety, Self-Interest, Hope, etc.). In the long run the combination of ability and goodness, together, will prevail. There can be negative structures in the short term, but they cannot sustain in the long run (due to the Safety and Self-Interest needs of others that will prevail over time to punish threats and dismantle negative pecking orders). Managing this force is important, with merit-based goodness prevailing. Thus, meritocracies have innate value in nature.

A major element often associated with the Social drive is to "keep up with the Joneses." This is a means to protect our status and power (Safety and Self-Interest), and our ability to have strength in numbers-based Safety. (Note: anthropology studies about early humans' Sociability drives, both for the men hunters (in teams usually) and for the women in the Social cave or village, are very compelling (and are overviewed in chapter 8).

Altruism is centered in the Sociability arena. There is Safety strength in numbers by helping others, and getting the rewards indirectly by contributing to causes others will reward. Note, however, this force is far down the power list versus other Primal Drives, so in general cannot be depended on consistently versus stronger Primal Drives such as Safety, Self-Interest, Hope/Transcendence, etc. Altruism often fades quickly when higher order Primal Drives are controlling, which is a special challenge to volunteer and charity organizations (see chapter 8 for some action insights).

To repeat, Sociability has a genes perpetuation purpose far beyond just being nice.

Always figure out how to get Sociability working for you, and not against you. Judo-leverage it!

Summary

As business leaders we are after results, and are on a constant quest to better achieve those results. The *combination* of understanding the importance of the Primal Drives (that enable the Primordial Drive to perpetuate our genes), envisioning, and values, and executing this understanding via the Judo Principle is a 1 x 1=4 combination. Each without the other is incomplete. The combination is essential to optimal results. Weak insights/ideas, even well executed, cause weak results. Good ideas poorly executed cause weak results. Together, good insights and ideas that are very well executed are powerful and provide a path to success. *That* is the mission! As Drucker noted, "Do the right things first, then do things right."

The Primal Drives:

1. **Safety**
2. **Self-Interest (including greed)**
3. **Hope and Transcendence**
4. **Honesty and Trust**
5. **Energy and Time Optimization**
6. **Sociability**

Appendix B

MORE ON LEADERSHIP ASSESSMENT

Independently Assess Yourself

Assessing your self-leadership potential, and challenges (aka opportunities) is critical. Either leveraging or overcoming one's own Values and challenges takes total self-awareness, understanding of the need to self-manage, and Values. How do we know if we have those Values and drives to be a leader, and where the gaps might be so we can tackle them? To do so, we can solicit 360-type feedback with a promise of no retribution (anonymously perhaps). *Primal Leadership* suggested the ECI-360 assessment.

For values insights, let's look at a leadership profile from my favorite psychological battery, the Hartman Values Profile (in which I have no financial interest, but I have found it to be especially insightful, once understood). I have used it since 1987 very effectively for self-analysis, team building, hiring, promoting, and organizing. It may exist, but nothing has been found by me that comes close to getting "between the ears" of the test taker related to true leadership insights (by role) and Values, and an online report is ready the next day. It is not expensive either. As noted, other assessments can be used.

Any assessment must be job specific per profiles, EEOC validated, and just one tool.

The Hartman test uses two sets of eighteen statements that are each rank ordered by the testee as to most pleasing to least pleasing. Then, a complex "Axiology" set of mathematics is applied to categorize the test taker on many important values and attitudes dimensions, including potentials and actuals. Axiology was first developed by Swedish psychologists and mathematicians in the 1930's.

Below are example Hartman Profiles for a general leadership role, and how I have learned to read them from many experiences (and results after hiring compared to the scores) related to leadership success. While the technical answers used in the report are broad, use of this battery over the years has resulted in observational views of results as presented below.

The first is the adapted Motivations Page, with example scores for a good leader.

Criteria	Excellent	Very Good	Good	Fair	Poor
Being of Service	X				
Mission Achievement	X				
Sense of Belonging	X				
Money, Material Things		X			
Personal Development			X		
Status, Recognition				X	

These profile excerpts, slightly restructured from the actual report order, are very important to who the person truly is. The top three I classify as the "Giver" factors; and the bottom three the "Taker" factors. The absolute scores are very important (with Excellent/Very Good being very important for the Giver features). As importantly, how does the cluster of Giver factors relate to the cluster of Taker factors? Is there a positive gap, or a negative one?

As Covey noted, the mature leader (all leaders!) need to have a "balance" of consideration (for others) and courage (for their and the organization's needs).

In this example, this is a Leader. He is mission achievement dedicated, wants the mission to be of service to others, and wants to achieve the mission as a member of a successful team to which he belongs, contributes, and helps. All three are critical success factors for leadership, to energize the team's

Notice that the Giver cluster is well to the left of the Taker cluster here. This is important. It is fair to want reasonable rewards and to personally grow. The key one to be far right is the Status/Recognition need. If it is to the left, the person may tend to take credit and pass blame. This is the *opposite* is what is needed! Give credit, and take blame to Judo-leverage others' Primal Drives for you, and not against you. (In another Hartman report, Handling Disappointments will often reflect Giver versus Taker propensities. Givers will do better.)

The extraordinary importance of being a Giver as a leader, to stimulate the Primal Drives of followers, is reflected in the following excerpts from the Booz and Company article "Turning the Table on Success" (penned for Booz by Dr. Adam Grant, Wharton University):

"(In collaborative teams) Givers...are the teammates who volunteer for unpopular projects, share their knowledge and skills, and help out by arriving early or staying late...takers stick out. They avoid doing unpleasant tasks and responding to requests for help...I've found that changes (in the workplace) have set the stage for takers to flounder and givers to flourish...*recent research has shown that employees with the highest rates of promotion to supervisory and leadership roles, exhibit the characteristics of givers...* Matchers' hover in the middle of the give-and-take spectrum, motivated by a deep seated desire for fairness and reciprocity...a wealth of research shows that in teams, givers earn more respect and rewards than do takers and matchers... employees will be evaluated not only on the basis of their individual results, but also in terms of their contributions to others...In fact, when givers become leaders their groups are better off...*employees work harder and more effectively for leaders who put others' interests first...*(this) motivates group members to give back to the leader and contribute to the group's interests...the more frequently employees give help and share knowledge, the higher their units' profits, productivity, customer satisfaction, and employee retention rates...*The single strongest predictor of leadership was the amount of compassion that members expressed toward others in need...compassionate people were not only viewed as caring: they were also judged as more knowledgeable and intelligent...*"

Thus, givers energize most or all of the Primal Drives in followers, and/or team members. *The beast in others is best unleashed by this process._*

In some industries the clusters can be closer as long as the Giving cluster is strongly to the left. Such industries might embody pure competition, high volume product turnover, and situations where selling is not inclusive of personal relationships with the customer. Also, having the Giver cluster dominate is important for leading all organizations of people, be they employees or others.

If the clusters are reversed from this graphic, with the Giver factors cluster to the center or right and the Taker cluster to the left, the leader is often narcissistic, not emotionally giving enough and puts off people. Figuratively, bodies may be strewn everywhere. Turnover will be high. EEOC complaints and product liability lawsuits will make the attorneys very powerful in the company. The term "turkey" is often whispered at the cooler, or worse. There is no loyalty or personal emotional commitment. A visitor to the company will see everyone with their heads down with no glee, spontaneity or otherness. Survival Safety in a hostile world is the employees' controlling Primal Drive; at least until they can bail out and extend a hand gesture as they go out the door (even if the exit interview is watered down for reference reasons, as is the norm). We have all seen such places, and often turnarounds have a flavor of this initially. The problem is often exacerbated because employees quickly mirror the CEO tangibly and intangibly. Mirroring a Giver is good; and vice versa. As noted, companies take on the leadership's personality and values.

The second (of several) Hartman Profile reports I pay attention to is the "ProForg." An example is below. For six key attributes it simultaneously assesses potential (Capacity) and actual practice ("- -" or "-" or "+" or "+ +") at the time. Varying combinations will exist, and practice scores can change over time with experiences. Profiles will also vary <u>by position/role type</u>. A strong, successful leader's profile is below.

Criterion	- -	-	Capacity*	+	+ +
Empathy		X	Excellent		
Practical Judgment		X	Excellent		
System Judgment			Excellent	X	
Self-Esteem		X	Excellent		
Role Awareness			Excellent	X	
Drive			Excellent	X	

* Can be Excellent, Very Good, Good, Fair, Poor

The center "Capacity" column is for potential, and I have come to believe is a surrogate for IQ. I have found the Capacity column rating from Excellent to Poor to be a very good surrogate for native Intelligence. Do they have "gray matter" or not? I cannot think of a time when the test was materially wrong. In marginal hires (often for that archenemy, expediency) where Good or Poor existed in more than two of six rows, the person sometimes did not successfully grow with the company over time. They just seemingly could not cognate enough in new ways as events inevitably changed, and then adapt to add value in "Newco." Desire alone was not sufficient. At some point they could not sufficiently "get it." At best they would get passed over. Sometimes they would be terminated, or be caught in a rightsizing reduction or leave in frustration, almost always blaming the company versus understanding the underlying truth (owing to the power of avoiding "cognitive dissonance," probably). EEOC or discrimination suits become more possible.

(Repeat note: The test alone is not sufficient to take specific actions (hiring, promotion by-passing, non-raises, or terminating), so careful, fair, and job performance specific evaluations are needed. The employees' or candidate's Safety, Selfishness and Hop will drive reactions and compel reactions if not rewarded with raises or bonuses, hired, or if demoted or terminated. Specific, defendable criteria are needed.

Thus, "due process" is needed to assure that EEOC–type exposure is limited; especially for "protected class" employees (women, minorities, males over forty, etc.). For terminations or promotion by-passes (and possibly for non-hires) very specific, written if-then prior "due process" criteria and documentation will often be required for protected groups. This may not stop an initial complaint, but an EEOC officer or plaintiff's lawyer will be positively impacted by proper, written pre-action due process. So, keep your motives right, processes tight, and all well documented. The employee has a right to know all aspects of the situation, including consequences of continued poor performance or inadequate attributes vs. others as applicable.

The other four columns are for present-day practice, from very low practice ("- -") to over-practice ("+ +"). These four situational columns can change over time with new experiences. I have not seen the center Capacity potential change much over time, however.

The six criteria in the rows are expansive in defining key values in regard to any job. The mix will vary by job type, so it is important (and EEOC compliant) to effectively profile proven successful people in a role as the basis for evaluating others relative to that role. Leaders do have the right to discriminate…as long as it is truly job performance related only.

Empathy is other directedness. A leader needs to intrinsically be in tune intuitively and attitudinally with the needs, feelings, aspirations and concerns of those around him; internally and externally. Thus, an Excellent or Very Good Capacity score is essential. Without that capacity the leader will not be empathetic when it counts, when the pudding has hit the fan and the effective leader needs to be part of the solution and not part of the problem. A low Empathy Capacity is a challenge. It can lead to poor sympathy with others' Primal Drives and how to harness them, even if inconvenient to do so.

A "+ +" score can be a challenge. This can be a too-softie profile; often a non-decision maker or sets standards that are too low so as to avoid corrective discipline being needed, or is a protector of weak people. When it comes time to draw a line in the sand, as leaders often have to do, the "+ +" leader disappears. Confrontation is nauseating. Decisions that affect others are not made. It just too uncomfortable and perhaps avoided until a crisis state evolves into which others have to get involved. Then an action is finally implemented only because it is the lesser of the evils. We have all seen this type. In reality their guts are figuratively in knots due to stress.

A "- -" score is equally a concern, in reverse, even with a high Empathy Capacity. When a problem occurs negative reactions and comments can be just below the surface. If the Capacity is low and a "- -" exists, you might be meeting the modern-day Attila.

A high Capacity and a "+" is a teacher type. It is net positive, but may not be results requiring enough, or too comfortable with the employee setting his own pace.

I believe an Excellent Capacity and a "-" score is optimal. The capacity is there, but the leader will decisively act when needed, even if someone is pained as a result. I call it "constructive toughness," or "fair but firm." Explain the Whys.

(In the coming *Primordial Marketing and Sales,* we will delve into how to find sales closers versus "professional visitors," or those with high call reluctance. The right profile will differ by selling situation. Matching selling skills to selling needs will also be covered. We will also review how to hire a right-brained marketing strategist versus just a good marketing communications person; there is a material difference.)

Practical Judgment seems reflective of detail orientation and left brain thinking strength. Does the person have the capacity for detailed thinking and is he practicing it? My bias is that leaders can't be excellent at both left and right brain thinking, and can hire detailed people, so the score of an Excellent or Very Good capacity and a "-" is acceptable (if the below System Judgment is strong in Capacity and practice also). The details can be delegated and then acted on; and it will be delegated if at all possible because the details are not natively as fun as conceptualizing. A low capacity or an extreme "- -" or "+ +" scores are red flags and should be delved into for senior leadership positions (not necessarily true for the Payroll Manager in Accounting with a "+ +," who must get details right). Of course, the leader of a technical team will have a different profile than the leader of a marketing or sales team.

System Judgment may be the most critical for policy level leaders. From direct observations I believe it reflects right-brain, spatial, holistic, end-in-mind thinking capability, and its intrinsic use (or non-use) for envisioning. An Excellent capacity and a "+" are good. If the Capacity is lower the leader had better surround himself with a spatial thinker, and listen to and support that person.

The key is to always be envisioning new potentials that are implementable, driven by any combination of increased Safety, Self-Interest rewards, Hope and Transcendence, and other Primal Drives. A "+ +" score is toward being too impractical at the "dreamer" end, and must be watched. Ideas and visions can become decoupled from positioning/implementation realities.

The old saying "Luck is preparation meeting opportunity" is anchored in the ability to correctly and practically envision the future, inclusive of all the causal power forces and how they will (always) change the status quo; and to "be there" at the right time with the right program. Once we get those visions right we then have a chance to figure out what to do to Judo-leverage the coming changes for us versus being harmed by them. We can be on the balls of our feet versus others being on their heels, and not vice versa.

We have all met people that "If they did not have bad luck they would have no luck at all." It is likely that these people have low spatial skills in capacity and/or practice, and are just in the wrong place at the wrong time too often...with the wrong "stuff."

A person with high System Judgment capacity but a "- -" practice may recently have been, or is in, a situation where independent, out-of-the-box thinking and taking calculated risks are criticized by peers and perhaps even other leaders or the board. This is a great resource that is not being taken advantage of by higher leadership. Some new hires might come with this because they recently left a punishing environment. The leader's job is to bring them out of their defensive shell, to be all they can be; including making reasonable mistakes and professionally learning and then to tell about it to all.

In summary, from direct observation this "spatial"-based System Judgment area is where I believe many types of leaders struggle. Covey noted that about 1 percent are spatial. We will cover these areas more in chapter 6, with some helpful ideas. Leaders need to continually grow in this area.

Self-Esteem. Self-Esteem is related to self-worth as a personality trait. The consultants I use for the Hartman consistently says that leaders have a high Self Esteem Capacity but often have a "- -" practice score. He attributes this to our competitive society of "be all you can be," "keep up with the Joneses," and other "you can be better" drives. I believe they have a very high Hope and Transcendence Primal Drive that keeps them constructively dissatisfied at all times. Also, I believe it is tied to the Drive factor reviewed below, perhaps from Nurture training as well. Such unmet needs are the mother of invention...and goals focused energy.

Role Awareness. This attribute helps to make sure there is not a square peg in a round hole. Make sure you understand the position well beforehand and it fits your "brand image" of yourself. The same goes for others. A mismatch can, and likely will, cause "cognitive dissonance" problems over time. A high Capacity is an important attribute because it helps correctly define the role. A "- -" score is a red flag of potential fit problems. A "+ +" often means a hard-headed person that will not take direction well because they are fixated on a view that cannot be changed. They might say "Yes," but when they leave the office the boss is quietly called non-positive names because in the employee's eyes the boss does not "get it." Follow-up actions do not change very much. If the person has other important attributes a "tight leash" has to be applied.

Drive. Author and speaker Dennis Waitley correctly commented that "Success is almost totally dependent upon drive and persistence. The extra energy required to make another effort or try another approach is the secret of winning."

President Calvin Coolidge wisely stated that "Nothing in this world can take the place of persistence. Talent will not; nothing is more common than unsuccessful people with talent. Genius will not; unrewarded genius is almost a proverb. Education will not; the world is full of educated derelicts. Persistence and determination alone are omnipotent. The slogan 'press on' has solved and always will solve the problems of the human race."

The Drive attribute is about the "need" to achieve goals versus just a "want" to do so. This Drive is where "perseverance" and related attributes exist. Long hours, creative thinking, rule breaking, risk taking, and other success factors are the result.

The strength of Drive relates to how strong the Primal Drives are in the aggregate. Any combination of needing (versus just wanting) Safety, Self-Interest, Transcendence, etc., are the sources of Drive energy.

A strong, Excellent or Very Good Capacity is important as a starting point. A "+ +" can be a workaholic that is out of balance. A "steamrolling" style can result. Often it correlates to a " - -" in Self Esteem.

A "- -" suggests a strong Energy saving Primal Drive, with a resulting lazy aspect to it; only doing what has to be done to get by, or not to get caught. An "-" score can mean that things that are enjoyed will be addressed, but other needs may get short-changed.

An Excellent Capacity and a "+" practice are optimal. Strong energy will exist, with some balance and perspective. A ++ score can be too strong, with burnout potential eventually.

Overall, the above two Hartman profile graphics generally represent an optimal leadership values and capabilities profile for most businesses. We are all complex beings and a blending of the key factors will exist. Capacities need to be strong, and System Judgment needs to be strong and well used, with street-savvy common sense applied. The need to achieve the mission by being of service to others and doing so via the team (belonging) is important (aggregating into a "Giver"). Not needing credit is very important, as well as a high Drive capacity that is balanced with surrounding realities. A high Empathy capacity but the ability to be direct when needed are important to have, together.

This Hartman profile's example elements are important for self-understanding and for self-improvement; and for executive team building and possibly selection. Counseling may be needed. Regardless of the assessment used, the leader must share his profile and that of other leaders as well. Facilitated discussions are also a potential help. Leadership team members will better understand themselves and others. Each can then build on strengths and work on weaknesses, in themselves and in others. I have seen this work.

Many possible profile tools exist. Any such profile(s) needs to be just one element of an excellence program, must be job situational and provide action guidelines only. Profiling successful individuals first is important to avoiding potential discrimination on any basis other than job performance for the specific role and its requirements. Third-party, experienced facilitators can also help assure proper application.

Handling Pain and Fear

Another rating by the Hartman Profile is the ability to handle disappointments. Do you absorb them and keep "ice water in the veins" and make good decisions? Or does "your hair get on fire" and cause you to make the wrong decisions and worsen things?

I once had a Sales EVP reporting to me that was the latter. He would run in and declare a crisis, with mostly the whites of his eyes showing. I'd say (let's call him Pete here), "Pete, a crisis is a rocket-propelled grenade coming at you. This is just an issue to deal with that we need to determine how to Judo-leverage into an opportunity." He would then smile, calm down and usually come up with the right answer.

Remember: who gets mad, or scared, last wins!

INDEX

Printed in the USA
CPSIA information can be obtained
at www.ICGtesting.com
JSHW022221140824
68134JS00018B/1194